Evidence-Based Medicine

While doctors through the ages have thought that they had based their practice on evidence, a new movement based on the ideas of the Scottish doctor Archie Cochrane has shown that this might not be the case.

The core of evidence-based medicine is the formulation of a question relevant to a clinical problem, then researching around this problem selecting the best type evidence from explicit criteria, and finally the making of decisions based on patients' values. This approach has received a mixed response in the medical community. This book focuses on its limitations as well as its strengths.

With contributions from recognised experts across many disciplines, this volume will prove to be of great interest to medical professionals, health planners and health science students across the world.

Ivar Sønbø Kristiansen is Senior Researcher at the Research Unit of General Practice at the University of Southern Denmark. **Gavin Mooney** is Professor of Health Economics at Curtin University, Australia and Visiting Professor at Aarhus University, Denmark.

Routledge international studies in health economics

Edited by Charles Normand

London School of Hygiene and Tropical Medicine

and Richard M. Scheffler

School of Public Health, University of California

1 **Individual Decisions for Health**
Edited by Björn Lindgren

2 **State Health Insurance Market Reform**
Toward inclusive and sustainable health insurance markets
Edited by Alan C. Monheit and Joel C. Cantor

3 **Evidence-Based Medicine**
In its place
Edited by Ivar Sønbø Kristiansen and Gavin Mooney

Evidence-Based Medicine

In its place

Edited by Ivar Sønbø Kristiansen and Gavin Mooney

Routledge
Taylor & Francis Group
LONDON AND NEW YORK

First published 2004
by Routledge
2 Park Square, Milton Park, Abingdon, Oxfordshire OX14 4RN

Simultaneously published in the USA and Canada
by Routledge
270 Madison Ave, New York NY 10016

Routledge is an imprint of the Taylor & Francis Group

Transferred to Digital Printing 2005

Typeset in Times by Wearset Ltd, Boldon, Tyne and Wear

British Library Cataloguing in Publication Data
A catalogue record for this book is available from the British Library

Library of Congress Cataloging in Publication Data
A catalog record for this book has been requested

ISBN 0-415-28321-3

Dedicated to Archie Cochrane's values

Archie Cochrane (1909–88).

Reprinted with kind permission of the Cochrane Collaboration.

Contents

Illustrations

Figures

Tables

Boxes

Contributors

Stephen Birch and **Amiram Gafni** are professors in the Department of Clinical Epidemiology and Biostatistics and members of the Centre for Health Economics and Policy Analysis at McMaster University, Canada. Their research interests are in methods for economic evaluation of health interventions, equity in health care resource allocation and policy analysis.

Arthur Elstein is Professor Emeritus in the Department of Medical Education, University of Illinois College of Medicine, USA. His research has focused on the psychology of clinical reasoning and decision making.

Helle Ploug Hansen is Associate Professor at the Faculty of Health Sciences at the University of Southern Denmark. She has a PhD degree in anthropology and a background in nursing, and has been involved in several ethnographic studies in Denmark.

Uffe Juul Jensen is Professor of Philosophy at Aarhus University, Denmark.

Ivar Sønbø Kristiansen is Senior Researcher at the Research Unit of General Practice at the University of Southern Denmark and at the Institute of Health Management and Health Economics at the University of Oslo, Norway. His research interests lie in risk communication and economic evaluation of medical interventions.

Gavin Mooney is Professor of Health Economics at Curtin University in Australia and Visiting Professor at Aarhus University in Denmark. His current interest lies in research and teaching in Aboriginal health.

Kjeld Møller Pedersen is Professor of Health Economics and Health Policy at the University of Southern Denmark. His research interests are valuation of health, economic evaluation, transaction costs economics applied to health economics, and the design and evaluation of health care systems.

Aileen Plant is Professor of International Health at Curtin University of Technology in Perth, Australia. She is a key player in the recently established Australian Biosecurity Cooperative Research Centre for Emerging Infectious Disease.

Knut Rasmussen is Professor of Cardiology at the University of Tromsø, Norway. His research interests are in cardiology, ethics and health policy.

Dag Steinar Thelle is Professor of Cardiovascular Epidemiology and Prevention at Göteborg University, Sweden, and of Epidemiology at the University of Oslo, Norway. His current research project is directed towards the interaction between susceptibility genotypes and external factors in the aetiology of common chronic disorders such as cardiovascular disease, diabetes and chronic obstructive pulmonary disease.

Preface

Gavin Mooney had the great pleasure of meeting Archie Cochrane on several occasions. Archie informed him, after their first meeting in south Wales, that he had revised his opinion of economists. On the basis of the evidence of an afternoon with Gavin, he now placed them second bottom, with sociologists at the bottom. There was much on which they agreed.

Despite his being a Scot, Archie's generosity was legendary. On hearing that Gavin needed £1,000 (little short of a year's salary for Gavin then) to get his first book published (the publisher had indicated that it was unlikely to be a best-seller), Archie arranged for a 'trust' that he 'chaired' to pay. Gavin is certain that the money came from Archie's own pocket.

Fond memories of a man of stature, humour and generosity . . .

One can only wonder what he would have made of the Cochrane This and the Cochrane That. Certainly then he was all too well aware that evidence depended very much on how it was presented and the values brought to its interpretation. As at that time a very junior member of staff at the Department of Health in London, Gavin recalls how Archie presented evidence from a randomized controlled trial (RCT) on treatment of heart attacks. The learned doctors nodded sagely when he reported that the evidence showed that treatment in hospitals was superior to treatment in the community. It was only when Archie 'confessed' to having got the figures round the wrong way that the learned nodders sought to question the study design!

In 1974, Ivar Sønbø Kristiansen started his medical career as a GP in a remote area of Norway. He soon upset his senior hospital colleagues by asking awkward questions about the 'evidence' for therapies that were at that time mainstream. For example: 'Why should we make young girls subject to unpleasant radiology examinations and possibly subsequent urinary surgery when they have had two or three urinary tract infections?' Hospital colleagues angrily responded that it would be better for the girls to experience some unpleasant procedures than suffer renal failure and death as a result of recurrent infections. Some of these procedures are now seen as obsolete.

For a sceptical doctor, it was a memorable moment to open the first issue of the Cochrane Database of systematic reviews. This revealed that many commonly used procedures related to pregnancy and childbirth were based more on beliefs than on evidence. However, attending a Cochrane Colloquium in 1995 was surprising and somewhat reminiscent of a religious meeting at which adherents gather together to renew and strengthen their faith. Ivar's surprise was no less when, soon afterwards, he joined a team of researchers, some of whom were also imbued with an 'evidence-based' fervour. These experiences created Ivar's interest in evidence-based medicine (EBM) and eventually sparked the idea of this book.

It is with great pleasure that we have co-edited the book. It has given us the opportunity to work with old friends and make new ones, and we thank them all for their ready cooperation.

In so much of what now passes for modern medicine, some of the values that Archie Cochrane brought to this noble discipline are too often missing, especially the values of justice and equality. These Uffe Juul Jensen dwells upon in his contribution to this book. He writes:

> [Cochrane's] book [*Effectiveness and Efficiency*] contains a strong critique of traditional clinical freedom. He seeks support to strengthen the pressure on medicine to use effectiveness and efficiency as indices in assessing therapy *and to get equality respected as a basic ethical principle of health care*. [Emphasis added]

The book does not attempt to provide a comprehensive analysis of EBM. Over the past ten years the use of the term 'evidence based' has mushroomed; it pops up in all sorts of contexts. The terms 'evidence based' and 'evidence-based medicine' are not copyright protected. They seem frequently to be used simply to try to give credibility to some idea or activity. Rather, the objective is critically to address some issues around EBM. We hope this will make the reader better able to understand the limitations of EBM, but also its strengths. We hope this book will place EBM in a proper context: EBM, in its place.

Ivar Sønbø Kristiansen and Gavin Mooney
Odense and Perth
December 2003

1 Evidence-based medicine

Method, collaboration, movement or crusade?

Ivar Sønbø Kristiansen and Gavin Mooney

Summary

In 1972 the Scottish epidemiologist Archie Cochrane (1909–88) suggested that critical, updated summaries by specialty of all randomised controlled trials (RCT) should be organised. The idea was adopted by a group of 77 doctors who in 1993 co-founded the Cochrane Collaboration. During the subsequent years the collaboration has expanded enormously, with several thousand people engaged in Cochrane centres, review groups, fields and networks. The collaboration promotes evidence-based medicine (EBM), which can be defined as 'the conscientious, explicit and judicious use of current best evidence in making decisions about the care of individual patients'. While the Cochrane Collaboration initially focused on clinical issues, its scope has been widened to encompass educational methods, health services research, health policy analysis, etc.

This introductory chapter first argues that because core methods of EBM are taken from medicine, including biostatistics and epidemiology, they may have limitations in analysing non-clinical issues, which may require much broader theories and methods than those offered by EBM. Second, while Archie Cochrane acknowledged the limitations of RCTs and meta-analyses, the Cochrane Collaboration in practice seems to overlook these limitations in the pursuit of 'best evidence'.

Established to promote epidemiological methods, the Cochrane Collaboration seems to be moving in the direction of becoming a movement or a crusade. Epidemiologists seem to keep the movement at a distance, whereas it is embraced by wide groups in other parts of medicine. Despite the widespread use of the term 'EBM', it is uncertain whether broad groups of doctors see themselves as soldiers in the EBM crusade.

The EBM movement has promoted a more systematic search for medical information, more demand for randomised trials and a critical attitude towards the effectiveness of medical interventions. There is little documentation, however, at least at the level the Cochrane Collaboration would require, that EBM improves patients' health. The more the scope of the movement is broadened, the more difficult it becomes to prove its own effectiveness. Nevertheless, EBM deserves a cautious welcome.

Introduction

When medical doctors read scientific journals or attended medical meetings in the early 1980s, they would have been surprised to come across the term 'evidence-based medicine' (EBM). They would probably have considered it somewhat odd because, they would have thought, doctors do base their practice on evidence. The most commonly used database for medical literature, Medline, has no hits for the term 'evidence-based medicine' in 1980, nor in 1985 nor in 1990. Indeed, it does not appear until 1992, when two papers were cited. For 1995 the number of citations was 77, while the numbers were 1,929 for 2000, 2,562 for 2001 and 2,691 for 2002. Today, the term 'evidence based' appears in all sorts of word combinations and contexts: evidence-based medicine, surgery, gynaecology, practice, nursing, health care, policy making, health economics, education, social policy, curricula, courses, etc.

Evidence-based medicine and other 'evidence-based' undertakings have taken the medical community and health care by storm. Many positive, even enthusiastic commentaries and analyses have appeared in the medical press and elsewhere. EBM 'came as a gift from the gods', in the words of Sir David Weatherall (Greenhalgh 2001).

More questioning and even critical pieces have also been published. While numerous books on the topic of EBM have appeared, to our knowledge there has been no attempt to publish a more comprehensive set of analyses or critiques of EBM or of the EBM movement. This book aims to fill that gap. In this introductory chapter, for those not familiar with the concept, we briefly explain what is meant by EBM. Subsequently, we put the concept in a wider context before taking a critical look at some of the key approaches of EBM. Finally, we discuss other aspects of the concept and of the EBM movement.

Evidence-based medicine: what is it?

The following definition of EBM is frequently quoted:

> Evidence based medicine is the conscientious, explicit, and judicious use of current best evidence in making decisions about the care of individual patients. The practice of evidence based medicine means integrating individual clinical expertise with the best available external evidence from systematic research. By individual clinical expertise we mean the proficiency and judgement that individual clinicians acquire through clinical experience and clinical practice. Increased expertise is reflected in many ways, but especially in more effective and efficient

> diagnosis and in the more thoughtful identification and compassionate use of individual patients' predicament, rights and preferences in making clinical decisions about their care.
>
> (Sackett *et al.* 1996: 71)

We suspect that most doctors, even before EBM became established with capital letters, would have said that this was not much different from how they had always practised medicine.

The Cochrane Collaboration Brochure (www.cochrane.org) provides a fuller idea of the enterprise. It started with the Scottish doctor and epidemiologist Archie Cochrane (1909–88), who was much concerned with people's health and health care. As a prisoner of war, he spent four years in German camps caring for thousands of fellow prisoners with often serious diseases. To his surprise, there were few fatalities, despite the fact that he could offer his patients only aspirin and a few other basic remedies. He saw this as a 'demonstration' of 'the relative unimportance of therapy' and from this developed a critical view of the real benefits of modern medicine. He thought that doctors as well as the public overstated the importance of modern therapies. Their benefits had not been properly assessed. He advocated the randomised controlled trial (RCT) as a means of achieving unbiased measures of effectiveness of medical therapies. This type of trial had been developed as an epidemiological tool before the Second World War, but was still in limited use when in 1972 Cochrane wrote, 'It is surely a great criticism of our profession that we have not organised a critical summary, by specialty or subspecialty, adapted periodically, of all relevant randomised controlled trials.'

This idea of undertaking more RCTs and systematic reviews was taken forward by various doctors in the United Kingdom, the United States and Canada. The first 'Cochrane Centre' was opened in Oxford in the United Kingdom in October 1992. One year later, at the first 'Cochrane Colloquium', 77 people from 11 countries co-founded the 'Cochrane Collaboration'. During the subsequent years the collaboration has expanded enormously. There are 50 Cochrane collaborative review groups, 11 Cochrane Methods groups, 10 Cochrane fields and networks and 15 Cochrane centres around the world. Importantly, the Cochrane Library (http://www.update-software.com/clibng/cliblogon.htm) provides databases for systematic Cochrane reviews (3,100 entries), other reviews (4,100), results of controlled trials (375,000), methodological issues (4,600), health technology assessments (3,800) and economic evaluations (11,800).

In parallel with the development of the Collaboration, the concept of EBM has crept into all corners of medicine and health care. Two major medical journals (the *British Medical Journal* and the *Journal of the American Medical Association*) have run series of articles on EBM and have broad coverage of themes related to EBM. Several medical journals, such as *Evidence Based Gynaecology*, have entered the market to offer brief updates on published papers and systematic reviews. EBM is an integral part of the curriculum in most medical schools in the United States, and probably in most other countries. EBM is thus very clearly 'on the agenda'. We would doubt that any medical doctor today would dare to state that he or she does not aim to practise evidence-based medicine.

According to the Cochrane Brochure (www.cochrane.org), tens of thousands of premature babies probably died unnecessarily because no systematic review had been performed of the effect of corticosteroids given to women who were about to give premature birth. In fact, the collaboration's logo depicts a review of the first seven clinical trials. The corticosteroid case is 'just one of many examples of the human costs resulting from failure to perform systematic, up-to-date reviews of health care'. What a great enterprise – to get the reviews done and save lives! How could anybody question a collaboration with such great promise?

In fact, this is exactly what this book is about. EBM has taken the world by storm, has received enormous attention and has gained a very strong footing in a surprisingly short period of time. Sceptical comments have appeared in the medical press (Kernick 1998), some published even by advocates of EBM (Anon. 2002), but in general EBM and the Cochrane Collaboration have received a warm welcome from most of the medical community. Yet EBM has its limitations. We believe that doctors and society more generally should be aware of these. It is therefore time to shed some critical light on EBM and its methods. In doing this, we emphasise that the Cochrane Collaboration and EBM have achieved a lot, based, in our opinion, on some very reasonable ideas. The question is not whether EBM is useful but whether all aspects of EBM and the EBM movement should be embraced uncritically.

What started off as a movement targeting purely clinical decisions has broadened its scope. The aim is now not only to inform clinical decisions but also to influence health care in general, including nursing, health policy, social policy and education. What began as a fairly well-defined enterprise has moved to become somewhat unfocused. This poses a problem for those who seek to analyse EBM because the EBM target is moving. In this book, we restrict attention to EBM applied to health care and health care policy making. Some readers may want to claim that we have – in the words of Bob Evans – moved the target to hit the bullet. We have, however, to restrict ourselves to keep the task feasible. Fortunately, this focus fits the focus of EBM as it is described in the Cochrane Brochure. Finally, we do not aim to cover all aspects of EBM, but rather to focus on those we consider important.

EBM in broad perspective

As long as the aim of EBM is to provide clinicians with systematic reviews on biomedical issues and assist doctors in their clinical decision making, its theoretical underpinning, as presented for example in the Cochrane Brochure or in Dave Sackett's handbook on EBM (Sackett *et al.* 2000), might be by and large adequate, even though there would still be some problems, as we shall see. As soon as the aim is extended to helping to create better medical education, better health care, better health policies, an array of new issues need to be addressed. What is health? How should it be measured? Whose values should count in designing health care systems? What is meant by evidence? What is meant by 'good decisions about health care'? It is not surprising that a movement that is born of clinicians in academic positions, epidemiologists and statisticians does not address such difficult issues (see Chapters 2, 4 and 5). It is inevitable perhaps that it is restricted to being a product of the methods they master. What *is* surprising is that the EBM movement aims to influence issues that lie some distance from its medical foundation. In fact, it can be argued that medicine is not a single coherent theory but rather a mixture of statements about practical skills and pieces of theory drawn from biology, psychology and elsewhere. In other words, EBM has quickly become a large edifice built on a relatively limited theoretical basis.

According to Sackett *et al.* (2000), EBM is the integration of best research evidence with clinical expertise and patient values. The synthesis of 'best research evidence' is at the core of biostatistics and epidemiology. What, however, is the scientific basis for 'clinical expertise'? Sackett *et al.* define it as 'the ability to use our clinical skills and past experience to rapidly identify each patient's unique health state and diagnosis, their individual risks and benefits of potential interventions, and their personal values and expectations'. The content of their handbook, however, deals mainly with searching and processing evidence. It contains little about clinical expertise. It seems as if EBM in reality offers no methods for improving clinical skills, or takes it for granted that doctors obtain clinical expertise by practising medicine. This is surprising, because studies of clinical decision making tend to demonstrate that clinicians are not handling information in a consistent and comprehensive way. Rather, they use heuristics and base their decisions on parts of the available information because to cope with the totality is in practice too difficult (see Chapter 8). One of us (I.S.K.) used to demonstrate the problems of medical decision making by asking clinicians to decide on therapy for 20 'paper patients' and subsequently identify what patient factors were important for the decisions. It turned out that many doctors seemed to be unaware of what factors they used in their decision making. They claimed that certain factors were important, yet regression analyses pointed to some totally different ones. Perhaps Archie Cochrane's concept 'the relative unimportance of therapy' may explain why 'clinical expertise' is considered relatively unimportant. To judge by the programme for the 2003 Cochrane Colloquium (http://www.colloquium.info/2003/), clinical expertise does not appear as a major issue in EBM in that none of the sessions covers this topic explicitly.

It is also of note that patient values, while claimed to be a core issue in EBM (Sackett *et al.* 2000), in practice attract less interest among practitioners of EBM. No methods for eliciting patient values or preferences are presented in the EBM handbook (Sackett *et al.* 2000). Further, patient values were implicitly deemed to be of little importance at the 2003 Cochrane Colloquium in that the topic was not listed for any of the sessions (http://www.colloquium.info/2003/).

In a paper that addressed the issue of 'when an effective treatment should be used' (Sinclair *et al.* 2001: 256), the authors present an EBM-based method for valuing outcomes. They suggest that '3 deaths are equivalent to 5 severe strokes or 5 severe intracranial haemorrhages', while '15 mild strokes or mild intracranial haemorrhages are equivalent to 7.5 episodes of serious gastrointestinal bleeding, or approximately 400 episodes of minor bleeding'. These statements are based on values extracted from studies by others. Clearly, the valuation of these various outcomes depends *inter alia* on the time duration involved, yet that was not considered at all in the paper. While there is a rich literature on difficulties in valuing outcomes and treatment effects, the EBM approach seems to take the line that elicitation of such values is so simple that doctors need no specific method other than their own experience and knowledge of the patient. It also endorses universalism. Might this algebraic 'x of A equals y of B' not vary from Iran to Ireland? And might some societies not also value C?

The medical way of thinking is very influential in the EBM movement. Who other than doctors would say that 'the results of reviews *must* [our emphasis] be integrated with the clinicians' expertise' or 'the results of the reviews *must* [our emphasis] also be integrated with the patients' expertise' (Cochrane Brochure). These statements sound as if they were expressed by a surgeon of yesteryear. We further learn that 'In operating in synchrony, these complementary forms of expertise are reflected in more efficient diagnosis and a more thoughtful identification and compassionate use of predicaments.' Ironically, such statements have much in common with doctors' confidence in therapies that do not have proven effectiveness. They create a dualism in the message. On the one hand: 'be sceptical until you are provided with evidence'; on the other hand: 'you need no evidence – put your trust in EBM!'

In discussions about the role of EBM in a health services research unit, the physician and social scientist Tor Inge Romøren in 1997 presented ten theses about EBM (Box 1.1). Here, Romøren warns that 'one should be careful not to research issues for which one is not competent. Graduation from medical school does not qualify one for every task. For most research topics, our bookshelves are already filled with scientific reports.' Seven years on, his analysis of EBM seems no less relevant.

Box 1.1 'Ten theses about evidence-based medicine' (EBM)

These 'theses' were pinned on a notice board in a research institute during a period of discussion of research strategies.

1 EBM is a set of methods to improve clinical decisions.
2 It is the responsibility of clinicians to apply these methods. Regrettably, they don't to the extent they should, but it is not an obligation for health services research to assume this responsibility on behalf of the clinicians.
3 EBM lies at the periphery of the primary purpose of health services research: research on the structure and function of health care services.
4 EBM is based on the paradigm of the randomised controlled trial. This is suitable for clinical practice. It can also successfully be applied to other restricted areas of organisational issues of health care. As a basis, however, for analysing or developing health care services in general, the paradigm is too narrow and 'one-eyed'.
5 EBM is based on a kind of rationalism for which clinical medicine should strive. However, health care and other important institutions in society either cannot or should not be organised on the same principles. Those who do not understand that what is going on in society in general is by nature different from medical care should not be involved with health services research.
6 As a basis for decision support to health authorities, EBM is in no different a position than other methods or professional insights. To the extent that such choices are made at the policy level, EBM should play a pivotal role when it comes to choice of therapy. In other cases, EBM can provide the clinical premises on which to base more complex policy decisions.
7 Systematic reviews are worthy undertakings. It is, however, important to realise that their necessity arises only because medical doctors read scientific literature to too limited an extent. Systematic reviews are also necessary because medical research all too seldom starts by placing itself in the context of the valid information in the area to be studied. This would lead social scientists to say: 'OK, but only after us.'
8 Studies of barriers to use of evidence could be an interesting topic, but are of limited importance as a research question. We already know the answer. People use the information that suits them. If this issue were to be put on the research agenda, one would use organisational theory and social psychology to

explore it. One should be careful not to research issues for which one is not competent. Graduation from medical school does not qualify one for every task. For most topics, bookshelves are already filled with research reports. If researchers do not realise this, and start researching barriers to use of evidence, they will fall victim to the EBM principle of conducting a systematic review before embarking on a research programme.

9 Studies by and for the 'informed consumer' may be 'cosy and beneficial' for well-educated people in the middle of their lives. Studies of the 'informed consumer' might be relevant in market-oriented health care systems, but not in the welfare systems of Northern Europe. The latter ought to be paternalistic. If the 'consumer' should be empowered, one should do the opposite: influence the professions' attitude to the patients. Consumerism is radical in market-oriented North America, not in social democratic Northern Europe.

10 It is unfortunate that EBM has been allowed to colonise the health services and public health research at this institute.

Presented with the permission of Tor Inge Romøren.

EBM in a narrower perspective

Now that we have raised some doubts about EBM in a broader perspective, is EBM free from problems when it is considered in the context of its initial focus, i.e. searching into, sorting and synthesising evidence? Not necessarily, it would seem. Some of the problems go to the core of EBM: for example, the methods proposed for obtaining 'the best research evidence'. Chapters 6 and 7 offer detailed discussion, and here we mention just a few aspects.

The randomised controlled trial

EBM advocates have told their disciples that 'if you find [a] study that was not randomized, we'd suggest that you stop reading it and go on to the next article' (Sackett *et al.* 1997: 94). Dag Thelle explores the wisdom of this suggestion in Chapter 6. Let us discuss a few issues here. First, and most important, the superiority of the RCT is based on dogma, not proof in any scientific sense. There are good reasons to believe that an experiment in which patients are allocated randomly (to avoid selection bias) to modes of intervention, and in which both patients and evaluators are blinded as to what intervention the patient is receiving (to avoid bias in measuring effects, i.e. information bias), will reduce the likelihood of results being distorted. This is eminently reasonable, but it is not proven. Clearly, observational studies may be subject to selection bias as well as information bias. However, randomised trials may also be subject to bias. The fact that individuals know that they are being observed in a trial may change the effect of an intervention (Kaptchuk 2001). In some cases, it is impossible or nonsensical to blind individuals to the interventions. For example, it makes no sense to 'blind' doctors to the payment they receive in studies of effects of financial incentives. Knowing that one is involved in a trial may induce strategic behaviour on the part of the participants, and consequently distort the results. It is, then, conceivable that results from observational studies are less distorted because strategic behaviour is avoided. Since experimental as well as observational studies may be subject to bias, one would need some external 'gold standard' to establish which method is least biased. Since no gold standard exists, it follows that there can be no empirical proof. Some might want to argue that the RCT constitutes the gold standard. This, however, involves a circular argument. As it happens, we believe in the dogma, but our beliefs do not constitute a scientific proof.

In principle, an RCT is based on a random sample of individuals from a pre-specified population and the results of the trial are claimed to be (internally) valid for this population. If we examine the EBM and relevant epidemiological literature, it is clear that the focus of interest is that of concerns for internal validity and, in turn, measures to try to safeguard internal validity. Usually, little if anything is said about external validity, i.e. the extent to which results from one population can be generalised to others. In one textbook, it is simply stated that 'concerns about external validity do not lend themselves to quantification and will not be addressed' (Kleinbaum *et al.* 1982: 188). It seems reasonable that a type of cancer surgery that 'works' in France will also 'work' in the United States or China. The extent to which it 'works' may vary, however. It is even possible that what constitutes 'works' may vary culturally. Whether an osteoporosis drug with proven effects in white Americans also works in black Americans may be questioned on the basis of differences in bone metabolism. Even more questionable, will the effectiveness of financial incentives as shown in American doctors work for those in the United Kingdom or Japan? The external validity is most often taken for granted without requiring 'evidence'.

There may also be limitations associated with the RCT from a practical point of view. One important one may be feasibility: that is, ethical or practical considerations may make the RCT infeasible. An EBM advocate was once asked what to do when in practice it is impossible to undertake a randomised trial. The evangelical response was simple: 'Undertake a randomised trial!' Interestingly, this argument seems not to apply when EBM advocates are asked for evidence that the use of EBM improves patients' health. In a commentary on common criticisms of EBM, two observers state that 'no investigative team has yet overcome the problems of sample size, contamination and blinding that such a trial raises' (Straus and McAlister 2000: 839).

Against the background of these theoretical and practical problems, and other issues raised in Chapters 2 and 9, there is reason to feel less certain about the 'truths' found in RCTs. The superiority of the RCT rests on dogma. Archie Cochrane, we and many others *believe* that the design of RCTs is superior in many instances. But belief is not proof or evidence. In fact, Cochrane did not want to 'give the impression that it [the RCT] is the only technique of any value in medical research' (Cochrane 1972: 25).

Meta-analysis: the core of the truth?

It would be possible to argue that medical textbooks and traditional review articles in medicine used to be based on opinion and prejudice rather than knowledge (Bjorndal *et al.* 2000). To the extent that that statement is correct, it may be so because expert clinicians who write review articles draw on publications and information in some less than systematic way. In contrast, EBM requires explicit statements about the aim of the review, its strategies for searching information, and explicit criteria for including and excluding the results of studies identified. In any scientific work, there can be no argument against working systematically and being explicit about aims and methods. In fact, the Cochrane movement should be congratulated for drawing so much attention to systematic principles in conducting reviews. EBM, however, goes further than that. It also requires a synthesis of the 'evidence' to be made, and preferably that this synthesis be presented in terms of numbers ('meta-analysis') such as odds ratio or other measures of effectiveness. Meta-analysis can be defined as a systematic review of the literature that uses quantitative methods to summarise the results. The logo of the Cochrane Collaboration depicts what is meant

THE COCHRANE
COLLABORATION®

by a meta-analysis. Here, the results of seven different randomised trials are presented in terms of odds ratios, and each horizontal line represents the confidence interval for the odds ratio of the studies.

An odds ratio of 1 is indicated by the central vertical line. The results to the left of this indicate that patients in the intervention group fare better than the controls. While two of the studies resulted in 'significant' improvements from therapy, the others were not 'statistically significant', and raise doubts about the effectiveness of the therapy. This resulted in few obstetricians using corticosteroids until a meta-analysis made a numerical synthesis of the seven studies. This synthesis is represented by the diamond in the lower part of the logo: the horizontal length of the diamond represents the confidence interval of the effect size. This interval is very small, and well to the left of the vertical 'no-effect line'. In other words, there is little doubt that there is a positive effect when all seven studies are 'boiled down' in one meta-analysis. On the basis of this, the Cochrane Collaboration claims that 'tens of thousands of premature babies have probably suffered ... from failure to use systematic reviews' (www.cochrane.org). This argument is compelling, but the limitations of meta-analysis are worth noting.

First, when the meta-analyst has identified studies by various search strategies, he or she has to exclude studies that either are irrelevant or do not meet certain criteria of quality. If only randomised trials are included, quality criteria are available to judge whether the studies are worthy of being included or not. Here, the choice of a different set of criteria may result in different trials upon which the meta-analysis is based (Juni *et al.* 1999). There is, however, discussion in the scientific environment as to whether or not to include a wider range of study designs. Depending on the decision here, this will again influence the results.

Second, a basic principle in science is to compare like with like, but this is open to challenge. Trials may be different with respect to the patient groups included, patients may not be treated in exactly the same way, etc. Several factors may create heterogeneity in the analysis. This may be detected by statistical tests, but such tests tend not to be very sensitive.

Third, some relevant studies may be left out because they are not identified in the literature search or because they are published in a language that is not understood by the meta-analyst. Also, relevant studies may be left unpublished because the researchers or the funding body prefer that the work remains unpublished. Unfortunately, non-publication may be selective (Krzyzanowska *et al.* 2003), thus creating bias in the results of the meta-analysis. Publication bias may be suspected if the distribution of the effects in the meta-analysis is skewed, but cannot otherwise be remedied. A meta-analysis of the effects of passive smoking on lung cancer could leave the impression that the effect of passive smoking was exaggerated by publication bias (Copas and Shi 2000). This has been strongly denied by others (Glantz 2000). A recent study of passive smoking published in the same journal (the *British Medical Journal*) found no effect of passive smoking on lung cancer. If this large study were included in an updated meta-analysis, the overall result would be that passive smoking has a small and 'non-significant' effect (Enstrom and Kabat 2003). Because the authors of that study had received research grants from the tobacco industry, many would argue that its results should not be included. Our point here is not to draw any conclusions about passive smoking but rather to draw attention to the problems that authors and users of meta-analyses inevitably face.

Meta-analyses are supposed to be particularly useful when individual trials are too small for firm conclusions to be drawn. The meta-analysis presented on the Cochrane logo is a nice example. The extent to which such numerical syntheses represent unbiased effect estimates may be judged on the basis of later larger clinical trials. A classic example is the use of magnesium for acute myocardial infarction. A meta-analysis had indicated a positive effect on survival but a trial of 58,000 (!) patients did not indicate any effect (Anon. 1995b). More generally, meta-analyses seem to predict the results of subsequent large clinical trials only in two out of three cases. Interestingly, different meta-analyses of the same subject may reach different conclusions, even when the studies included are about the same (DerSimonian and Levine 1999; Lindbaek and Hjortdahl 1999).

Even if we disregard the problems mentioned above, the user of meta-analyses should be cautioned about the variation in interpretation of the results once the reviews are published. In a study of 160 completed Cochrane reviews, the inter-rater agreement between two experienced readers of the reviews was about 0.70 (when 0 indicates no agreement and 1.0 perfect agreement), while it was 0.32 for one reader and the authors (Ezzo *et al.* 2001). In general, the authors of the reviews were more optimistic about the therapy in question than the independent readers. The authors of this 'review of the reviews' conclude that 'inter-rater disagreements suggest a surprising degree of subjective interpretation involved in systematic reviews'.

Alchemists aimed to make gold out of base metals but they failed. The late editor of the *Journal of Clinical Epidemiology*, Alvan Feinstein, claimed that meta-analysis was 'statistical alchemy for the 21st century' (Feinstein 1995), and the editors of the *Lancet* claim they were 'unaware of the gold in [our] pages awaiting discovery by intellectual processes more intense than those of [our] own editors, referees, etc.' (Anon. 1995a: 785). No wonder, then, that meta-analyses do not always resolve disagreements, even within the Cochrane Collaboration. While Olsen and Gotzsche at the Nordic Cochrane Centre conclude that 'the currently available reliable evidence does not show a survival benefit of mass screening for breast cancer' (2001: 1), the editors of the Cochrane Breast Cancer Group (ibid.: 39) maintain that

> at this stage the editorial group has elected to publish the review of outcomes on mortality and breast-cancer mortality but defer presentation or discussion of results on changes in treatment (mastectomy, radiotherapy, etc.) until further editorial review has been completed.

Whatever one's opinions, the shortcomings of systematic reviews and meta-analyses are real.

Level of evidence

Those who subscribe to EBM often apply systems of 'level of evidence' to tease out decisions about interventions. There exist various scales for grading evidence, and, not surprisingly, the level of evidence for a specific policy or clinical issue will depend on which grading system is used (Ferreira *et al.* 2002). They all tend, however, to put the results of meta-analyses of several well-performed randomised trials at the top of the evidence hierarchy, while expert opinion or anecdotes are left at the bottom.

From Chapter 6 of this book, and from what we have said here about meta-analyses, we would maintain that there is no scientific proof that meta-analyses necessarily provide less biased results than, say, cohort studies. From arguments about likely bias in different study designs, we believe – in line with EBM advocates – that RCTs represent less bias. RCTs, however, have important limitations, and may on occasion yield more biased results than do other designs. There exists, to our knowledge, no proof either in logic or empirically of what is the best method for grading evidence. The fact that RCTs may yield results different from those of observational studies does not constitute a proof – unless one accepts the RCT as the gold standard. Therefore, the concept of 'level of evidence' is also based on dogma, not scientific proof.

A further relevant concern here arises over the practice of equating level of evidence with level of recommendation. Whether a specific intervention should be implemented – the normative question – should be answered not by scientists or clinicians but by patients or policy makers. The decision should be based not only on the likely outcome of an action – i.e. the issue addressed by EBM methods – but also on value judgements. The values of EBM practitioners and other professionals should not count more than the values of anyone else. For example, EBM methods can be used to judge the 'evidence' that passive smoking results in heart attacks and lung cancer. When politicians decide on policies to protect non-smokers against passive smoking, that decision should rest on an array of factors in addition to the evidence, and there is no reason to 'grade the recommendation' in line with any grading of the evidence.

Quantifying effectiveness

While EBM, in the narrow sense, rests on clinical expertise (best research evidence and patient values (Sackett *et al.* 2000)), the contribution of EBM to improving clinical expertise lies in its ability to help to interpret data from clinical trials better. In Chapter 8, Elstein claims that EBM rests on the notion that doctors are skilled decision makers, but need simple tools to improve their performance. One of these tools is the number needed to treat (NNT), which was introduced as a simple measure that would help doctors and patients to make better decisions. It was seen as a 'measure of immense clinical value' (Massel and Cruickshank 2002). It turns out that this 'evidence-based' tool is not easy to understand, nor is there much evidence that it helps doctors or patients to make better decisions than do other measures of effect. Rather, Chapter 7 describes how NNT has repeatedly been misunderstood by those who advocate using it, as well as by its potential users. There are several problems with NNT, but two are particularly pertinent. First, while NNT is most often used to express the effect of interventions for chronic disease processes in which *timing* of adverse events is crucial, NNT is measured at *one single point in time*, and is thus unable to capture aggregate effects over time. Also, NNT may vary considerably from time to time if it is measured repeatedly, a factor that will further reduce its utility. Second, the term 'number needed to treat' can leave the impression that adverse events are totally avoided. In chronic conditions it is more likely that adverse outcomes are postponed. This is certainly the case with respect to fatal outcomes! For the patient and/or the doctor, the distinction between avoidance and postponement may be crucial when making a decision. Research papers have drawn potentially misleading conclusions because of the misunderstandings surrounding NNT (Laupacis *et al.* 1988; Massel and Cruickshank 2002), and the metric has been used to develop new methodologies that make little sense (Sinclair *et al.* 2001).

There is no direct evidence that NNT helps patients, clinicians or others in making better decisions (see Chapter 7). In contrast, surveys of doctors and, in particular, lay people indicate that they do not understand NNT, certainly not fully. Interestingly, while NNT has become widely accepted in the medical community without any 'evidence' that it is better than other measures of health benefit, it is difficult to get papers that question NNT published, even in journals that specifically promote EBM.

EBM: method, collaboration, movement or crusade?

The Cochrane Collaboration is based on ten principles:

- collaboration;
- building on the enthusiasm of individuals;

- avoiding duplication;
- minimising bias;
- keeping up to date;
- ensuring relevance;
- ensuring access;
- continually improving the quality of its work;
- continuity;
- enabling wide participation.

Some of these principles imply that EBM is a scientific method (avoiding duplication, minimising bias), others that it is a collaboration (continuity, participation), while others still that it is a movement (enthusiasm, access). In Chapter 8, Arthur Elstein goes a step further and uses the term 'crusade'. This would be in line with the declaration 'I have joined the Cochrane Collaboration' expressed with the same type of enthusiasm as others use when they speak of 'the day Christ came to me'. The evangelical tone is even observed by the EBM advocates themselves. In a humorous piece about EBM in the *British Medical Journal*, the authors, who belong to the Cochrane movement, warn crusaders about 'retaliation from the grand inquisitors in the new religion of EBM' (Anon. 2002: 1496). Clearly, this crusade-like zeal is a reason why EBM and the Cochrane Collaboration have achieved so much in ten years. At the same time, it represents a problem for those who have yet to see the beauty of the method. It risks posing a threat to the movement itself.

Just as interesting as the items on the list of Cochrane principles are those that are not there. Why not 'be sceptical' when that is part of the judgement about 'evidence', whether in court or in science? Why not 'oppose the pharmaceutical industry' when the anti-industry sentiment is so clear? Even though the Cochrane Brochure promotes some drug therapies specifically, EBM advocates are more often critical of pharmaceuticals. In a paper about the interaction between physicians and the pharmaceutical industry, advocates of EBM condemned the use of relative risk reduction when expressing benefits from drug therapy because it 'overstates' the benefits (Moynihan *et al.* 2000). Nevertheless, the authors recommend using relative risk reduction when implementing certain public health policies. Recently, the *British Medical Journal* published a discussion within the Cochrane Collaboration about problems associated with receiving money from commercial sources, but no mention was made of the potential that other sponsors may have to influence the movement (Moynihan 2003). There are good reasons to be concerned about the influence of commercial interests on health policies, but anti-industry ideologies would be better stated explicitly. The movement may well learn from its founding father, Archie Cochrane, who stated his own ideology very explicitly: 'I am emotionally in favour of the idea of an NHS [National Health Service]' (Cochrane 1972).

A potential side effect of the crusade flavour may be that it deters some practitioners who would otherwise support the basic ideas. Interestingly, many of the better-known advocates of EBM do not have backgrounds in biostatistics or epidemiology, which are the scientific disciplines that are closest to the core of the EBM methods. Conversely, many of those who do have such backgrounds are not involved in the Cochrane Collaboration, even though they may teach RCT methodology or meta-analysis. Typically, such scientists share Archie Cochrane's fundamental scepticism and have difficulties in being faithful, whether it is to a belief in 'wonderful medical progress' or in EBM.

The crusades of the twelfth and thirteenth centuries brought large numbers of people to the holy wars against the 'infidels'. The success of the EBM movement has been remarkable in the sense that the term is on everybody's lips, and all sorts of evidence-based enterprises have emerged. The number who actually enrol in the army is more limited. The number attending the annual Cochrane Colloquium is about 1,000, and a few hundred abstracts are submitted. This modest interest stands in contrast to other 'world conferences' of general medical interest. The annual meetings of North American societies for cardiology or rheumatology gather typically 10,000 participants, with thousands of scientific abstracts submitted. Industry sponsoring of doctors attending the latter types of conferences may explain in part the contrast in size, and doctors may fancy 'world congresses' more than 'colloquia'. Nevertheless, the great majority of medical doctors remain at arm's length from the EBM movement. The slow production of the Cochrane reviews may also be an indication of a lack of enthusiasm among the many. Of about 3,100 entries of Cochrane reviews, as many as 1,300 are protocols, and not yet finished reviews. Searching the Cochrane Library for Cochrane reviews, using for example the search term 'osteoporosis' in the title, results in 8 completed reviews and 11 in process (February 2003). For the 8 completed reviews, the most recent update was as of February 2002 and the earliest from 1998. The 'mean age' of the reviews was 34 months. Taking into account the fact that reviews in practice experience difficulties in including papers that have been published later than 6–12 months prior to the publication of the review, users of the Cochrane Library will inevitably find outdated or uncompleted 'evidence'.

Final comments

EBM and the Cochrane movement represent some excellent ideas and practices (see Box 1.2). They also have limitations and shortcomings. A frequent criticism is that EBM advocates 'cookbook medicine'. We do not agree with this criticism. First, it has been repeatedly shown that medical practice varies greatly, and more than can be justified in terms of variations in patient preferences (for a review, see Andersen and Mooney 1990). Since two or more different ways of treating a medical condition

Box 1.2 Some key points about EBM

Most will be sympathetic to the ideas that:

- literature searches should be systematic rather than non-systematic;
- decision makers could use existing information better than is currently the case;
- clinicians should use updated databases when seeking medical information interventions;
- more experimental empirical research is needed, especially in the context of clinical medicine.

Not everyone is convinced that:

- RCTs are always superior to observational studies;
- meta-analyses will always provide the 'truth';
- EBM will necessarily improve patient outcomes – at least until there is evidence for it;
- EBM is useful in health policy or that medicine alone is a good theoretical foundation for health policy;
- doctors have great training or expertise in making decisions about complex phenomena or eliciting patient preferences.

Some will oppose the ideas that:

- there is *one truth* – and it is found in RCTs and meta-analyses;
- improving health is all that matters in health care.

cannot each be best in terms of outcome and costs, some sorts of guidelines are needed. Second, anybody interested in good food would know that goodness is dependent upon a combination of tastes on the part of the consumer, and art, excellent raw materials and skilful processing on the provider's side. A good recipe will be of great help to most cooks. Our concern about EBM is not rooted in the idea of collecting recipes in a 'cookbook', but rather in the ingredients themselves.

Important ingredients are the randomised controlled trial, the meta-analysis and doctors' clinical expertise. These are dogmas to which many patients, health practitioners and policy makers will subscribe. Rather than explicitly warning about the limitations of the EBM methods, the Cochrane Collaboration in its web-based brochure invites people to subscribe to its principles. This seems to have been successful in creating a movement or a crusade. The crusade strategy may, however, prove disadvantageous when clinicians and others learn the methods' limitations and loose faith in the dogmas.

While Archie Cochrane and initially the Cochrane Collaboration aimed at improving clinical decisions, the scope has been widened to education, health care and health policy in general. With this wider scope, EBM is leaving an area where it has its core expertise, and moving into territory that requires more than biostatistics, epidemiology and faith. It is likely that social scientists and others have relevant theories and insights that are not learned in medical school or on courses in biostatistics or epidemiology. It would be unfortunate if the wider scope and ambitions that now seem to drive EBM were to move the focus away from those areas where EBM has a real contribution to make to those where other scientists are better equipped. Modest ambitions and more modest attitudes, more in line with Archie Cochrane's personality, among advocates of EBM would benefit the movement and public spending, as well as people's health.

Finally, but most important, we need to see convincing evidence that EBM improves patients' health. Knut Rasmussen's reflections are not promising in this respect (see Chapter 11). By better health we mean longer life or better quality of life. We suppose that everybody would reject the idea that blood pressure, doctor behaviour or other proxy variables should be accepted as measures of improved health. What we are looking forward to see, is real evidence. While we are awaiting such evidence, the 'gift from the gods' needs to take its rightful place.

References

Andersen, T.F. and Mooney, G. (1990) *Medical Practice Variations: Where Are We?* London: Macmillan.

Anon. (1995a) Evidence-based medicine, in its place, *Lancet*, 346: 785.

Anon. (1995b) ISIS-4: a randomised factorial trial assessing early oral captopril, oral mononitrate, and intravenous magnesium sulphate in 58,050 patients with suspected acute myocardial infarction. ISIS-4 (Fourth International Study of Infarct Survival) Collaborative Group, *Lancet*, 345: 669–85.

Anon. (2002) EBM: unmasking the ugly truth, *British Medical Journal*, 325: 1496–8.

Bjorndal, A., Flottorp, S. and Klovning, A. (2000) *Management of Medical Knowledge* (in Norwegian), Oslo: Gyldendal Akademisk.

Cochrane, A.L. (1972) *Effectiveness and Efficiency: Random Reflections on Health Services*, London: Nuffield Provincial Hospitals Trust.

Copas, J.B. and Shi, J.Q. (2000) Reanalysis of epidemiological evidence on lung cancer and passive smoking, *British Medical Journal*, 320: 417–18.

DerSimonian, R. and Levine, R.J. (1999) Resolving discrepancies between a meta-analysis and a subsequent large controlled trial, *Journal of the American Medical Association*, 282: 664–70.

Enstrom, J.E. and Kabat, G.C. (2003) Environmental tobacco smoke and tobacco related mortality in a prospective study of Californians, 1960–98, *British Medical Journal*, 326: 1057–60.

Ezzo, J., Bausell, B., Moerman, D.E., Berman, B. and Hadhazy, V. (2001) Reviewing the reviews. How strong is the evidence? How clear are the conclusions?, *International Journal of Technology Assessment Health Care*, 17: 457–66.

Feinstein, A.R. (1995) Meta-analysis: statistical alchemy for the 21st century, *Journal of Clinical Epidemiology*, 48: 71–9.

Ferreira, P.H., Ferreira, M.L., Maher, C.G., Refshauge, K., Herbert, R.D. and Latimer, J. (2002) Effect of applying different 'levels of evidence' criteria on conclusions of Cochrane reviews of interventions for low back pain, *Journal of Clinical Epidemiology*, 55: 1126–9.

Glantz, S.A. (2000) Lung cancer and passive smoking: nothing new was said, *British Medical Journal*, 321: 1222–3.

Greenhalgh, T. (2001) *How to Read a Paper: The Basics of Evidence Based Medicine*, London: BMJ Books.

Juni, P., Witschi, A., Bloch, R. and Egger, M. (1999) The hazards of scoring the quality of clinical trials for meta-analysis, *Journal of the American Medical Association*, 282: 1054–60.

Kaptchuk, T.J. (2001) The double-blind, randomized, placebo-controlled trial: gold standard or golden calf?, *Journal of Clinical Epidemiology*, 54: 541–9.

Kernick, D.P. (1998) Lies, damned lies, and evidence-based medicine, *Lancet*, 351: 1824.

Kleinbaum, D.G., Kupper, L.L. and Morgenstern, H. (1982) *Epidemiologic Research*, New York: Van Nostrand Reinhold.

Krzyzanowska, M.K., Pintilie, M. and Tannock, I.F. (2003) Factors associated with failure to publish large randomized trials presented at an oncology meeting, *Journal of the American Medical Association*, 290: 495–501.

Laupacis, A., Sackett, D.L. and Roberts, R.S. (1988) An assessment of clinically useful measures of the consequences of treatment, *New England Journal of Medicine*, 318 (26): 1728–33.

Lindbaek, M. and Hjortdahl, P. (1999) How do two meta-analyses of similar data reach opposite conclusions?, *British Medical Journal*, 318: 873–4.

Massel, D. and Cruickshank, M.K. (2002) The number remaining at risk: an adjunct to the number needed to treat, *Canadian Journal of Cardiology*, 18 (3): 254–8.

Moynihan, R. (2003) Cochrane at crossroads over drug company sponsorship, *British Medical Journal*, 327: 924–6.

Moynihan, R., Bero, L., Ross-Degnan, D. *et al.* (2000) Coverage by the news media of the benefits and risks of medications, *New England Journal of Medicine*, 342: 164–50.

Olsen, O. and Gotzsche, P.C. (2001) Screening for breast cancer with mammography, *Cochrane Database Systematic Review*, no. 4: CD001877.

Sackett, D.L., Richardson, W.S., Rosenberg, W. and Haynes, R.B. (1997) *Evidence-Based Medicine: How to Practice and Teach EBM*, New York: Churchill Livingstone.

Sackett, D.L., Rosenberg, W.M., Gray, J.A., Haynes, R.B. and Richardson, W.S. (1996) Evidence based medicine: what it is and what it isn't, *British Medical Journal*, 312: 71–2.

Sackett, D.L., Straus, S.E., Rosenberg, W. and Haynes, R.B. (2000) *Evidence-Based Medicine: How to Practice and Teach EBM*, New York: Churchill Livingstone.

Sinclair, J.C., Cook, R.J., Guyatt, G.H., Pauker, S.G. and Cook, D.J. (2001) When should an effective treatment be used? Derivation of the threshold number needed to treat and the minimum event rate for treatment, *Journal of Clinical Epidemiology*, 54: 253–62.

Straus, S.E. and McAlister, F.A. (2000) Evidence-based medicine: a commentary on common criticisms, *Canadian Medical Association Journal*, 163: 837–41.

2 Evidence, effectiveness and ethics

Cochrane's legacy

Uffe Juul Jensen

Introduction

Recent adherents of evidence-based medicine recognise varieties of evidence(Sackett *et al.* 1997). It is, however, manifest that epidemiology and statistics in general and randomly controlled clinical trials (RCTs) in particular have shaped the ideal of evidence-based medicine that has dominated the discussion about rational health care during the past 30 years. Some elevate the RCT to a gold standard of rational medical practice.

Philosophers of science in general have abandoned the idea that there is only one particular method, which deserves to be called *the* scientific method. Sometimes such an idea is even ridiculed as *methodological fetishism.*[1] The canonisation of the RCT as the gold standard of scientific medicine appears to be a revival of an old methodological fetishism within medicine.

In 1972 A.L. Cochrane, physician and director of the MRC Epidemiological Unit, Cardiff, published his 'random reflections on health services', *Effectiveness and Efficiency*. It is a small book but rich in content. It is a defence of the United Kingdom's National Health Service (NHS) but also a critical examination of its performance, with ideas for improving it. Cochrane praises the introduction of the RCT and tells how his turning to epidemiology provided him with new and important means for analysing and critiquing medicine and health care. In this chapter I shall argue that Cochrane's advocacy of the RCT must be seen in the context of a philosophy of medicine and health care. The content of this philosophy and Cochrane's ways of arguing are, it appears, opposed to methodological fetishism. Understanding his complex perspectives opens our eyes, I shall argue, to important challenges facing modern health care systems, challenges that cannot be met only by canons of scientific rationality.

Cochrane ends his reflections by quoting Agatha in T.S. Eliot's *The Family Reunion*, who wanted action 'Not for the good that it will do / But that nothing may be left undone / On the margin of the impossible.' It is Cochrane's expectation that future clinicians will abandon the pursuit of the 'margin of the impossible'. Instead, they should settle for 'reasonable probability'. By that time, there would be, Cochrane ends, 'a whole rational health service to gain'. To achieve this, his reflections make clear, much more than rigid scientific methods are needed.

Effectiveness and Efficiency is a personal but carefully argued examination of a health care system built upon ethical ideals but, according to Cochrane, on a dangerous route to decline. Thirty years later, in 1992, James Le Fanu published his *The Rise and Fall of Modern Medicine*, a book much larger than Cochrane's, but also based upon personal experiences and critical examination of modern medicine and health care. Le Fanu's conclusions are, however, in some crucial respects completely contrary to Cochrane's.

For Cochrane, medicine at the beginning of the 1970s was close to running amok – driven by a desire to offer still more therapies to patients desiring still more therapies. In Fanu's retrospective gaze, there were no severe symptoms of clinical crisis at the beginning of the 1970s. What to Cochrane were symptoms of a fatal disease of the health care system, to Le Fanu were signs of a glorious future. 'By the close of the 1960s', he writes, 'medicine's astonishing progress over the previous quarter-century was building to a climax' (ibid.: 241). He recalls 'the optimism and enthusiasm' of the period around 1970. The hospital expanded, recruiting specialists with an interest in new treatments. 'Medicine had matured into a highly sophisticated enterprise, with an intellectual energy and resources to deal with the whole range of human illness' (ibid.: 242). What went wrong, according to Le Fanu? During the 1970s and through to the end of the century, there was a declining interest in medical research. Epidemiology and social science during this period had gained a still more central role in medicine and medical thinking.

Cochrane had based his expectations on epidemiology. Le Fanu, almost 30 years later, wanted to expel epidemiology from medicine. Cochrane as well as Le Fanu salutes the RCT as an indispensable tool for developing a rational medicine So, their different and in some respects even contradictory assessments of medicine at the end of the twentieth century – and in the period when RCT came to play a central role in medicine – demand close scrutiny. I shall argue that their contradictory assessments of medicine are due to their having completely different philosophies of medicine – that is, different perspectives, first, of what disease is, the place of disease in nature and in human life; and second, of human and social life in general. I shall further argue that in any serious discussion about evidence-based medicine or rational health care, such broader frameworks should be made explicit and made the subject of critical examination.

Are doctors superfluous?[2]

Cochrane's book has a special importance, partly because he so explicitly articulates his philosophy (without calling it such). Le Fanu tends to mask his perspectives as those of medical science *per se*. By contrasting the two accounts, I hope to lay open to closer examination the philosophical perspectives that they embody.

Cochrane does not ground his plea for a more rational NHS in any abstract principle of rationality or universal scientific method. He openly presents his own biases. 'I am', he admits, 'emotionally in favour of the idea of an NHS' (1972: 4). He is quite explicit about the causes behind this attitude: the social injustices he witnessed in the 1930s. Later, Cochrane travelled widely. In 1971, he still believed that the NHS was 'the best of a very poor lot'. His account of efficiency and effectiveness is, however, not only rooted in general ethical-political principles. He also reveals his views on medicine and human disease in particular and human suffering in general. These are, it appears, shaped by very personal experiences. Cochrane was for four years a prisoner of war in German hands. As a senior medical officer he took care of 20,000 other prisoners of war in a camp at Salonika. The diet provided only 600 kilocalories a day. All had diarrhoea. The camp was ravaged by various epidemics. Cochrane had few interventions at his disposal: some aspirin and a few other things. Under the best conditions, one would, he says, have expected 'an appreciable mortality'. There were, however, only four deaths (and three of these were due to gunshot wounds). Cochrane does not appropriate the credit for this to himself. On the contrary, he sums up his experience as follows: 'It demonstrated . . . very clearly the relative unimportance of therapy in comparison with the recuperative power of the human body' (ibid.: 5). In the following, I shall refer to this hypothesis as RuT (the relative unimportance of therapy).

This claim is a key to understanding what I would call his philosophy of medicine. But what does he mean by 'demonstrate'? He cannot be using the word in a strictly logical sense. It is clearly not possible on the basis of a particular experience to deduce a general conclusion about the relative unimportance of therapy.

Cochrane was certainly not a methodologically naïve person who used epistemologically loaded terms in a loose way. The reader needs then to ponder: what could Cochrane possibly mean by talking about experience *demonstrating* his radical conclusion?

Different kinds of evidence

Cochrane dedicates a whole chapter to the question of how to evaluate evidence. He contrasts opinion and evidence, and complains about striking changes in word usage during the 1950s and 1960s. Opinion, he claims, has been upgraded in comparison with other types of evidence. 'Experiment', on the other hand, has been downgraded. He blames television interviewers for this development. When, Cochrane asks polemically, did we ever hear a television interviewer ask anyone what his evidence was for some particular statement?

It is clear to Cochrane, as it should be to anybody else who is interested in medicine, that the question of evidence is not something new and revolutionary in medicine.[3] He reminds us that the oldest 'and probably still the commonest form of evidence proffered, is clinical evidence' (ibid.: 20). Its value varies with the ability of the clinician and the breadth of his or her experience. In general, however, its value must be rated low, Cochrane stresses, 'because there is no quantitative measurement, no attempt to discover what would have happened if the patients had had no treatment' (ibid.: 20–1).

However, bearing in mind Cochrane's bold hypothesis about the relative unimportance of therapy, the reader may still be rather confused. The hypothesis seems to be based on rather limited clinical experience in the camp. Cochrane even admits that he has rather limited clinical experience in general.

Having expressed his views on 'opinion', he then briefly discusses the value of observation in justifying general hypotheses. Moving to the observational level, he says that 'the main changes introducing improvements are the appearance of "comparison" groups, the introduction of measurement and the exclusion of possible bias from the measurements' (ibid.: 21).

As already indicated, Cochrane does not discuss the status of RuT and the evidence on which it is based. Referring to his own classification of evidence, we might interpret it as being based upon observation rather than opinion. Cochrane expected hundreds to die of diphtheria in the absence of specific therapy. This expectation was probably based on comparison with what he considered to be matching groups. In discussing the value of observation in general, however, he warns the reader against estimating its value too highly. Comparison groups are, he says, a 'very mixed lot'. This would be a relevant objection to RuT interpreted as an 'observation'. We do not know and cannot know with whom Cochrane tacitly compared the prisoners in the camp.

Cochrane would not fight hard to get RuT recognised as being based upon observation. Though better than opinion, observational evidence is thoroughly unsatisfactory (ibid.: 21). He draws from this the further conclusion that all research on effectiveness of therapy 'was in an unfortunate state until the early 1950s', only excluding from this harsh verdict drugs (such as insulin, sulphonamide and penicillin) whose effects on mortality were so manifest that no trials were necessary. According to Cochrane, the turning point came in 1952. He associates it with the publication of Daniel and Hill's famous paper 'Chemotherapy of pulmonary tuberculosis in young adults: an analysis of the combined results of three Medical

Research Council trials.' The victory over loose clinical evidence based upon opinion and feeble observational evidence is won by means of one powerful weapon: the RCT.

Cochrane's sceptical claim about therapy (RuT) is certainly not based on the RCT. Nor it appears, is it based upon opinion, observation or experimental evidence. RuT is a claim of a more general, philosophical kind, a way of summing up critical reflections on medical practice in both a historical and contemporary perspective. He refers to 'the straightforward story of the ineffectiveness of medical therapy historically' (ibid.: 8). To support this claim, he refers to McKeown and Lowe and their demonstration that 'environmental factors themselves were important in improving vital statistics up to the end of the nineteenth century and until the second quarter of this century therapy had very little effect on morbidity and mortality' (ibid.).

Cochrane's critical attitude to therapy is not just based upon therapeutic shortcomings. He refers explicitly to *the recuperative power of the human body* and later, when critically discussing 'laymen's uncritical belief in the medical profession', he explicitly reminds us of 'the tendency of many diseases to disappear spontaneously or improve with time'. In the same context he talks about 'the general placebo effect', and while, strangely enough, he does not discuss the possible interrelationship between the natural recuperative power and the clinically constructed placebo effect, the moral is clear.

Cochrane's critical examination of clinical practice is based upon some general philosophical assumptions. These (including RuT) are presuppositions of his analysis and are not themselves the object of analysis. When Cochrane talks about demonstrating RuT from his experiences in the camp, he is not, of course, pretending to have proved the claim deductively. He is, I think, using 'demonstration' in a straightforward, ordinary way. Teachers demonstrate scientific laws or principles in the classroom. This does not imply that they are engaged to justifying or corroborating laws or principles. It is already presupposed that the laws or principles being demonstrated embody our knowledge about some part of physical nature. Cochrane is in a similar way demonstrating a philosophical perspective – that is, giving examples of general medical knowledge. In the following, I shall contrast his philosophy with another philosophical approach to medicine and clinical practice.

Contrasting philosophies of medicine

Cochrane's call for randomly controlled clinical trials is not motivated by any aspiration to pave the way to a golden land of absolute medical truths – a land in which biomedical therapy will eventually free us all from disease and misery. On the contrary, his critical gaze is directed primarily against therapeutic optimism – that is, the belief that if medicine were to adhere to the canons of science, it would free us from the grip of disease. He puts the burden of proof on the shoulders of those who represent biomedical knowledge. He apparently accepts as 'common knowledge' that diseases come and often go without biomedical intervention. Taking this as a given, we then have good reasons for demanding evidence from those who claim to provide effective therapy. Cochrane is a sceptic, but not in a radical epistemological sense – that is, a person who questions the possibility of knowledge at all. According to my interpretation, his sceptical examination is carried out in the light of and under the presupposition of his implicit philosophy of medicine. This philosophy implies that we share a body of medical knowledge: not knowledge articulated in deductively structured theories, but a knowledge embodied in and accumulated through our dealings with ailments and diseases throughout history.

To clarify my interpretation of Cochrane's position further, let me contrast it with another perspective on medicine and the RCT. In that contrasting perspective, results of RCTs are interpreted as preliminary, and in some respects problematical, steps to rational treatment. The RCT cannot in itself disclose causal mechanisms. If an RCT is carried out and interpreted carefully, we can, however, rely on its results *until* we get causal knowledge.

Such an interpretation presupposes in its most radical form an essentialist conception of disease, i.e. diseases understood as specific entities or malfunctions caused by specific biological conditions. I take Le Fanu as a spokesman of such medical essentialism ([1992] 1999: 382). He does not explicitly connect his hesitant advocacy of the RCT with a radical essentialist and mono-causal conception of human disease. Nor, however, does he leave the reader much in doubt about his general outlook. In a chapter called 'The unsolved problem: the mysteries of biology revisited', Le Fanu correctly points out that medicine's post-Second World War success was won without understanding 'the nature or the causation of the disease' (ibid.: 383). He compares contemporary medicine with the situation of mid-nineteenth-century medicine. There were a whole series of diseases (anthrax, gonorrhoea, cholera, diphtheria, etc.) whose causes were unknown. Robert Koch and his colleagues a few decades later 'discovered the precise bacteria responsible for each and every one'. Continuing this, Le Fanu, without much ado, predicts that 'Similarly, it has to be presumed that some types of as yet elusive biological agents must explain why one person gets multiple sclerosis, another rheumatic arthritis and a third schizophrenia. But what are they?' (ibid.: 383). It would not have been especially interesting if Le Fanu had only predicted that future discoveries would reveal how biological mechanisms play some role in the diseases mentioned. But Le Fanu is actually advocating a strong, mono-causal conception of disease.

In contrast to medical essentialism, Cochrane's position can be characterised as *medical pluralism*. Diseases have multiple causes. Sometimes we can, if we are lucky, cure them by therapy. Sometimes they just come and go. There are good reasons for characterising medicine as the art of making decisions under uncertainty. We should not hope for absolute knowledge. But less can do.

Cochrane does not refer only to his experiences at the camp in Salonika. He reveals to the reader another experience from his life as a prisoner of war. In a camp at Elsterhost, all the prisoners had tuberculosis. For most of them, it was far advanced. The conditions were not too bad. Because of Red Cross parcels, all got sufficient food. It was possible to screen all patients and do sputum 'smears'. Cochrane collaborated with a French physiologist. They were together with the patients day in and day out. Even during the nights, they were in the same building as the patients. Thus, they had an intimate knowledge of the patients and their condition. Cochrane tells how he was presented with pamphlets assumed to be suitable for medical officers who were prisoners of war, pamphlets that praised 'clinical freedom and democracy'. But Cochrane would happily have given up some of his freedom for more knowledge. 'My trouble was', he says, 'that I did not know which [therapy] to use and when' (1972: 6). At that time, Cochrane had never heard about controlled clinical trials. He knew, however, that there was no evidence that anything they had to offer had any effect on tuberculosis. He was even afraid that he shortened the lives of some of the patients by unnecessary intervention.

Later in the chapter on effectiveness and efficiency, Cochrane mentions drug therapy of tuberculosis as an example of a therapy supported by RCT. This does not, however, contradict Cochrane's general attitude to disease and health care. Above, I have labelled his approach pluralist. I have done this because Cochrane understands human diseases as complex phenomena to be accounted for within a framework of interrelated biological, social and cultural processes. This implies a rejection of classical essentialist and ontological conceptions of disease which interpret disease as breaks in the natural order. Further, it implies a rejection of monocausal conceptions and a defence of multi-factorial understanding of disease. Under specific circumstances and under the presupposition of relevant and adequate results of RCTs, it is rational to treat diseases by biomedical intervention, e.g. by drugs. Preventive strategies attacking other causes of the disease might, however, be shown to be more rational.

Cure and care

Will acceptance of effectiveness and efficiency as indices of therapy in the long run not result in denying care for the elderly and the disabled, including the mentally ill, psycho-social rehabilitation, etc.? How would it remain possible to defend and sustain services composed of activities or interactions that defy assessment in accordance with canonised standards?

Cochrane is quite aware of this problem. To resolve it, he points to an important distinction between cure and care. In the introductory chapter of his book, he points out that the NHS on the one hand supplies therapy, on the other hand 'board and lodging and tender, loving care' (Cochrane 1972: 3). He further stresses that the two indices which are his main focus (effectiveness and efficiency) are relevant when assessing therapy, but only to a limited extent when assessing care. To compare the two branches and 'to add a little humanity' to his approach, he needs a third standard: *equality*.

Here, as in other contexts, Cochrane gives explicit reasons for the standards he recommends. His enthusiasm for equality goes back to his experiences in the 1930s. He recalls differences in the medical care of the rich and the poor. While reminding us of the limitations of curing therapies, he stresses that 'the need for care is widespread' (ibid.: 7). In that light, his views on equality become especially important.

What, according to Cochrane, is equality? What kinds of evidence are relevant in controversies about equality of care? Cochrane is not very explicit about this. He does not present a general account, let alone an analysis of equality (as he does of effectiveness and efficiency). He makes it clear, however, that equality is a complex concept that means different things in different contexts. He is most explicit about the meaning of equality in the context of therapy and cure. He addresses briefly the question of social class inequalities in the NHS (ibid.: 70). There undoubtedly used to be gross inequalities, he says. Over the years, however, things have improved a lot. In that context, he mentions the British government's *Surveys of Sickness*. From 1945 to 1952 they showed an important increase in the use of GPs by the lower-income groups. He briefly discusses inequalities between geographical regions in the allocation of hospital beds. The examples illustrate inequalities in the use of and in access to service. These kinds of inequalities are, however, not the main interest when focusing on care as something over and above the therapy provided. How should quality of *care* – understood in this basic sense of the word – be assessed?

Cochrane is quite aware that we face this problem in the hospital setting. The hospital does not only offer the patient therapy. The patient also gets food, heating, lighting, decoration and comfort (ibid.: 73). Cochrane points to inequalities 'between the standard of living in an acute hospital on the one hand and psychiatric, geriatric, and mentally deficient institutes on the other' (ibid.: 73).

I cannot here get into a discussion of the relevance of this problem in the real world of heath care. Let us assume, however, that there are inequalities of the kind mentioned by Cochrane. On what kind of evidence or reasons could such inequalities be justified? According to Cochrane, effectiveness and efficiency are not adequate standards for assessing care. So, we can conclude that he would not base his assessment upon statistical evidence (i.e. evidence showing that care would contribute to prolonging the lives of fatally ill patients). It appears that his critique of existing inequalities is based on experience. 'The longer I stay anywhere the more careful I am about accommodation. I can put up with practically any hotel for one night, but I am fussy when it comes to two weeks. If the rest of the life came in question I would be very fussy indeed' (ibid.). He appeals to personal experience or attitudes. But he assumes, apparently, that this is a common human experience, not a private, idiosyncratic one.

Cochrane demonstrates, through a brief recourse to history, *why* there are inequalities of the sort mentioned here. The hospitals for the chronically sick, he points out, are descendants of the poor-law institutions. The general hospitals, on the other hand, were formerly honorary hospitals ruled by 'honoraries'. Owing to their wealth and power in the royal colleges, they were able to secure higher standards of living in the hospitals where they worked compared with those in local authority hospitals. These reflections, though brief, show that Cochrane considers it a myth that structure and organisation of health care systems are the result of scientific reasoning under the guidance of high ethical standards. He is very much aware of the role of power (especially the power of physicians and their organisations) in the development of health care systems. His struggle to get effectiveness, efficiency and equality recognised as governing standards in health care systems is very much motivated by his wish to limit the power of his own profession.

Equality and human vulnerability

Cochrane espouses his commitment to equality in care just as strongly as he articulates his support for effective and efficient therapy. But he does not discuss or analyse equality as carefully as these two indices. Though Cochrane does not say so explicitly, the reader may suspect that he conceives of equality as a less rational or universally binding principle than effectiveness and efficiency. In one particular context he seems directly to subordinate equality to these principles. He considers a possible defence of higher standards of living in general hospitals compared with other hospitals. The general hospital, his defence claims, merits this because it is more effective. It alters the natural history of disease and thereby allows people to return to productive work (Cochrane 1972: 73). If district general hospitals were 'powerhouses of effective treatment efficiently administrated there would be something to be said for this argument', Cochrane says.

Such a conclusion, however, would contradict Cochrane's own understanding of the principle of equality of care. As we have seen, he argued that care should be distributed according to need (as illustrated by his defence of the view that the longer we stay in an institution, the more continuous care we need).

In another context, Cochrane articulates more explicitly ethical reasons for a principle of equality. Criticising the view that patients in long-stay hospitals, on average, are not as sensitive to standards of living as those in district general hospitals, Cochrane adds that these people are 'our brothers and sisters, our cousins and our aunts', and may very likely someday be ourselves (ibid.: 75).

This defence of equality fits well into what I have called his general philosophy of medicine. We are vulnerable not just as possible victims of diseases, understood as malfunctionings that occasionally hit some of us, but also as independent and autonomous agents. Vulnerability and dependency on other people are part of the basic human condition.[5] This contributes to explaining why it is rational to adopt equality as a principle for organising health care.

Evidence-based medicine: scientific awakening or bureaucratic control?

The call in recent years for evidence-based medicine has generated elements of strife among those concerned with health care and the organisation of health care systems. Critics connect the demand for evidence-based medicine and the RCT with recent attempts by politicians and bureaucrats to limit the freedom of physicians by implementing standards and programmes and abandoning procedures that are not based upon scientific evidence. It is widely accepted that the RCT is a necessary scientific tool to be used by medical researchers and clinicians struggling to raise the scientific status and credibility of medicine. From this perspective, however, the RCT and other epidemiological procedures create problems when social scientists and bureaucrats, without the medical insight and ethical stance of the physician, appropriate the physician's tools, thereby limiting his or her clinical freedom. This is Le Fanu's diagnosis of what he considers to be a crisis in and fall of contemporary medicine.

Cochrane's book makes it clear that things are more complex and mixed than they might at first appear in any picture portraying in black and white the good guys of medicine and the bad guys of social science, administration and politics. The book contains a strong critique of traditional clinical freedom. He seeks support to strengthen the pressure on medicine to use effectiveness and efficiency as indices in assessing therapy and to get equality respected as a basic ethical principle of health care.

When Cochrane wrote his book, the RCT was already recognised as a gold standard in assessing the quality of drugs. However, this had not come about as a result of a peaceful process within the scientific community. During long periods in the twentieth century, there was much struggling and striving around medicine, on the one hand to get the RCT recognised and on the other to limit its influence.[6]

Cochrane addressed his colleagues, physicians, continuing to believe that they would be able to develop the NHS in a more efficient and equitable way. One part of his legacy, his insistence on experimental documentation of efficiency of therapies, has been widely acclaimed. The other part, his plea for a health care system that cares for patients even when no efficient therapy is available, has not been a part of the ethos of the medical profession in the late twentieth century.

Cochrane tried to sustain and later to revive a classical medical ideal: that the physician should be modest. The physician has only limited methods and means for cure and must also rely on nature's own healing powers. In the last decades of the twentieth century, however, this classical ideal was gradually replaced by an idol of biomedical almightiness supported by predictions of forthcoming biomedical breakthroughs.

Rational health care presupposes more than clinical skills, experimental knowledge and a justifiable ethical stance. Rational practice must also be self-critical and self-reflexive to reveal old myths and prejudices. One such myth is that medicine until recently has been governed by physicians guided only by clinical experience and inherited medical ethics. The truth is that medicine has always been deeply embedded in social and political practice and influenced by economic interests. The power of physicians was never grounded only in knowledge (clinical or experimental) and ethical principles; there were much more mundane forces too. This is not at all a new insight. For example, Immanuel Kant, one of the greatest philosophers of all time, discussed the role of medicine and medical knowledge in relation to political power.

Medicine and political power: a fragile harmony

In one of his later works, *The Conflict of the Faculties* (1979),[7] Kant discussed the role of medicine as a profession and a science. As with law and theology, medicine belongs to the higher faculties. These are faculties which the government can use to achieve its own ends of influencing people (ibid.: 31): 'first comes the eternal well-being of each, then the civil well-being as a member of society, and finally his physical well-being (a long life and health)'. By teaching the first of these, the government can exercise great influence and guide the intentions of its subjects. This is the task of theology. Law manages teachings that help to keep public conduct 'under the reins of public law'. Medicine is taught to make sure that the government will have 'strong and numerous people to serve its purposes'.

According to Kant, there is no conflict between the interest of government or state and the interest of citizens. People consider medicine to be the most important of the three higher faculties because it contributes to prolonging their lives.

Kant has a very realistic view of the role and the authority of the higher faculties, including medicine. The physician practises in accordance with reason, 'but bases itself on the command of an external legislator'. This means that 'the professor of medicine does not draw his method of therapy as practised on the public from physiology of the human body but from medical regulations' (ibid.: 35). Since physicians deal with people's health, this must be of great interest to the government. The government is therefore entitled to supervise physicians' practice, through, for example, a board of public health. But this board should, according to Kant, be composed of practising doctors. In other words, Kant presents the way health care was organised and had been organised in most European nations until recently as the rational way. No external control should interfere with this board of medical doctors, but the government must help medical practitioners to be of service to the public by establishing dispensaries and hospitals.

The medical faculty, according to Kant, is and should be freer than those of theology or law (e.g. free with regard to determining the content of the teaching of doctors). There are good reasons for allowing medicine this special status among the higher faculties: though medicine is an art, it is an art 'that is drawn directly from nature and must therefore be derived from a science of nature' (ibid.: 41). Conflicts within medicine and between medicine and politics could still – in the eighteenth century – be ignored. But Kant was an acute observer of practice. He pointed to contradictory tendencies that only became manifest in the twentieth century. Cochrane's work, with its implicit philosophy of medicine, can be seen as a revival of Kantian perspectives on medicine but also as a correcting of Kant's view of the art of medicine.

People approach physicians as if they were soothsayers and magicians. We easily forget the precepts of reason: to be moderate in our pleasures, patient in our illnesses and rely primarily on the self-help of nature (ibid.: 49). But if medicine is a rational undertaking, an art deriving its knowledge from nature, we assume that physicians will be able to reject immodest demands from people. It should be possible for medicine to keep its status as a self-governing practice provided it follows rational, scientific principles. It is interesting that Kant – though pointing to the autonomy of medicine – did not believe that.

Medical professionals (as well as 'businessmen' in theology and law)

> will always be such miracle-workers, unless the philosophy faculty is allowed to counteract them publicly, not to overthrow their teachings but only to deny the magic power that the public superstitiously attributes to these teachings and the rites connected with them.
>
> (ibid.: 51)

Rational scientific and methodological principles are not sufficient for securing rational and humane health care. A philosophy reminding us of both our limited scientific possibilities – limited in principle – and our personal responsibility is needed. It is of one of Cochrane's great merits to have provided just that. It is to be regretted that many more people seem to have adopted his more technical advice concerning effectiveness and efficiency than have grasped the philosophical framework within which these standards are situated.

Notes

1 For a general critique of methodological fetishism, see, for example, Putnam (1981). I have exemplified and criticised versions of methodological fetishism in medicine in *Practice and Progress* (Jensen 1987).
2 Cochrane quotes a German *Oberartzt* (chief physician) in the camp for that radical claim. 'I was furious and even wrote a poem about it; later I wondered if he was wise or cruel; he was certainly right' is Cochrane's polemical comment (1972: 5).
3 For an interesting account, see Hacking (1975).
4 For a detailed critique of medical essentialism, see my *Practice and Progress* (Jensen 1987).
5 Marthe Nussbaum articulates and defends this philosophical perspective in various works. See especially her *Fragility of Goodness* (1984). In *Practice and Progress* (Jensen 1987) I have shown the relevance of this perspective to medicine and health care.
6 For a detailed account of parts of this fascinating story, see Marks (1997).
7 Translated from German (*Der Streit der Fakultäten*, first published in 1789).

References

Cochrane, A.L. (1972) *Effectiveness and Efficiency: Random Reflections on Health Services*, London: Nuffield Provincial Hospitals Trust.

Daniel, M. and Hill, A.B. (1952) Chemotherapy of pulmonary tuberculosis in young adults: an analysis of the combined results of three Medical Research Council trials, *British Medical Journal*, 1: 1162–8.

Hacking, I. (1975) *The Emergence of Probability*, Cambridge: Cambridge University Press.

Jensen, U.J. (1987) *Practice and Progress: A Theory for the Modern Health Care System*, Oxford: Blackwell Scientific.

Kant, I. (1979) *The Conflict of the Faculties*, Lincoln: University of Nebraska Press.

Le Fanu, I. (1999) *The Rise and Fall of Modern Medicine*, London: Little, Brown.

Marks, H.M. (1997) *The Progress of Experiment: Science and Therapeutic Reform in the United States, 1900–1990*, Cambridge: Cambridge University Press.

Nussbaum, M. (1984) *The Fragility of Goodness: Luck and Ethics in Greek Tragedy and Philosophy*, Cambridge: Cambridge University Press.

Putnam, H. (1981) *Reason, Truth and History*, Cambridge: Cambridge University Press.

Sackett, D.L., Richardson, W.S., Rosenberg, W. and Haynes, R.B. (1997) *Evidence-Based Medicine: How to Practice and Teach EBM*, New York: Churchill Livingstone.

3 Evidence-based nursing

Must or mantra?

Helle Ploug Hansen

Introduction

Evidence-based nursing (EBN) is relatively new. The aim is continually to develop and strengthen the quality of nursing interventions. It is tiptoeing in the wake of the movement for evidence-based medicine (EBM) and evidence-based practice (EBP). Much of the past 20 years has focused on the identification and consideration of strategies to overcome barriers to EBP. Those barriers that nurses have identified include substantive variations in nursing practice and nursing results; lack of guidelines for nursing practice; time constraints; limited access to the research literature; lack of skills in clinical appraisal; lack of coordination between the different health care sectors; and lack of skills in information seeking. On top of this, nurses claim that the prevailing professional ideology emphasises practical skills rather than intellectual knowledge, and that their work environment does not encourage information seeking (Royle *et al.* 1996; Mulhall 1998; DiCenso *et al.* 1998).

Challenging these barriers has resulted in different initiatives such as national and international conferences, journals, books, teaching programmes and centres. These activities often share a positive but largely uncritical approach, stating directly or indirectly that EBN is something we must have, and that it is something we must have now. While the interest among nurses in nursing practice, in education and in research – nationally and internationally – has increased, at the same time many nurses do not embrace EBN with enthusiasm, probably because it appears to hold such limited relevance for their everyday practice needs (Blomfield and Hardy 2000: 123).

The aim of this chapter is to stimulate debate about some of the underlying assumptions in EBN and to argue for a new understanding of it. The debate here is from an anthropological perspective. This means that the perception of the texts on EBN is from a particular point of view where 'understanding is an event, implying a human agent or a mediation by a subject' (Hastrup 1995: 165). There is no fixed relation between words and sentences and objective reality and meaning are not givens but occur in practice (ibid.: 163).

The chapter is divided into five parts. First, a brief overview of definitions and research designs within EBN is presented. Next, a close look is taken at the concept of evidence. Thereafter, some assumptions are examined about truth and the nature of reality inherent in randomised controlled trials (RCTs), meta-analyses and systematic reviews, followed by a close look at nursing practice. In conclusion, the future of EBN is discussed.

Definitions and designs

The international journal *Evidence-Based Nursing* began in January 1998 'as a direct response to a dilemma of practitioners who want to use research, but are thwarted by overwhelming clinical demands, an ever burgeoning research literature, and for many, a lack of skills in critical appraisal' (Mulhall 1998: 1). The journal is published quarterly, and is a joint venture of the BMJ Publishing Group and the United Kingdom's Royal College of Nursing. It has the aim 'to select from the health related literature those articles reporting studies and reviews that warrant immediate attention by nurses attempting to keep pace with important advances in their profession' (*Evidence-Based Nursing* 2002: 1).

The Centre for Evidence-Based Nursing (CEBN), part of the Department of Health Sciences at the University of York, is concerned with furthering EBN through education, research and development.[1] Its research activities are listed on the Centre's home page (www.york.ac.uk/healthsciences/centres/evidence/cebn.htm (accessed 21 September 2002)). Its first aim is to generate reliable research evidence for clinical nursing through primary research and systematic reviews of the efficacy of caring methods and nursing interventions. Its ongoing projects include systematic reviews of wound care (through the Cochrane Wounds Group), support for carers of people with Alzheimer's disease, and a multi-centre RCT of compression bandages for people with leg ulcers. Second, its staff are researching into how nurses in practice use their clinical expertise alongside both research evidence and patient preferences in making decisions. Third, they are evaluating the impact of teaching EBN on nursing practice and organisations. The Centre's definition of EBN is related to that given by DiCenso *et al.* (1998: 1): 'Evidence based nursing is the process by which nurses make clinical decisions using the best available research evidence, their clinical expertise and patient preferences, in the context of available resources' (www.york.ac.uk/healthsciences/centres/evidence/cebn.htm). This understanding of EBN has considerable parallels with EBM and the definition given by Sackett *et al.* They write:

> Evidence based medicine is the conscientious, explicit, and judicious use of current best evidence in making decisions about the care of individual patients. The practice of evidence based medicine means

> integrating *individual clinical expertise with the best available external clinical evidence* from systematic research. By individual clinical expertise we mean the *proficiency and judgement* that individual clinicians acquire through clinical experience and nursing practice. Increased expertise is reflected in many ways, but especially in *more effective and efficient diagnosis* and in the *more thoughtful identification and compassionate use of individual patients' predicament, rights and preferences* in making clinical decisions about their care.
>
> (Sackett *et al.* 1996; emphasis added)

The last sentence indicates that individual patients *have* knowledge about themselves (experiences and preferences), which health professionals can *use* compassionately, assuming they can *identify* them, and *integrate* them with the best available evidence, if they are relevant to making clinical decisions about treatment and care. The italicised words bring out the assumption that words and sentences correspond to objective reality. Patients' experiences and preferences are separate entities in their own right, which can be identified through specific research methods.

DiCenso *et al.* (1998) state that the evaluation of nursing interventions and the understanding of patients' experiences have to be investigated by different research methods. RCTs, meta-analyses and systematic reviews are the best designs for evaluating nursing interventions, while qualitative studies (interviews) are to be preferred to gain a better understanding of patients' experiences. The latter are particularly useful in exploring and explaining the barriers to patient compliance, how a treatment affects patients' everyday life, the meaning of illness to the patient, etc. The idea of RCTs, meta-analyses and systematic reviews as the 'gold standard' methods of assessing the effectiveness of treatment methods and nursing interventions is based on the assumption that rigorous systematic reviews provide nurses with a summary of all the methodologically sound studies related to a specific topic. Further, 'The reason that the RCT is the most appropriate design is that through random assignment of patients to comparison groups, known and unknown confounders are distributed evenly between the groups ensuring that any difference in outcome is due to the intervention' (ibid: 4). This picture of EBN is based on the assumptions that knowledge is autonomous and cumulative (in the sense of being additive) (Gordon 1988: 30); that words can be taken at face value; and that nursing interventions are fixed in time and space – that is, they can be considered 'context free'. Before challenging these assumptions, it is necessary to take a closer look at the concept of evidence.

Evidence – and evidence in nursing

The word 'evidence' is first and foremost an Anglo-American legal term that covers such meanings as documentation, the production of evidence, the giving of evidence. For instance: 'There wasn't enough evidence to prove him guilty'; 'We cannot condemn him on such slight evidence'; 'Mr. X was the first witness called on to give evidence in the law court'; 'A piece of evidence'. Evidence is used about anything that proves a statement to be true. It can involve the presentation of *documentary evidence*, the presentation of things; *real evidence*; or *examining witnesses* or playing of *tape or video transmissions* (Hornby *et al.* 1963: 339). When a person is summoned as a witness, he or she takes the oath declaring, 'I shall tell the truth, the whole truth and nothing but the truth.' Here evidence is strongly connected to truth and, as is shown later in this chapter, *truth* has an appeal because it corresponds to reality in the general understanding of EBN.

Evidence in nursing

Throughout the literature on EBN, it seems that researchers take it for granted that the word 'evidence' has only one distinct meaning, namely the one derived from evidence as a legal term. As far as searches have been able to ascertain, there are no references in the literature to the Latin word *evidentia*, which means the quality of being obvious, evident and clear (Hårbøl *et al.* 2000).

EBN gives priority to 'knowledge' that can be understood as:

- *documentary evidence*, through 'meta-analyses' and 'systematic reviews';
- *real evidence*, through for instance results of RCTs and other kinds of intervention studies;
- *examining witnesses*, through expert committees, audit, interviews with patients and their relatives (JLP 1996: 151).

In EBM and EBN, the documents are attributed with different degrees of evidence, depending on the kind of research methods used.[2] It is not surprising that EBM is strongly connected to RCTs and meta-analyses. Medical research has a long and strong tradition in the natural sciences, where the only kind of valid inference is deductive, and where repeated experiments are the only solid ground for reaching 'the truth'. At the same time, it is surprising and yet not surprising that EBN follows the EBM line.

It is *surprising* because at least within the past 20 years there has been a movement in nursing practice and in nursing theories away from instrumental reasoning in nursing to caring (the individual patient in the centre) reasoning. Furthermore, a part of nursing research nationally and internationally has moved away from the ideals of natural science to more interpretative research ideals, based on the social and humanistic sciences (Martinsen 1989; Benner and Wrubel 1989).

It is *not surprising* because a great part of nursing research is derived from medical research (the ideals of natural science) and because the nursing profession seeks to achieve the same academic level as the medical profession. In a Danish text about EBN, the author claims that EBN will change nursing practice from 'think and feel' to 'knowledge and documentation' (M.N. Hansen 2000: 104). This claim is based on an optimism that surrounds natural science and on the comforting view that natural science is progressing towards the correct description of reality (Johnson 1987: 197). The belief is that experts can find solutions to major health care problems through instrumental reasoning and that natural science still offers the best sources of long-term security. Furthermore, nurses in general are not educated in examining epistemological assumptions, for instance about truth and context.

Trusted ideas

It is my belief that one major reason why EBN until now[3] has followed the line of EBM and the dominant understanding of evidence is found in a 'trusted idea' about truth as correspondence to an objective reality (the ideal of natural science). Trusted ideas are those that survive repeated use, that we trust and on which we no longer feel a need to reflect critically. They become consolidated or 'hard-programmed' (Bateson 1972: 501, 502). The extent to which an idea can survive is determined by its connections to other ideas, and it is commonly more generalised ideas that survive repeated use. Hard-programmed ideas become premises upon which other ideas depend. Frequency of validation of an idea, however, 'is not the same as *proof* that the idea is either true or pragmatically useful over a long time' (ibid.: 502). Trusted ideas are handled in a specific way that differs from the way in which the mind handles other, especially new, ideas:

> The phenomenon of *habit formation* sorts out the ideas which survive repeated use and puts them in a more or less separate category. These trusted ideas then become available for immediate use without thoughtful inspection, while the more flexible parts of the mind can be saved for use on newer matters.
>
> (ibid.: 501)

The trusted idea within EBN is continually produced and reproduced in RCTs, meta-analyses, systematic reviews and, as shown later in this chapter, in different nursing contexts. It values objective truth and instrumental reasoning, and seeks to establish rationality, objectivity and science as synonyms. Rationality is supposed to be stripped of value. It presents only 'facts'. Truth is neutral and universal and beyond time and space (Gordon 1988: 30). The common perception of RCTs, meta-analyses and systematic reviews appeals to truth as correspondence to objective reality

(Sackett *et al.* 1996; 1997; DiCenso *et al.* 1998). Within the underlying scientific paradigm, reasoning is instrumental. This means that scientific procedures such as protocols fulfilling basic criteria such as the random allocation of participants to comparison groups, outcome measures of known or probable clinical importance, reproducibility of results, etc., are valid (Gregson *et al.* 2002: 26). This builds, however, on a narrow epistemology that gives precedence to instrumental reasoning and to establishing true knowledge about the patient. The survival of this frequently used trusted idea 'is further promoted by the fact that habit formation tends to remove the idea from the field of critical inspection' (Bateson 1972: 501). The weight placed on instrumental reasoning is, however, problematical. As the American philosopher Rorty puts it,

> We tend to identify seeking 'objective truth' with 'using reason', and so we think of the natural sciences as paradigms of rationality. We also think of rationality as a matter of following procedures laid down in advance, of being 'methodical'. So we tend to use 'methodical', 'rational', 'scientific' and 'objective' as synonyms.
>
> (Rorty 1991: 35)

The neglect of context

To give precedence to instrumental reasoning and to objective truth means that questions about time, space and contexts are left behind. This is problematical because patients and nurses are living, thinking, feeling and acting individuals, relating to one another in different ways and situations, where communication[4] in a broad sense always take place in time and space. The trusted idea about truth as correspondence to objective reality does not take into account that acting is contextual, that interpretation always is at stake and that it is difficult (impossible) to produce generalisability from one group of nurses or patients to another (external validity). External validity would, for example, be less of a problem when studying pharmaceuticals, where the effect is more constant across patients whatever the place and time of the intervention.

The RCT is born of a mechanical natural science view, where cause–effect relationships form the agenda, where time ideally can be fixed and where contextual factors are understood as biases. It follows that it is not an appropriate research method with which to evaluate nursing interventions, because such interventions involve social relations and take place in time. Although the advocates of EBN indicate that patients' preferences and experiences are important components of most clinical decisions and that the best design to gain knowledge of this is qualitative, too often their good intentions fail.

The qualitative design[5] within EBN shares, in a more blurred and therefore in a potentially more dangerous form, the same problems as the RCT.

Of course, one can get other kinds of answers from patients using a semi-structured or an open-ended questionnaire instead of a closed questionnaire. This, however, does not solve the main problem, which is that within EBN, patients' preferences and experiences are viewed as something static, independent and unchanging over time, space, contexts and nursing intervention. As long as the design is not separated from the mechanical natural science paradigm, where cause–effect relationships form the agenda, interpretations will have shortcomings (Gregson *et al.* 2002).

The trusted idea and nursing practice

The reproduction of the trusted idea has consequences not only for research within EBN, but also for nursing practice, because it is 'stripping out any elements of rational thinking that might be thought to be value oriented, intuitive, or ethnocentric' (Gregson *et al.* 2002: 26). Knowing how to practise nursing is also a matter of expertise, and the practice of nursing always takes place in contexts. Although nurses within EBN express the view that patients have preferences and experiences, this is phrased within the context of what amounts to a specific trusted idea. The nurse is an active agent who first can *identify* and second *take* the patient's experiences through dialogues and interviews, and thereafter *use* them in various ways. She (or he) is placed outside and above the object (the patient), in a privileged position, where she does not form part of what she observes, describes, evaluates and documents. Her gaze floats over the patient. Metaphorically, one can say that the nurse is placed on a pedestal at a suitable distance to form a general view of the object (the passive patient).

However, to paraphrase Mark Johnson (1987: 197), it is difficult to stick to the comforting view that science is progressing toward the correct description of reality. Knowledge expands with language (Hastrup 1995: 62). It is not connected to an agent (patient, nurse, doctor, etc.). Knowledge is always positioned. This means that the understanding of patients' preferences and experiences involves events, implying a human agent (ibid.: 165). Truth can be understood as a matter of convention, of conceptual relativity and not a 'property' (ibid.: 170).

In relation to EBN, the trusted idea with respect to truth as correspondence to objective reality becomes powerful because, as a generalised and abstract idea, it tends to be a relatively inflexible premise upon which other ideas depend (Bateson 1972: 502). It becomes a premise for the understanding of the nurse as active and the patient as passive. It provides epistemological justification that beliefs based on valid scientific procedures (the RCT, meta-analyses, systematic reviews, critical pathways, clinical practice guidelines and clinical guidelines for nursing) correspond to reality. They are true (Gregson *et al.* 2002: 26). Of course, trusted ideas in general are necessary. If nurses do not have reference points, they cannot act as nurses. Trusted ideas are the fundament of nurses' ways of understanding nursing. They are, however, problematical because they can result in blindness to new ideas and new acknowledgements and thereby be difficult to change (Bateson 1972: 502).

From this general and superficial view on nursing practice, we now take a closer look at some characteristics of nursing practice in order to prepare the ground for a discussion of EBN in the future.

Nursing practice

Here the focus is only on that part of nursing practice that is related to meetings between patients and nurses. Research within EBN is most often focused on nursing interventions; such interventions always include a patient.[6] Encounters between nurses and patients are meetings between bodies. We have a body and we are a body, which means that the body is always ascribed meaning (Douglas 1966; Lock and Scheper-Hughes 1990). From an analytical perspective it is possible to isolate four main areas to which nursing practice is related. These can be called *to treat*, *to nurse*, *to service* and *to take care of*. In relation to each of these four areas, nurses are engaged in different kinds of tasks that involve different kinds of social relations. The categories are constructed against the background of my own anthropological research about cancer nursing practice (Hansen [1995] 2003),[7] literature on nursing, and from a model developed by Jens Erik Kristensen, a researcher into the history of ideas. The following presentation is short and of course simplified because it is assumed that it is possible to delimit and focus on only one category at a time. In daily nursing practice the areas are interwoven. Analytically, one can say that when one area appears as a figure (text), another area recedes into the background (context). Nurses struggle all the time to make sense of complex practice situations and interpersonal relations (ibid.).

To treat

The category *to treat* frames the kind of tasks for which nurses are handling patients' symptoms and diseases. To treat is generally connected to the work of doctors. They diagnose, they treat and they make prognoses. Often nurses are seen as assistants to doctors, but nurses also independently carry out different tasks characterised as treatments – for instance, wound care, injections and intravenous infusions. In Denmark, nurses (and doctors) need to be authorised by the National Health Service before they can practise. The tasks are at a level of necessity (Hansen [1998] 2002: 10–11). It is a criminal offence to give wrong kinds of infusion, to prescribe medicine to the wrong patient, or to switch off the oxygen supply to a patient with severe respiratory problems.

The tasks set the scene for social relationships, where the nurse is an agent observing and treating various parts of the patient's biological body: organs, eyes, muscles, skin, etc. The patient is decontextualised and atomised into organs, symptoms and diseases that become the object of the nurse's clinical gaze (Gordon 1988: 26; Hansen [1995] 2003: 101–4). The nurse is placed on a pedestal at a suitable distance to form a general view of the body parts of the patient. The relationship between the nurse and the patient is *subject to object*. The nurse's role is active while the patient's role is passive. Techniques and procedures in relation to *to treat* are primarily about typical, general, routine acts. The nurse does not have to invent eye dripping, oxygen treatment, etc., every time a patient needs eye drops, oxygen support, etc.

To nurse

The category *to nurse* frames the kind of tasks for which nurses are handling and supporting patients' limited bodily competences. The tasks include a long list of techniques and procedures such as bed baths, oral hygiene, footbaths and transference from bed to chair (Hansen [1998] 2002, [1995] 2003). The concept *bodily competences* refers to the knowledge and skills necessary for a person to control important bodily functions (biological, psychological and social) in work and in daily life. The necessary knowledge and skills are not natural bodily competences. Different societies value different bodily competences. They result in different *normal* claims to persons. In a Nordic context, this means that a person should be able to:

- control the intake of food, and excretion;
- control feelings, language and gesture;
- move freely and without help at home, in traffic and at work (Damkjær 1998).

The tasks are at a level of possibility and appropriateness, which means that nurses are not punished if they do not perform a bed bath or administer oral hygiene to a patient in the prescribed way (Hansen [1998] 2002: 11). The tasks set the scene for social relationships in which the patients are dependent on the nurses. They provide nursing care through specific techniques and procedures first and foremost on the patients' biological bodies (objects). The patients, with their limited bodily competences, are understood as cases to be dealt with (Hansen [1995] 2003: 83). The body is looked at as something objective, as an autonomous unit. Again the nurse is the acting agent placed on a pedestal at a suitable distance for forming a general view of the patient. The relationship between the nurse and the patient again is *subject to object*. The nurse's role is active while the patient's role is passive, or active under the command of the nurse (H.P. Hansen 1998: 118–20). Techniques and procedures in relation to *to nurse* are again primarily about typical, general, routine acts. The nurse does not have to invent bed bathing, giving an enema, etc., every time a patient needs a bed bath, an enema, etc.

To service

The category *to service* frames the kind of tasks for which nurses provide services to the patients (Timm 1997). It is rather new within nursing. It stems from the idea of health care consumption that arose after the Second World War. In the 1990s the idea gained more and more ground in the health care systems of Western countries. The patient became a consumer and a user, and in Denmark the notion of 'the user-friendly hospital' was created. Among other things, patients organised themselves into patients' unions and self-help groups. Patients' hotels came into being. In Denmark, patients are allowed to read their medical records. They can complain about treatment and care to a specific patients' complaints board. They give informed consent to certain kinds of investigations and treatments, and they have the right to choose among different treatments. The tasks are set at a level of possibility and appropriateness, which means that nurses are not punished if they do not, for instance, inform a patient in the way prescribed (Hansen [1998] 2002: 11).

Within this category, the role of patients has changed from passive to active. The ideal is that patients become customers and consumers with free choices. They are understood as rational, autonomous agents exercising freedom, choice and personal responsibilities, who have the rights to be given or to obtain optimal information about disease, treatment, side effects, prognoses, etc. They are encouraged to 'express themselves'. The nurses' role as active agents has changed as well. They have become communicators of knowledge. The idea of shared decision making has developed within this market-oriented category (Charles *et al.* 1997).

The relationship between the nurse and the patient is one of subject–subject. The nurse empowers the patient through information and education and facilitates patient compliance. The nurses are no longer placed on a pedestal at a suitable distance but are part of the landscape together with the patients. Nurse and patient are not, however, equal. The patient is sick; the nurse well. The nurse, as a professional agent working in the highly bureaucratised and institutionalised hospital system, has the power to make decisions, while the patient is powerless. The relationship between nurse and patient is thus asymmetrical in relation to power (N.G. Hansen 1998; J. Littlewood 1991; R. Littlewood 1991).[8]

To take care of

> 'I went into his room and he yelled at me, "Are you listening?" I said yes pretty calmly, and he began crying softly and talking. He knew I was listening.' *Mary Culnane, RN, MS.*
>
> (Benner and Wrubel 1989: 1)

The category *to take care of* frames the kind of tasks for which nurses provide caring to patients. Within this category the word 'tasks' should be understood in a very broad sense, because caring is always specific and relational and has to be understood in a context (Benner and Wrubel 1989: 3, 5). In Western countries, nursing has historically been close to caring, humanity, sacrifice and vocation. Caring and humanity are still among the basic values of nursing (Martinsen 1989; Henderson 1995). Within this category, patients are understood as individual persons with experiences, hopes, wishes and preferences, needs of caring and information and needs of help to cope with an illness. They have their own life histories and histories of illness, which nurses try to understand through empathetic listening, and by being 'in tune' with the patient. Interpretative skills are at the heart of any caring situation (Benner and Wrubel 1989: 17). *To take care of* involves a social relationship in which one subject (the nurse) cares for the other subject (the patient): 'Caring is the most natural and the most fundamental aspect within human existence' (Martinsen 1989: 69).[9] Within the literature on caring, there is a profound critique of instrumental reasoning, mechanistic assumptions and the dominance of natural science (Benner and Wrubel 1989: 29–30; Martinsen 1989; Henderson 1995). The role of the nurse is to give caring and the role of the patient is to receive the caring (Hansen [1995] 2003: 95–7). The tasks are at a level of possibility and appropriateness, which means that nurses are not punished if, for example, they do not listen empathetically (Hansen [1998] 2002: 11). The nurses are part of the landscape together with the patients. As within the category *to service*, the relationship between nurse and patient is asymmetrical in relation to power (ibid.: 12), and it is the nurse's task to turn power into caring (N.G. Hansen 1998).

The four categories and the trusted idea

The trusted idea about truth as correspondence to reality is continually produced and reproduced not only in RCTs, meta-analyses and systematic reviews, but also in nursing practice, most obviously within the categories *to treat* and *to nurse*. It becomes a premise for the understanding of the nurse: 1) as active and the patient as passive; 2) as a subject and the patient's body or parts of the patient's biological body as an object; and 3) as a pedestal at a suitable distance from the patient making objective observations independent of time, space and context. The nurse can provide an accurate explanation of objective reality (the patient's symptoms, etc.), and knowledge is autonomous (Gordon 1988: 30): '[D]iseases are considered to have an identity separate from their specific hosts and are located and treated in the "atom" of society – the individual, his/her body divided into parts and parts which are approached as autonomous units' (ibid.: 26).

Within the category *to service*, the roles of the patient and the nurse have changed. The trusted idea is, however, still at stake. The idea of the patient as a rational, autonomous consumer and the customer is close to the idea that truth is neutral and universal and beyond time and space (ibid.: 30). Within the category *to take care of*, the patient is not considered rational and autonomous. Caring is related to context, to relationships and to coping (Benner and Wrubel 1989: 5), and truth is understood as contextual. Summarising, one can say that the tasks within the categories *to treat*, *to nurse* and *to service* understand patients as *having* individual experiences and preferences, which they can *give* to the nurses or which the nurses can *take* from them. The tasks within the category *to take care of* understand the patient as someone *producing and reproducing* individual experiences and preferences in social relationships, for instance together with nurses.

EBN in the future

Nursing practice must be understood as a complex and ambiguous matter (J. Littlewood 1991). With the rise of EBN, an inherent dilemma, or paradox, in nursing practice becomes more apparent, namely the dilemma between *the will to generalise* and *the will to understand specific and individual expressions* of health-threatened, sick and dying persons (Hansen [1995] 2003). As with other kinds of dilemmas, the dilemma in nursing cannot be solved, but it can be acknowledged and explored. Practice is not only value laden; it is at the same time predictable and unpredictable.

It is predictable in the sense that there are general, routine and typical nursing tasks based on knowledge, skills and professional attitudes (first and foremost within *to treat* and *to nurse*), and unpredictable in the sense that every meeting between a nurse and a patient is creating a new situation (first and foremost *to take care of*) (Martinsen 1989). We can never be in the same situation twice. Time, space and context are matters that cannot be fixed. Nursing practice cannot be reduced to exact cumulative (additive) knowledge. Of course, nurses do encounter patients who cannot urinate, breathe, eat or drink by themselves. In the discovery and definition of a 'fact' for instance 'severe side effects to apoplexia cerebri', there are, however, always biases and prejudices involved. It is not possible to establish facts without values. What becomes a fact requires scientific agreement (Hastrup 1995: 176).

Trammels

If EBN is to be more than a mantra, it is necessary that it be lifted out of the trammels binding it to medicine and to the juridical understanding of evidence, and the claims of a neutral, almost contextless stance: 'There are real dangers for nursing if it unquestioningly adopts the medical-model definition of evidence-based practice, a problem evident in previous attempts to raise status and recognition' (Blomfield and Hardy 2000: 128). It is evident that the tasks within the category *to treat* and in some degree within the category *to nurse* can and must be based on evidence in a broad sense. It is important that general, routine and typical nursing tasks are based on sound knowledge and skills. Systematic reviews, meta-analyses and RCTs can very well be an important part of a research programme, but not *the* most appropriate programme. One has to be extremely aware, first, that statistical data still need to be interpreted within a relevant context, and second, that any task takes place in the context of nursing practice and involves social relations (*to take care of* and *to service*). If the tasks within the categories *to treat* and *to nurse* took place between nurse robots and patient robots, it would be possible to create totally objective, measurable and context-free nursing situations, fixed in time and space. If nurses rely on one source of evidence – for instance, RCTs or meta-analyses – this can be compared with watching black-and-white television: 'A core of information might be present, but in wide screen technicolour the impression may be totally different' (ibid.: 124).

Research programmes must include theories and methods from the social and humanistic sciences that are able, first, to grasp the complexity and the ambiguity of nursing practice, the dilemma between the general (the predictable) and the particular (the unpredictable), and second, to deal with ongoing and changing experiences of the individual patient. It is a big challenge for nursing as a practice, a profession and a discipline to insist that knowledge is always positioned (Hastrup 1995:165). Neither within research nor within nursing practice is it possible to: ' "know" individuals as subjects; nor can we "understand" them, as if they were truly objects; what we, as ethnographers, can know, is the space that they are prepared to share with us' (ibid.: 156–7). Nurses are themselves a part of what they observe, what they act in relation to what they evaluate and what they document. The patient, the consumer, a part of the body, a symptom, etc., cannot be looked at and considered independent of the observer. And the other way around: the patient is also an active observer and agent. Knowledge can never be free from interpretation and contexts. Science can never guarantee the truth of its conclusions.

From inflexibility to flexibility

> As a Japanese Zen master once told me, 'To become accustomed to anything is a terrible thing.'
>
> (Bateson 1972: 503)

EBN could be a *must* in the future if nurses, researchers, health care planners, etc., are ready to give up the trusted idea of truth as corresponding to reality. It is not enough to broaden the definition of EBN or to broaden the research perspective in EBN. If this trusted idea continues to become the premise upon which other ideas depend, nothing will have changed. It is necessary that inflexible ideas be replaced by flexible ones that acknowledge that there is no fixed relationship between sentences and objective reality, and that meaning is not given but occurs in practice. Therefore, I would propose that research in EBN in the future has nursing practice as its reference point, because nursing interventions always include at least one human agent. Furthermore, I suggest that research programmes within EBN should be multidisciplinary. Theories and methods from the social and humanistic sciences must be recognised as appropriate for facing the dilemma between the will to generalise and the will to understand the particular.

Meta-analyses, systematic reviews and RCTs will still take their places in decision making in EBN but they will have *a* position, not *the* position. The methods are not in themselves the problem. Rather, the problem lies in the idea of RCTs, meta-analyses and systematic reviews that are 'derived from a narrow view of epistemology where science is regarded as the application of instrumental reason and the picture of truth as correspondence' (Gregson *et al.* 2002: 27).

To end on a positive note, the statement that doctors and nurses should use 'the current best available evidence' at least implies that evidence will always be incomplete and subject to revision.

Acknowledgement

Many thanks to Associate Professor Helle Johannessen and Ph.D. student Niels Buus for valuable comments on an earlier draft of this chapter.

Notes

1 The Joanna Briggs Institute for Evidence-Based Nursing and Midwifery is a multicentre collaboration of supporting centres in Australia, Hong Kong and New Zealand (http://www.joannabriggs.edu.au/)

2 There are different models that outline a hierarchy of methods for evaluating treatment effects (e.g. Guyatt *et al.* 1995):

   1 Systematic reviews and meta-analyses.
   2 Randomised controlled trials with definitive results.

3 Randomised controlled trials with non-definitive results.
4 Cohort studies.
5 Case-control studies.
6 Cross-sectional studies.
7 Case reports.

3 Within the last few years, more critical articles about EBN have been published (Gregson *et al.* 2002; Blomfield and Hardy 2000; Trinder 2000).
4 Communication is understood as something that can be verbal and/or non-verbal, texts, behaviour, actions, passivity and silence (Bateson 1972; H.P. Hansen 2001).
5 The qualitative design within EBN has first and foremost been understood as qualitative interviews. There are, however, a few new initiatives arguing for the use of 'narrative review', 'meta-ethnography' (Forbes and Griffiths 2002) and 'interpretative research' (Blomfield and Hardy 2000).
6 *EBN Online* has published a list of articles with findings applicable to nursing practice (2001).
7 The author did one year full-time of ethnographic fieldwork (participant observation and ethnographic interviews) as part of her Ph.D. project.
8 Relations in hospitals are a 'family', where the doctor is the father, the nurse the mother and the patient the child (R. Littlewood 1991; J. Littlewood 1991).
9 Translated by the author of this chapter.

References

Bateson, G. (1972) Ecology and flexibility in urban civilization, in G. Bateson (ed.) *Steps to an Ecology of Mind*, New York: Ballantine Books.

Benner, P. and Wrubel, J. (1989) *The Primacy of Caring: Stress and Coping in Health and Illness*, New York: Addison-Wesley.

Blomfield, R. and Hardy, S. (2000) Evidence-based nursing practice, in L. Trinder and S. Reynolds (eds) *Evidence-Based Practice: A Critical Appraisal*, vol. 6, Oxford: Blackwell Scientific, pp. 111–38.

Charles, C., Gafni, A. and Whelan, T. (1997) Shared decision-making in the medical encounter: what does it mean? (or it takes at least two to tango), *Social Science and Medicine*, 44 (5): 681–92.

Damkjær, S. (1998) Patient og sygeplejerske: et møde mellem kroppe, in H.P. Hansen (ed.) *Omsorg, krop og død: en bog om sygepleje*, vol. 7, Copenhagen: Gyldendal, pp. 136–46.

DiCenso, A., Cullum, N. and Ciliska, D. (1998) Implementing evidence-based nursing: some misconceptions [Editorial], *Evidence-Based Nursing*, 1: 38–9. EBN Online: http://ebn.bmjjournals.com/ (accessed 21 September 2002).

Douglas, M. (1966) *Purity and Danger*, New York: Praeger.

EBN Online (2001) Other articles noted. *Evidence-Based Nursing*, 4: E1–11, at http://ebn.bmjjournals.com/cgi/content/full/4/4/E1 (accessed 21 September 2002).

Evidence-Based Nursing (2002) Purpose and procedure, 5: 66–7. EBN Online: http://ebn.bmjjournals.com/ (accessed 21 September 2002).

Forbes, A. and Griffiths, P. (2002) Methodological strategies for the identification and synthesis of 'evidence' to support decision-making in relation to complex healthcare systems and practices, *Nursing Inquiry*, 9 (3): 141–55.

Gordon, D. (1988) Tenacious assumptions in Western medicine, in M. Lock and D. Gordon (eds) *Biomedicine Examined*, London: Kluwer Academic, pp. 19–57.

Gregson, P.R.W., Meal, A.G. and Avis, M. (2002) Meta-analysis: the glass eye of evidence-based practice?, *Nursing Inquiry*, 9 (1): 24–30.

Guyatt, G., Sackett, D., Sinclair, J. *et al.* (1995) Users' guides to the medical literature 9: a method for grading health-care recommendations, *Journal of the American Medical Association*, 274: 1800–4.

Hansen, H.P. (1998) Renlighed i sygeplejen, in H.P. Hansen (ed.) *Omsorg, krop og død: en bog om sygepleje*, vol. 6, Copenhagen: Gyldendal, pp. 118–36.

Hansen, H.P. (2001) *Hvordan har du det? Kommunikation i sundhedssektoren ud fra Gregory Bateson*, Copenhagen: Munksgaard Danmark.

Hansen, H.P. ([1998] 2002) *Teknikker og procedurer i sygeplejen*, 2nd edn, Copenhagen: Munksgaard Danmark.

Hansen, H.P. ([1995] 2003) *I grænsefladen mellem liv og død: en kulturanalyse af sygeplejen på en onkologisk afdeling*, 3rd edn, Copenhagen: Munksgaard Danmark.

Hansen, M.N. (2000) Vidensbaseret sygepleje og referenceprogrammer, in I. Egerod *et al.* (eds) *Dokumentation og kvalitetsudvikling*, vol. 5, Copenhagen: Nyt Nordisk Forlag Arnold Busck, pp. 92–110.

Hansen, N.G. (1998) Løgstrups etik og sygeplejens praksis, in H.P. Hansen (ed.) *Omsorg, krop og død: en bog om sygepleje*, vol. 2, Copenhagen: Gyldendal, pp. 33–59.

Hårbøl, K., Schack, J. and Spang-Hanssen, H. (2000) *Dansk Fremmedordbog*, Copenhagen: Gyldendal.

Hastrup, K. (1995) *A Passage to Anthropology: Between Experience and Theory*, London: Routledge.

Henderson, V. (1995) *The Nature of Nursing*, Copenhagen: Munksgaard.

Hornby, A.S., Gatenby, E.V. and Wakefield, H. (1963) *The Advanced Learner's Dictionary of Current English*, London: Oxford University Press.

JLP (1996) *Den store danske encyklopædi: Danmarks Nationalleksikon*, vol. 6, Copenhagen: Gyldendal, p. 151.

Johnson, M. (1987) *The Body in the Mind: The Bodily Basis of Meaning, Imagination and Reason*, Chicago: University of Chicago Press.

Littlewood, J. (1991) Care and ambiguity: towards a concept of nursing, in P. Holden and J. Littlewood (eds) *Anthropology and Nursing*, vol. 10, London: Routledge, pp. 170–90.

Littlewood, R. (1991) Gender, role, and sickness: the ritual psychopathologies of the nurse, in P. Holden and J. Littlewood (eds) *Anthropology and Nursing*, vol. 9, London: Routledge, pp. 148–70.

Lock, M. and Scheper-Hughes, N. (1990) A critical-interpretative approach in medical anthropology: rituals and routines of discipline and dissent, in T.M. Johnson and C.F. Sargent (eds) *Medical Anthropology: Contemporary Theory and Method*, vol. 3, New York: Praeger, pp. 47–73.

Martinsen, K. (1989) *Omsorg, sykepleie og medisin*, Otta, Norway: Tano.

Mulhall, A. (1998) Nursing, research, and the evidence, *Evidence-Based Nursing*, 1: 4–5. EBN Online: http://ebn.bmjjournals.com/ (accessed 21 September 2002).

Rorty, R. (1991) *Objectivity, Relativism and Truth*, Cambridge: Cambridge University Press.

Royle, J.A., Blythe, J., Ingram, C. *et al.* (1996) The research utilisation process: the use of guided imagery to reduce anxiety, *Canadian Oncology Nursing Journal*, 6: 20–5.

Sackett, D.L., Richardson, W.S., Rosenberg, W. and Haynes, R.B. (1997) *Evidence-Based Medicine: How to Practice and Teach EBM*. New York: Churchill Livingstone.

Sackett, D.L., Rosenberg, W., Gray, J.A., Haynes, R.B. and Richardson, W.S. (1996) Evidence based medicine: what it is and what it isn't, *British Medical Journal*, 312: 71–2.

Timm, H.U. (1997) *Patienten i centrum*, Copenhagen: DSI.

Trinder, L. (2000) A critical appraisal of evidence-based practice, in L. Trinder and S. Reynolds (eds) *Evidence-Based Practice: A Critical Appraisal*, vol. 10, Oxford: Blackwell Scientific, pp. 212–42.

4 Evidence-based health economics

Answers in search of questions?

Stephen Birch and Amiram Gafni

Introduction

Over the past 20 years, increasing attention has been given to the development of evidence-based approaches to decision making in health. The underlying principle of the evidence-based approach is that decisions about which health care interventions to provide should be based on the evidence about the clinical effectiveness of interventions (Sackett and Rosenberg 1995). The evidence-based approach has incorporated both methodological components concerning guidelines for the design of high-quality research and empirical components concerning the use of these guidelines in the identification of high-quality studies and the systematic review of such studies. In recent years this evidence-based approach has attracted the attention, interests and participation of health economists (Birch 2002). Partly this stems from the interests of decision makers being concerned with more than just the clinical effectiveness of treatments. The impact of clinical outcomes of treatments on the well-being of individuals and populations and the costs of those treatments also contribute in important ways to the evidence base for decision makers. This has led researchers in the evidence-based movement to include economists in studies of treatment effectiveness and the introduction of the notion of 'evidence-based health economics' (EBHE) (Donaldson *et al.* 2002a).

In this chapter we consider the contribution of the evidence-based approach to providing evidence to decision makers facing problems of an economic nature (i.e. where the decision maker is concerned with making the best use of resources). We start by considering the foundations of the evidence-based approach and show how the approach results in satisfying the curiosity of the researcher as opposed to meeting the needs of the decision maker. We then consider the application of the evidence-based approach in health economics. We examine the role and contribution of EBHE to the evidence-based approach. We show how, to date, EBHE has failed to provide the appropriate application of economic concepts to the challenges facing health care decision makers. As a result, EBHE, as currently applied, fails to reflect the social scientific roots of the economics discipline. Instead, EBHE uses economics 'topics' such as costs and well-being in non-economics ways to serve the interests of the clinical epidemiologists as opposed to the needs of individuals and populations. We review one recent example where EBHE has been applied in health care decision making. The outcome of this application is presented and provides 'evidence' of the failure of current applications of EBHE to lead to more efficient use of health care resources.

The evidence-based approach

The evidence-based approach is based on the premise that the findings of high-quality research studies ought to be useful to, and hence used by, decision makers (Sackett and Rosenberg 1995). Considerable resources have been devoted to the development of guidelines for the design and conduct of research studies, the timely dissemination of research findings to decision makers and facilitation of the use of research findings in the decision-making process. In this way, the evidence-based approach is characterised by researchers providing information about interventions that decision makers 'should' use, based on the assumption that the interests of the researchers satisfy the needs of the decision makers (Birch 1996).

The development of the evidence-based approach in health can be traced back to Cochrane's work on the effectiveness of clinical interventions (Cochrane 1972) and the subsequent development of the discipline of clinical epidemiology (Sackett *et al.* 1985). Attention tends to be focused on, and confined to, the relationship between exposure to a health care intervention and responsiveness (i.e. health status changes) in individuals with a disease or condition of interest to the researcher (i.e. the study population). The (implicit) question asked by the researcher is 'Does this intervention work on average, in this population?' Other possible explanations of observed changes in health status in the study population confound or confuse the estimation of the intervention–outcome relationship. By excluding certain types of individuals from the population selected for study and randomising the selected population between those who receive the intervention and those who do not receive it, researchers seek to minimise the probability of observed changes in health status being explained by other factors (Birch 1996).

Decision making, however, does not take place in such 'context-free' circumstances. Instead, decision makers need to know 'under what conditions will individuals with the health problem benefit from this intervention?' and 'Will the intervention work given the circumstances of the subjects for whom it is being considered?' (Birch 1996). So, abstracting research from reality in order to serve the intellectual curiosity of the researcher casts doubt on the ability of the studies to provide the information required to satisfy the needs of either the decision maker or the subjects.

Evidence-based health economics (EBHE)

In a recent book on the EBHE approach, Donaldson *et al.* (2002a) describe EBHE as the application of 'evidence-based principles' in the practice of economic evaluation. Although these principles are not identified, the important role played by systematic review as a 'cornerstone' of EBHE is clear from the subtitle *From Effectiveness to Efficiency in Systematic Review*, as well as from several contributions to the volume.

Two factors are identified that characterise EBHE and distinguish it from other evidence-based approaches. First, the scope of problems addressed by EBHE is much broader than for other areas of the evidence-based approach, such as evidence-based medicine (EBM). Under EBM, interest is focused on (and confined to) individual health care interventions and the clinical consequences of those interventions. EBHE complements EBM by contributing information on the economic consequences of interventions in the form of the net change in resources used and the impact, in terms of other benefits forgone as a result of taking resources from elsewhere in order to support a particular intervention. In economics, these forgone benefits represent the opportunity cost of the intervention. However, EBHE can also be applied to a wide range of economic issues beyond individual health care interventions concerning the production, protection and restoration of health in populations. So, the application of economics is not confined to whether a particular intervention represents an efficient use of resources. Economics can also be used to consider whether the current method of physician remuneration is the best way of ensuring that physicians prescribe this intervention, as opposed to alternative, less efficient interventions, to the right people at the right time.

Second, the authors note that under EBHE, the evidence-based principles used must be based on concepts of the economics discipline. In other words, the practice of EBHE must be compatible with the application of economics. In the absence of compatibility with economic concepts, we might ask: Where is the economics in evidence-based health economics?

Having established these defining characteristics, the authors return to the focus on economic evaluations of clinical interventions and the important notion of systematic reviews. In other words, although the inclusion of economics in the evidence-based approach provides a resource context to the evidence base, and broadens the focus of attention beyond clinical interventions, the nature of the question being considered remains academically driven. For example, EBHE would include consideration of the outcomes of different methods of paying health care providers, e.g. capitation versus fee for service. But the underlying question of EBHE remains acontextual – that is, from an economic perspective, does substituting capitation payment for fee-for-service payments 'work on average' in the population being studied? However, the application of economic principles would suggest that the impact of capitation in place of fee-for-service will depend on the preferences and circumstances of individual providers as well as the particular levels and forms of the two separate payment arrangements under consideration (Hutchison *et al.* 1996). In other words, the proposed application of EBHE seems to favour the acontextual even though the principles of the economics discipline emphasise the importance of context.

Two different approaches to EBHE are discussed: systematic reviews of effectiveness (i.e. the outcomes of EBM) as an input in economic evaluation studies, and systematic reviews of economic evaluations, presumably to include, but not be confined to, those economic evaluations in which effectiveness information is based on systematic reviews of effectiveness (Donaldson *et al.* 2002b). However, both approaches remain focused on the evaluation of 'the intervention' in isolation of the context in which the underlying problem is experienced. In this way, the EBHE process determines what are the questions to be addressed, instead of the prevailing problems facing the decision maker being used to determine the appropriate policy question to be asked and the method through which this question is to be answered. In other words, although the discipline of economics seems to offer an appropriate set of tools for analysing the problem facing decision makers, these tools are not used under EBHE.

Economics and evidence-based health economics

Although economics was not part of the initial thinking behind the evidence-based approach, the key theme of the approach, using evidence about which interventions do most good to take decisions about which interventions to provide, is compatible with the three fundamental concepts of economics: *scarcity*, *choice* and *opportunity cost*. Ageing populations, technological developments in health care and increasing public expectations all lead to increasing demands on the resources made available to health care services. Hence, there are never enough health care resources to satisfy all the possible uses of resources, and health care resources are *scarce*. As a result, *choices* have to be made about how to use the resources that are available for health care. Increasing the quantity of resources, whether that be through increased expenditures on health care resources or improving the efficiency with which existing resources are used, does not avoid the problem of choices; it simply changes the nature of the choices. Faced with these often difficult choices, decision makers have focused attention on considering what is achieved by the current practices and whether different practices would achieve more – essentially a matter of *opportunity costs*.

Clinical epidemiology focuses on what can be achieved (effectiveness) without comparing this with what resources are required and hence what has to be forgone (efficiency). Economists' participation in the evidence-based movement provides the 'resource' context into what is primarily a clinical epidemiology exercise (Birch 2002). Consideration of the impact on both clinical outcomes and health care resources of health care interventions is the basis for the economic evaluation of health care programmes. Economic evaluation is concerned with 'ensuring that the value of what is gained from an activity outweighs the value of what is sacrificed' (Williams 1983). The economic question underlying economic evaluation – whether an activity adds more to well-being than the alternative uses of the same resources – would appear to be relevant to health care decision makers. However, as with the clinical outcomes of interventions, the practice of economic evaluation has tended to approach the estimation of the impact of interventions on both well-being and health care resources in isolation of the problem context. In other words, the practice of economic evaluation has been focused on answering the question 'Is this intervention an efficient use of health care resources?' regardless of the context. However, this fails to reflect the underlying nature of the economics discipline and the social science traditions on which it is based.

Economic evaluation incorporates both objective (or technical) and subjective (or valuation) components (Birch and Gafni 1996). The objective component of economic evaluation is concerned with the estimation of an input–output relationship – that is, the relationship between the health care intervention of interest and health outcomes produced by that intervention. However, there are many influences on (or inputs to) the health of individuals. The health production function provides information on the association between all inputs (or health determinants), including health care interventions, and changes in health as measured by life expectancy adjusted for the health-related quality of life or quality-adjusted life years (QALYs). The presence and mix of these determinants may differ between settings. Moreover, the identification and measurement of the full range of influences on health may present many intellectual challenges. Nevertheless, there is an underlying technical relationship between inputs (determinants) and outcomes (health) that, although stochastic, is free of subjective considerations, and hence applies generally across individuals and populations. In other words, two populations of individuals with identical levels and mixes of health inputs will have the same distribution of health levels, *all other things being equal.* Economic evaluation of health care interventions focuses attention on the relationship between one input (or one group of inputs), health care interventions, with health outcomes. In reality, all other things are not equal among different populations. Hence, although the underlying health production function (input–output relationship for a particular intervention) might be the same, as would be the case where clinical developments are widely disseminated, there may not be equality in the levels of other determinants of health between populations. As a result, the health care resources required to achieve the same change in health status in two populations might be very different. But this means that the relationship between health outcomes and health care inputs, the basis of the cost-effectiveness ratio, cannot be established independent of the context or setting in which the intervention is being considered and is likely to vary among different contexts (Birch and Gafni 2002a).

The subjective component of economic evaluation is less straightforward. In principle, we are still dealing with a production problem: the production of well-being to the individual, from inputs of health and other commodities (e.g. leisure, education, housing, etc.). The challenges associated with the identification and measurement of the full range of influences on well-being are at least as great as for the production of health from health care and other health determinants. However, because well-being is a subjective concept, there is no reason why this production of well-being will be the same between different individuals, different groups or different populations. Two populations with the same levels and mixes of health and other commodities need not have the same distribution of well-being. They would have the same distribution of well-being only if the individuals in the two populations had the same underlying preferences. Moreover, even if the individuals do have the same underlying preferences, the additional well-being associated with an improvement in health status may depend on the circumstances of the populations (e.g. prevailing levels and distributions of education, income, etc.). Where these circumstances differ between populations, the additional well-being associated with a given health improvement will also vary. Only in the special case of identical underlying preferences and either equal distributions of all other commodities or health being separable from other commodities (i.e. the well-being associated with health is independent of all other circumstances) would the well-being of additional health be the same for both populations.

The notion of economic evaluation producing a cost-effectiveness ratio, a net benefits expression or a cost-effectiveness acceptability curve for an intervention (Drummond *et al.* 1996) is therefore inconsistent with both the problem context of the decision maker and the economics discipline on which economic evaluation is supposed to be based. As a result, interventions aimed at improving health that fail to address the context in which health problems occur risk leading to reductions in well-being for individuals.

In principle, EBHE might go so far as estimating separate cost-effectiveness ratios for each population setting to reflect between-population differences in the relationships between health care inputs, health outputs and improvements in well-being. For example, the incremental cost-effectiveness ratio (ICER) of, say, a smoking cessation programme in population A might be estimated to be $30,000 per additional QALY, and decision makers believe that this is sufficient to justify the programme.

Suppose population B has the same prevalence of smoking as population A; however, the ICER is found to be $40,000 per QALY. To base resource allocation decisions on the first study alone would overestimate the productivity of resources allocated to smoking cessation. EBHE would therefore imply that the programme is worthwhile in population A but not in population B. However, this would be inconsistent with the underlying principles of the economics discipline and the notion of efficient use of scarce resources.

The higher ICER in population B does not mean that the programme does not represent an efficient use of resources in population B; the ICER does not provide sufficient information to make this determination. The efficiency of using resources to support the smoking cessation programme cannot be determined by reference to only the costs and effects of the programme under evaluation (Birch and Gafni 2003). The opportunity cost of the these resources depends on two factors, neither of which is related to the smoking cessation programme: the total budget available to the decision maker for addressing the health problems of the population, and the marginal valuation of alternative uses of these resources. Hence, even if a programme has the same ICER (i.e. the same relationship between health care resources, health outcomes and improvements in well-being) in two populations, it does not follow that using health care resources to support the programme is of equal efficiency in the two populations (Birch and Gafni 2002a). Moreover, it is quite possible that a programme with a lower ICER in population A represents an inefficient use of resources, while in population B, where the programme has a higher ICER, allocating resources to the programme would be efficient.

Grossman (1972) developed an economic model of an individual's health behaviour, or demand for health, based on the household production model (Becker 1965). Using a utility-maximising framework, Grossman showed that an individual's behaviour with respect to expected health change is determined by the balancing of the benefits and opportunity costs of health change. One of many applications of this model over the past 30 years is Ehrlich's explanation of the systematic diversity in life expectancies across populations and the observed wide variability in empirical estimates of the valuation of life-saving programmes (Ehrlich 2000). Under Grossman's model, benefits incorporate two components: consumption (the direct change in well-being associated with the change in health – feeling healthier or less healthy) and investment (the impact of health change on other aspects of the individual's life – health change might affect an individual's income-earning capacity or the capacity to engage in leisure activities, etc.). These are measured in terms of the individual's valuation of these 'consequences' of health change.

Similarly, opportunity costs are measured by the impact on the individual's well-being of what he or she has to forgo or undertake in order to achieve the health change. Under this approach, there are many possible explanations of different individuals faced with *the same health changes* behaving differently. The health change could be associated with different impacts on earnings capacities, or change in earnings capacities might have different effects on the individuals' well-being. Similarly, the change in well-being associated with a given change in health status might differ between the two individuals. Even if the effect of the given health change on well-being is identical, the opportunity costs differ if what the individuals have to forgo for the health change differs or, where this is the same, if the effect of this sacrifice on well-being differs between individuals.

EBHE in practice: decision making about the drug formulary in Ontario, Canada

Ontario is one of several jurisdictions that have adopted an evidence-based approach to decision making about which interventions are to be supported by public funds. In particular, the Drug Quality and Therapeutics Committee (DQTC) of the Ontario Ministry of Health recommends to the Minister for Health which drugs are to be admitted to the provincial formulary of the drug benefit programme – the programme that provides public funds for ambulatory drugs prescribed for residents over the age of 65 years and those on social assistance (Laupacis 2002). The committee reviews submissions by pharmaceutical manufacturers who wish to have their drugs included in the provincial formulary.

Faced with continual increases in the cost of drugs under the programme and the need to make sure that resources were being used efficiently, the DQTC adopted an evidence-based approach to the development of its recommendations. The recommendations are based on the economic evaluation of the drugs under consideration, and follow guidelines for the economic evaluation of new technologies published a decade earlier (Laupacis *et al.* 1992). In this way, the work of the committee would seem to represent EBHE. The evaluation involves a comparison of the new drug with the current way of treating the patient group for whom the new drug is being proposed, and is summarised in the estimated value of the ICER. The ICER is calculated by dividing the difference in costs between new and old treatments by the difference in effects to give the additional cost per unit outcome (e.g. $50,000 per QALY).

The decision makers face the choice between the proposed drug and the current approach to dealing with the condition in question only in very specific and unusual circumstances: where the two alternative approaches use exactly the same resources. However, in such circumstances there is no ICER, since the difference in costs is zero and the decision can be taken based entirely on which treatment has better outcomes. More generally, comparisons result in the new drug offering the prospect of improved outcomes but costing more than the current intervention. This results in a positive ICER – that is, the resources used by the current intervention are not sufficient to cover the costs of the new intervention for the same patients. The decision maker needs to compare the *total cost* of the new drug in its proposed use with the outcomes produced by the range of other services and interventions that would need to be forgone, including the current intervention, in order to fund the new drug (Gafni and Birch 1993, 2003a).

Because the methods proposed by the economic evaluation guidelines focus exclusively on the characteristics of the current and proposed interventions, the information requirements to determine whether the new drug represents an efficient use of resources are not satisfied. Instead, a value judgement is made, either explicitly or implicitly, about whether a particular ICER value, e.g. $50,000 per QALY, represents a 'good buy'.

The use of the ICER as the basis for making recommendations about the drug in this way fails to acknowledge that the additional funds required for a new programme must come from other uses, i.e. cuts to unspecified programmes. However, by failing to consider how the resource consequences of the new drug are to be satisfied, the approach necessarily leads to increases in health care expenditures, other things being equal. As new drugs are recommended on the basis of subjectively acceptable ICERs, more resources are required to support the additional costs involved. But, as we explained above, an efficient use of resources requires that any given level of resources is used in ways that maximise the outcomes produced. Under the DQTC approach, outcomes are considered independent of any given level of resources.

Notwithstanding the use of this EBHE approach, the Chair of the DQTC reported in a recent paper that following introduction of the approach, expenditures on the drug programme rose by 10 per cent annually between 1997 and 2000 and by 15 per cent in 2001 (Laupacis 2002). Moreover, this growth in expenditures has led both the Provincial Premier and his Minister of Health to question the affordability of the programme, despite the recommendations being 'cost-effective' according to the EBHE approach followed by the DQTC. In other words, far from providing valid recommendations to the Minister of how to make the most productive use of the resources already devoted to the programme, the EBHE approach followed has put in question the continued existence of the programme. Charged with the task of finding ways of getting maximum output from existing resources (a question of efficiency), the DQTC has come up with recommendations that involve ways of using more resources without any evidence that these resources are to be used efficiently.

The experience of Ontario is not unique. More recently, the National Institute for Clinical Excellence (NICE) in the United Kingdom has followed a similar evidence-based approach to the development of recommendations concerning health care interventions under the National Health Service (National Institute for Clinical Excellence 2001; Taylor *et al.* 2003). It has been reported that recommendations made by NICE up to April 2002 concerning the adoption of new drugs implied additional resource requirements of £250 million (Taylor 2002). Because the programmes and interventions that need to be forgone in order to fund the new programmes are not considered by NICE, there is no way to judge whether the introduction of these new programmes results in an increase in the health gains from existing resources (Birch and Gafni 2002b). However, evidence presented to a recent Parliamentary Select Committee indicated that actual NHS expenditure on these drugs was around 60 per cent of this figure (House of Commons Select Committee 2002). The discrepancy is explained by the failure of some authorities to implement the NICE recommendations. Although NICE recommendations are deemed to be mandatory once approved by the Minister for Health, 15–20 per cent of health authorities could not confirm that they had introduced drugs recommended by NICE one year after publication of the recommendation. Moreover, fewer than half of all health authorities have a policy for monitoring local compliance with NICE recommendations (Taylor 2002). In other words, in the absence of any guidance from NICE about which programmes to cut in order to fund the new technologies, each health authority has taken its own decision about its ability and willingness to reduce or eliminate other programmes to accommodate the new drugs (Gafni and Birch 2003b).

Economics and informed decision making

The development of the notion of EBHE is interesting, given the important role played by information in the discipline of economics. The model of perfect competition is based on the assumption of perfect information being available to consumers and producers. The application of economic concepts shows that the behaviour of individuals and groups will be determined by, among other things, the information available to them. Recognition of the absence of perfect information has led to the development of approaches for dealing with imperfect information leading to 'market failure'.

We have shown that EBHE, and the approaches to economic evaluation on which it is based, are not concerned with informing the economic questions arising from the problems facing decision makers. On the contrary, it focuses attention on 'interventions in isolation' as opposed to 'problems in contexts'. Hence, EBHE, far from providing a strategy for dealing with the problem of imperfect information or its consequences, actually contributes to the problem.

It has been argued by others that the broadening of the evidence-based approach is a way of applying the same standards of justification to health care decision makers as are applied to clinical decision makers (Donaldson *et al.* 2002a). However, economics provides recognition of the complex nature of the world in which we live and the tools for exploring approaches to dealing with the problems occurring in that complex world. These matters generally lie outside the scope and/or interests of clinical epidemiologists. As a result, EBHE involves reducing problems to the exploration of simple input–output relationships – essentially a set of answers. But they are answers to questions that decision makers have not asked and relate to problems they do not face.

Instead of adopting the focus of attention and methods used under the evidence-based approach, none of which has been justified from an economics perspective, health economists can better serve decision makers by using the analytical framework of the discipline of economics to address the needs of decision makers.

References

Becker, G. (1965) Theory of the allocation of time, *Economic Journal*, 75: 493–517.

Birch, S. (1996) As a matter of fact: evidence-based decision-making unplugged, *Health Economics*, 6: 547–60.

Birch, S. (2002) Making the problem fit the solution: evidence-based decision-making and 'dolly' economics, in C. Donaldson, M. Mugford and L. Vale (eds) *Evidence-Based Health Economics: From Effectiveness to Efficiency in Systematic Review,* London: BMJ Books.

Birch, S. and Gafni, A. (1996) Cost effectiveness and cost utility analyses: methods for the non-economic evaluation of health care programs and how we can do better, in E. Geisler and O. Heller (eds) *Managing Technology in Health Care*, New York: Wiley.

Birch, S. and Gafni, A. (2002a) Economics and the evaluation of vaccination programmes: the importance of context, *Vaccinations: Children and Practice*, 5: 38–42.

Birch, S. and Gafni, A. (2002b) On being NICE in the UK: guidelines for technology appraisal for the NHS in England and Wales, *Health Economics*, 8: 185–91.

Birch, S. and Gafni, A. (2003) Economics and the evaluation of health care programmes: generalisability of methods and implications for generalisability of results, *Health Policy*, 64: 207–19.

Cochrane, A. (1972) *Effectiveness and Efficiency: Random Reflections on Health Services*, London: Nuffield Provincial Hospitals Trust.

Donaldson, C., Mugford, M. and Vale, L. (2002a) *Evidence-Based Health Economics: From Effectiveness to Efficiency in Systematic Review*, London: BMJ Books.

Donaldson, C., Mugford, M. and Vale, L. (2002b) Using systematic reviews in economic evaluations: the basic principles, in C. Donaldson, M. Mugford and L. Vale (eds) *Evidence-Based Health Economics: From Effectiveness to Efficiency in Systematic Review*, London: BMJ Books.

Drummond, M., O'Brien, B., Stoddart, G. and Torrance, G. (1996) *Methods for the Economic Evaluation of Health Care Programmes*, 2nd edn, New York: Oxford University Press.

Ehrlich, I. (2000) Uncertain lifetime, life protection and the value of life saving, *Journal of Health Economics*, 19: 341–67.

Gafni, A. and Birch, S. (1993) Guidelines for the adoption of a new technology: a potential prescription for uncontrolled growth in expenditures and how to avoid it, *Canadian Medical Association Journal*, 148: 913–17.

Gafni, A. and Birch, S. (2003a) Inclusion of drugs in provincial drug benefit programs: should 'reasonable decisions' lead to uncontrolled growth in expenditures?, *Canadian Medical Association Journal*, 168: 849–51.

Gafni, A. and Birch, S. (2003b) NICE methodological guidelines and decision-making in the United Kingdom National Health Service, *PharmacoEconomics*, 21: 149–57.

Grossman, M. (1972) On the concept of health capital and the demand for health, *Journal of Political Economy*, 80: 223–55.

House of Commons Select Committee (2002) *Health: National Institute for Clinical Excellence*, London: The Stationery Office.

Hutchison, B., Birch, S., Hurley, J., Lomas, J. and Stratford-Devai, F. (1996) Effect of a financial incentive to reduce hospital utilization in capitated primary care practice, *Canadian Medical Association Journal*, 154: 653–61.

Laupacis, A. (2002) Inclusion of drugs in provincial drug benefit programs: who is making these decisions, and are they the right ones?, *Canadian Medical Association Journal*, 166: 44–7.

Laupacis, A., Feeny, D., Detsky, A. and Tugwell, P. (1992) How attractive does a new technology have to be to warrant adoption and utilization? Tentative guidelines for using clinical and economic evaluation, *Canadian Medical Association Journal*, 146: 473–81.

National Institute for Clinical Excellence (2001) *Technical Guidance for Manufacturers and Sponsors on Making a Submission to a Technology Appraisal*, London: NICE.

Sackett, D. and Rosenberg, W. (1995) On the need for evidence-based medicine, *Health Economics*, 4: 249–54.

Sackett, D., Haynes, B. and Tugwell, P. (1985) *Clinical Epidemiology: A Basic Science for Clinical Medicine*, Toronto: Little, Brown.

Taylor, R. (2002) Generating national guidance: a NICE model? Paper presented at the Fifth International Conference on Strategic Issues in Health Care Management Policy, Finance and Performance in Health Care, St Andrews, Scotland, UK, 11–13 April.

Taylor, R., Hutton, J. and Culyer, A. (2003) Developing the revised NICE appraisal technical guidance to manufacturers and sponsors: opportunity or threat?, *PharmacoEconomics*, 20: 1031–8.

Williams, A. (1983) The economic role of health indicators, in G. Teeling-Smith (ed.) *Measuring the Social Benefits of Medicine*, London: Office of Health Economics.

5 Evidence-based medicine

Objectives and values

Gavin Mooney

Introduction

In deliberating on the merits of evidence-based medicine (EBM), there is a need to address the question as to whose values are to be used in setting objectives in health care. The nature of the good that is sought from health care is unlikely to be constant. It will be defined differently if we ask medical doctors, other health care professionals, patients or citizens (the community). It will vary from one country or culture to another.

Too often, EBM appears to operate in a largely value-free world or one where medical values dominate, even monopolise. Either can lead to an unquestioned view of the good of health care being about nothing other than health maximisation. This is not necessarily wrong; it is, however, a hypothesis, and as such should be tested. It is unlikely to be true in all contexts and all cultures. Further, the construct of health is not constant across all cultures.

I suggest that it is best to ask the community who it is that they would want to be the guardians of the values on which health care should be built. It follows that there is a need to establish whether such community preferences are constant across different decision-making arenas (such as the choice of the health care system's overall objectives, the question of which medical interventions to adopt in diabetes, who to screen – and how often – for cervical cancer, etc.). How EBM might move to embrace some of these wider value issues needs to be addressed.

This chapter suggests that there is a need to view EBM as just one part of a strategy for improving decision making. Set in these terms, this allows a focus on the objectives of health care, the influence of better decision making on the meeting of such objectives and, in turn, comparisons to be made of the value of EBM and other strategies for meeting these objectives. It is argued that there is a need for a better balance in such strategies. In achieving that balance, there is currently a relative over-investment in EBM as compared with, for example, implementation strategies.

The next section looks at the nature of the good of health care in the context of EBM. This is examined from different perspectives. Two specific value issues – equity and quantification – are discussed. The chapter then examines the question of where EBM sits in relation to improving health care decision making more generally. Finally, the chapter reaches certain conclusions regarding the future of EBM.

Values, objectives and EBM: what's the good of health care?

In much of the writing on EBM, there is at least by implication an assumption that the good of health services is restricted to health alone. There is, however, increasing evidence that that is too narrow a view. (See, for example, Ryan 1999 and Birch *et al.* 2003.) Just what it is that patients want beyond health or that doctors want to deliver to patients can be debated. Again, there is some evidence that citizens, as distinct from patients, want more than health from the health care system; precisely what is again a matter for greater debate. What is pertinent in the context of this chapter, however, is not precisely what that extra might be but the fact that there is extra and that someone needs to decide what that extra is or ought to be.

EBM has been defined by Sackett *et al.* (1996) as 'the conscientious, explicit and judicious use of current best evidence in making decisions about the care of individual patients'. Furthermore, Sackett *et al.* say, 'For family physicians, evidence-based medicine is also of value in making decisions about the care of families and communities.'

To make decisions about the care of individual patients requires some prior judgements about what the objective of such care is. There is also a need to determine who is to decide what that objective is. As indicated earlier, too often the presumption within EBM is that all that is relevant to the care of the patient is the health outcome. If that is accepted, then it follows that all the evidence that is needed is related to health. This helps to explain why epidemiology has dominated EBM to the extent that it has. It may also explain why it is primarily medical doctors who decide what the objectives of patient care are. Implied in the definition given by Sackett *et al.* is that it is the doctor who is making the decision about what the objective is.

With respect to the setting of objectives, when these are about individual patient care, some might find it acceptable that these should be determined by doctors. It is of note, however, that there is less clarity surrounding the objectives of patient care than is ideal. Why that is so is now discussed.

The doubts regarding the objective of patient care arise largely because few have seen the need to try to establish it. There is a belief, a faith perhaps, that health services are only about health. The vast majority of randomised controlled trials (RCTs) do not get beyond health. There is also a feeling that if health changes are captured, then these so dominate that others can be discounted. Unless that assumption is challenged, then it will remain the case that RCTs and other investigations into what is valued in health care will continue to be restricted to health.

Returning to the definition by Sackett *et al.*, there is a large jump from the first to the second of the sentences quoted. It is assumed that the stance for patients is applicable when families or even communities are considered. That seems unlikely, unless of course one takes the view that all that patients, families and communities want from their health services is health.

It is difficult intuitively to think that moving the focus from patients to families will result in no shift in the concerns with respect to outcomes or objectives. In, for example, care of the elderly, the family is involved in caring. There is a potentially complex situation for both what the person cared for seeks or gets and what the person caring seeks or gets. Being loved and loving are both potentially important and valued dimensions of care. Caring may involve costs or loss of benefit for the carer; there will often be positive feelings through caring, not only caring *for* but caring *about* (Wiseman 1997). If a health service intervention results in a son or daughter having reduced strain or stress, ought this not to be included as a part of the good of the intervention? If a carer does less caring in the wake of a health service intervention, is this positive with respect to the good that the intervention does (the carer has time freed up for other activities) or is it bad (the carer no longer has as much of an outlet for her compassion)? Both positive and negative aspects might be present in the same intervention. Whatever, there is a wider objective here if all the effects are included, and not just those that affect the patient. The extent to which EBM copes with this change seems limited.

On caring, Little (2000) argues:

> While 'good care' obviously needs guidelines and standards, they are not enough on their own to ensure good care. We may say that this performative kind of care is 'a caring for'. The moral dimension, however, refers to 'caring about'. We can *care for* people by following protocols, but to cope flexibly with the needs of the ill, we need to *care about* them in a more strictly moral sense. Management protocols provide rules that help us to care for. Our consciences and compassion provide guides to caring about.

It is not at all clear that EBM embraces caring about.

Moving to the community, and trying to continue to accept that the objective remains as for the individual patient, requires a yet bigger leap of faith. Communities are likely to be concerned about fairness or equity to a much greater extent than are individuals or families. As a result, there are repercussions for the health of the population as a whole. Indeed, economists argue that there can be trade-offs or conflicts between efficiency (which is about maximising benefits with the resources available) and equity or fairness (which is about distribution). Giving all women access to breast screening might be deemed fair; it is likely to be more efficient to restrict access to those aged over 50. Making services more decentralised may promote equity geographically but lead to less efficiency within a constrained budget.

Equity at a community level may be valued for its own sake. There is a universal public health care system in Australia (Medicare) with a goal, in principle at least, of equal access for equal need. This policy of universality may be valued simply because the community believes that it is a good thing to have fairness in health care. It can be an indicator of a good or decent society. Individual patients and families may also value equity, but this is less likely (see, for example, Mooney *et al.* 1999). Whatever, the extent to which EBM allows for equity in its concerns is very limited and often missing. (This is discussed in more detail on p. 67.)

The values and preferences that could lie behind the objectives of health care are many. Economists argue that in health care, patients are generally poorly informed, and as a result rely on the better-informed doctor as their agent to advise them. They thus get not just treatments from their doctors but also information. There is also the issue of what it is that the doctor-agent is trying to maximise on behalf of the patient. What does the doctor perceive as the objective? Various answers are possible: health; utility (satisfaction) more broadly than that from health but still restricted to outcomes such as information and reduced anxiety; or utility where values can also be attributed to processes such as respect for autonomy, being treated with dignity.

One issue that is little discussed is that different doctors may be trying to do different things. This may be part of the explanation of why medical practice variations exist. Indeed, even if not often recognised, one can see the beginnings of the EBM movement in the work of Jack Wennberg (1984) on such variations. Wennberg argued that the main reason why these variations exist is that doctors' knowledge of the effectiveness of their treatments is uncertain. The problem, according to Bob Evans (1991), is yet simpler: 'Knowing is not the same as doing.' This is almost certainly the nub. It may also be, however, that doctors have different objectives. If true, then this would explain why they do different things. If Evans is right, or if doctors are attempting to achieve different ends, then EBM is unlikely to do much for medical practice variations and may not do much for greater effectiveness, efficiency or equity from clinical practice. This is because there remains the problem of how to get clinicians (and others) to *act* on the basis of the knowledge gained from EBM. To make a difference, evidence has to be recognised as such, seen as relevant, interpreted and acted upon. No one can seriously oppose good evidence as a basis for practising medicine or plumbing or bus driving. One can question, however, how much good is optimally good and what good such good evidence creates. As discussed on p. 70, the perfecting of evidence may well not stand up to examination through the weighing up of marginal costs and marginal benefits.

There is, however, more to getting good or best practice than EBM. Evidence is good; it is not sufficient.

It is thus puzzling that as a movement, EBM seems not to be overly concerned about establishing the objectives of health care, whether at the level of individual patient care, from the perspective of families or at a systems level. Particularly on the last, the notion of a health care system as a social institution seems not to be recognised by EBM proponents. The objective of patient care, family care and community care is taken to be health maximisation.

On another front, there is the question raised earlier of who sets the objectives. It is possible to argue that it is appropriate to use individuals' values to guide what is the objective for interventions at the level of individual patient care. This is less likely to be the case at a community level. Of course, it might be argued that the community is simply an aggregation of individuals. It is also possible that community values might be just that, i.e. the values of the community, as an entity in its own right.

The question of values, including that of whose values, is crucial. Yet what is striking in the EBM literature is how little values are debated. Nowhere, for example, is the word 'values' or 'preferences' listed in the glossary of the *Cochrane Collaboration Reviewers' Handbook* (2003). In that same handbook it is stated that 'Recommendations that depend on assumptions about resources *and values* should be avoided' (emphasis added). The appearance of a 'value-free' world is maintained.

That lack of concern with values is exemplified within that glossary in a number of ways. One is that the question of different cultures and variations in culture across the world is dealt with in one sentence: 'For some health care problems, such as psychiatric problems, cultural differences sometimes limit the applicability of results.' The different cultural constructs of health, the variations culturally in what is important in quality of life, and different cultural attitudes to death are all but ignored, especially as regards physical health. There is no recognition of the differential barriers to care for some cultures in multicultural societies. There is little recognition that EBM is itself a cultural phenomenon.

The reductionism of EBM is thus not solely at the level of keeping things narrow, thereby simplifying the world and being able to explain it on the basis of just a few key variables. This reductionism extends to portray a largely value-free world and one which, when the presence of values is recognised, is universalist rather than relative and where one culture (essentially a UK/US culture) dominates, even monopolises.

One notes the emphasis in EBM of medical science and epidemiology, and to some extent that is justified. The almost total lack of philosophers and anthropologists in the area is, however, concerning.

A possible explanation of this 'value-free' space of EBM is that the questions of which evidence, about what and whose evidence are currently determined very much by the medical profession. They are seemingly the self-appointed guardians of the nature of the good that health care seeks to provide. EBM does support in principle the idea that patients might have some say as well. The reality is very different. It is important to look at health services not just as medical organisations but as, first and foremost, *social* institutions. Adopting that latter view suggests that the nature of good of health care is something that people as citizens have a right to determine or, as a minimum, influence.

Two value issues: equity and quantification

Accepting the focus of health care as a social institution means that equity in health care, which is so clearly a social phenomenon, merits attention. It is an attention that EBM signally fails to provide. This issue is debated here.

Equity can be seen as synonymous with notions of justice or fairness. It is generally defined as equality in the distribution of something. Equality *per se*, however, is seldom able to be equated with equity – that is, there is usually some caveat or qualification accompanying the equality statement (such as 'for equal need').

In the literature there is much discussion over the appropriate principle for equity policy. Some principles proposed are equal expenditure per capita, equal resources per capita, equal resources for equal need, equal access for equal need, equal use for equal need, and equal health. The debate over what might be deemed an appropriate equity principle to a large extent mirrors a wider debate over what the appropriate criterion for fairness is. This is not surprising, given that the issue of equity is driven by values – essentially *social* values.

Whatever, equity is an important goal in most health services. When the choice is between equality of health, of use and of access (Donaldson and Gerard 1992), the principle of equity that is most commonly adopted is equal access. Equal health is elitist. It is also unattainable in practice. Equal use is also elitist, and removes respect for variations in individual preferences from the scene. Equal access places responsibility for equity clearly where it should be: on the supply side of the equation in that the concern is with equal availability or equal opportunity to use and (if access is defined sufficiently widely) on the provision of information.

Where health includes notions of autonomy and self-determination, then if the focus of equity is purely on reducing disparities in health, this may create a potentially false separation between health *per se* and participation (both individual and community). This would suggest some role for the community in deciding what constitutes the benefits of various programmes and also how these are to be distributed equitably and according to what principles. This is especially important given that equity is likely to be construed and weighted differently by different populations and different cultures.

In the wake of this discussion, the difficulties for EBM with respect to equity are two. First, if, as seems most commonly the case, equity is defined in terms of access, i.e. opportunity to use or availability, then measures of health, which are the key focus of EBM, are not directly relevant to this definition. Second, the preferences that seem most relevant to equity are those of the community. Again, EBM is not strong on social preferences.

This discussion of equity exemplifies the two concerns discussed this far in this chapter with respect to EBM: the lack of explicit objective setting and the playing down of the relevance of values, especially social or community values, in health policy making. The extent to which EBM recognises equity as an objective of health care is all too limited. Ignoring equity in EBM, given how much of a hold the EBM school now has on health policy, creates a risk that equity is sidelined as a social goal of health care.

A related but more specific point on the question of values is the dominance of quantification in the evidence for EBM. This is perhaps a function of the 'value-free' environment of EBM. There can be, even if falsely, an impression that if something is presented in numbers, it is value free. Perhaps the negative is stronger. If one cannot measure it, it is seemingly more value laden. There is present here also a desire on the part of EBM adherents to worship at the altar of science, where science is defined in terms of rigour, and in turn rigour is seen as being encapsulated only in whatever is quantifiable. The science of medicine is very much wrapped up in epidemiology, and it is, then, little wonder that this discipline dominates EBM.

There are dangers here of overcooking. Clearly, epidemiology is a crucial part of the evaluation of health care and medical evaluation. That is not in dispute. It is also the case, however, and not adequately recognised, that epidemiology is not value free. Choosing, for example, the probability of five-year survival as a measure of effectiveness is an example of just how value laden it can be (all that count are life and death, and then only for five years, indeed exactly five years). The point is rather that the extent to which there is among EBM advocates a desire to see epidemiology as value free and a shuddering at the prospect of bringing in values to this scientific arena creates concerns about just how reductionist the reductionism of EBM can be.

As Little (1998) has written about the science that drives EBM,

> There is a danger that epidemiology may lose sight of the values which justify its existence as well as the existence of all the constituents of health services. It may lose this perspective because it moves so definitely in the computational domain, while the values that justify it

originate in the cultural and value-laden domain which is expressed in language rather than numbers. This dichotomy needs to be recognised and the relative incommensurability of the parameters of each domain needs to be respected and overcome.

EBM and priority setting

Even if we were to agree that the objective is health maximisation, in the EBM literature the link between EBM and this assumed goal is not made as strongly as one would wish. To return once again to the definition by Sackett *et al.*, the question to be asked is what the purpose is of any information or better information (evidence or whatever) in a decision-making context. It is to make better decisions. What is a 'better' decision? Presumably one that gets the decision maker closer to the goal to which she or he aspires. In terms of determining how best to improve decision making, then presumably the decision maker needs to look at the various options faced. There is, then, a need to weigh up the costs and benefits within some cost–benefit framework, choose how best to use the resources available to improve the decision and thereby meet the objective better.

Yet the *raison d'être* of EBM appears to be better information/evidence *per se*. That is somewhat absolutist, even abstract. It leaves open or even neglected the question of where EBM sits in the context of priorities for better decision making. How does one decide how to allocate (inevitably) scarce resources both *to* EBM and *within* EBM? Are the costs and benefits of a higher level of evidence always such that that higher level should be pursued? In what circumstances might one be better off settling for a lower level of evidence? Where should providers of evidence concentrate their energies? Is cancer EBM more worthy of extra resources than diabetes EBM? For which sorts of decisions can better EBM add most value? What are the priorities for EBM and between EBM and other aids to better decision making?

To me, as an economist, priority setting involves up to four questions:

1. Is this (intervention) worth doing in terms of doing any good? Is it effective?
2. Is it more worth doing this way rather than that? Which is more cost-effective?
3. Is it worth doing at all, given the opportunity cost involved? Are the benefits greater than the costs?
4. Is it worth doing more? Are the extra benefits of more, greater than the extra costs of more?

For the economist, crucial to any discussion on evaluation are two concepts: opportunity cost and the margin. The benefit forgone in the best alternative use of the resources is the opportunity cost. Cost defined in this way is thus also measured in terms of benefits, but in this case as benefits given up or sacrificed. So, the benefits obtained are compared with the benefits given up. Clearly, establishing benefit obtained and benefit forgone is enhanced through EBM. To that extent, then, EBM is welcome.

Yet equally clearly, benefits and costs are value-laden concepts. Take cost. There are three value judgements built into any costs:

1 What is the best opportunity forgone?
2 What is the size of the benefit forgone?
3 Who is to make these two value judgements?

These values and value judgements plague so much of health care decision making. Assume an additional $1 million is made available for health care. If we were all agreed, on the basis of 'fact', that spending $1 million on care of the elderly was the best way to use that money – that investing there provided the greatest benefit of all possible uses of that $1 million – then many of the difficulties that arise regarding choices in health care would be avoided. We are, however, seldom so agreed. This might be a function of poor evidence. Disagreement might well remain, however, even if we had perfect evidence. No decision can be reached about whether to spend on care of the elderly, on child care or on cancer patients without bringing in value judgements. There is no perfect evidence on values.

The second concept of the margin is about change – strictly, a change of one unit more or less. Thus, the marginal cost of treating the twentieth patient is the difference in cost between treating 20 patients and treating 19 patients. The concept is important, because so often what is of interest in resource allocation in health care is just this sort of question: treating more or fewer patients or employing more or fewer nurses or conducting more or fewer screening tests.

Now what has this discussion to do with EBM? What is sought here is to establish that information of the kind that EBM throws up has a purpose and that that purpose is to promote better decision making – in essence, more knowledgeable decision making. Such improvement in decision making is not an end in itself. It ought to lead in turn to better outcomes or greater benefits or higher efficiency or more equity or more or better of whatever it is that is sought from the allocation of society's scarce resources to the social end involved. EBM is, to quote Sackett *et al.* as earlier, about 'use of current best evidence in making decisions'. Certainly they add that these decisions are 'about the care of individual patients' – but to what end?

Where evidence is already good or non-controversial, or where there are no or few choices, or nearly everyone is practising good medicine (however defined) already – or, in other words, where the capacity to benefit through EBM or better EBM is low – then the extent to which investing more in EBM is likely to be justified will be smaller. The value added by EBM will not be as large. Investing in reviews is time-consuming; practising EBM at the clinical level may take the individual clinician more time. Yet the EBM literature seems not to have worked through any basis for priority setting for investing in EBM. At one level this is understandable, as EBM tends to be based on a view that uncertainty is to be avoided at all costs, that the idea that 'might' (as in uncertainty) might be right is anathema, that 'might' is wrong and that certainty is sought. It is not strictly that certainty is the target, more that uncertainty is the enemy. Aiming at the wrong target is clearly wrong; specifying the wrong target is also wrong; but the greatest EBM sin appears to be to fire without knowing all the evidence that is available. One might still hit the target. One might hit a lesser target. The goal, however, seems to be in the process – in informed decision making – rather than in the outcome.

When one is dealing with scarce resources, establishing how to use them is best done by looking at the question: if we spend an extra, say, $1 million on X and take that from Y, is the overall good achieved greater or less? To be able to judge whether we are better off requires first that we have some notion of the good that we seek to better. The sort of paradigm that EBM is built upon does not lend itself to this thinking. That is a pity, not for some obscure philosophical reason but because EBM is left looking somewhat purist, and there is then a risk that that is its undoing.

This is not just a question of how best (most efficiently) to achieve some acknowledged good or some sought-after better; it is a matter of what philosophy or set of values underpins the endeavour. To overstate the importance of evidence not only risks not achieving as much good as we might; it also risks changing the nature of the good sought.

It is this last point that is the most fundamental criticism that this chapter offers. It is not simply that EBM adherents have not bothered to find out what societies seek as the good of health care; they have by and large assumed they know: the maximisation of health. By so doing they risk reducing the amount of good provided by health care.

Conclusion

Values are an inevitable part of evaluation. Additionally, there are few if any resource allocation choices in health care that are not moral choices (Little 2000). It follows that in examining issues of choices in how to allocate scarce health care resources, issues of ethics arise, and in particular in how clinical freedom operates with respect to such resource allocation.

The idea of the doctor trying to do the best for his or her patient is one to which all can subscribe. Yet it raises many questions. While it is clearly the patient's best that is being sought, who decides what that is? Is that best to be defined purely in terms of health? Normally, the debate around this issue is set in terms of a balance between on the one hand the doctor deciding and acting on behalf of the patient, and on the other the doctor advising the patient and the patient then deciding.

Clearly, good evidence is important in this context – but to what end? The context in which evidence is presented and EBM is practised matters. The objective of the doctor matters not only in interpreting evidence but in how it is presented or even whether it is presented. It is to a large extent this contextual matter that is at the root of the concern in this chapter.

Caring *for* is what EBM is about, and such caring is a worthy endeavour. On caring *about*, EBM is silent. Yet that is also a worthy endeavour. In any assessment of EBM, there is a need to remember that there is more to appraising health care than the management protocols that EBM supports. Compassion, goodness, doing good should still count. For EBM, the challenge remains to define or to have defined the good in doing good.

References

Birch, S., Melnikow, J. and Kuppermann, M. (2003) Conservative versus aggressive follow up of mildly abnormal pap smears: testing for process utility, *Health Economics*, 12 (10): 879–84.

Cochrane Collaboration Reviewers' Handbook, The (2003) www.cochrane.org/resources/handbook/index.htm (accessed 13 November 2003).

Donaldson, C. and Gerard, K. (1992) *Economics of Health Care Financing: The Visible Hand*, Basingstoke: Macmillan.

Evans, R.G. (1991) The dog in the night-time: medical practice variations and health policy, in T.F. Andersen and G. Mooney (eds) *The Challenge of Medical Practice Variations*, London: Macmillan.

Little, M. (1998) Assignments of meaning in epidemiology, *Social Science and Medicine*, 47: 1135–45.

Little, M. (2000) Ethonomics: the ethics of the unaffordable, *Archives of Surgery*, 135: 17–21.

Mooney, G., Jan, S., Ryan, M., Bruggemann, K. and Alexander, K. (1999) *What the Community Prefers, What it Values, What Health Care it Wants: A Survey of South Australians*, Report to the SA Health Commission, Adelaide.

Ryan, M. (1999) Using conjoint analysis to take account of patient preferences and go beyond health outcomes: an application to in vitro fertilisation, *Social Science and Medicine*, 48: 535–46.

Sackett, D.I., Rosenberg, W.M.C., Gray, J.A., Haynes, R.B. and Richardson, W.S. (1996) Evidence based medicine: what it is and what it isn't, *British Medical Journal*, 312 (7023): 71–2.

Wennberg, J.E. (1984) Dealing with medical practice variations: a proposal for action, *Health Affairs*, 3 (2): 6–32.

Wiseman, V. (1997) Caring: the neglected health outcome? Or input?, *Health Policy*, 39 (1): 43–54.

6 Randomised clinical trials in assessing inferences about causality and aetiology

Dag S. Thelle

Introduction

> I took twelve patients with scurvy on board the Salisbury at sea. Their cases were as similar as I could have them. They all in general had putrid gums, the spots and lassitude, with weakness of their knees. They lay together in one place . . . and had one diet common to all.
>
> (James Lind 1753)

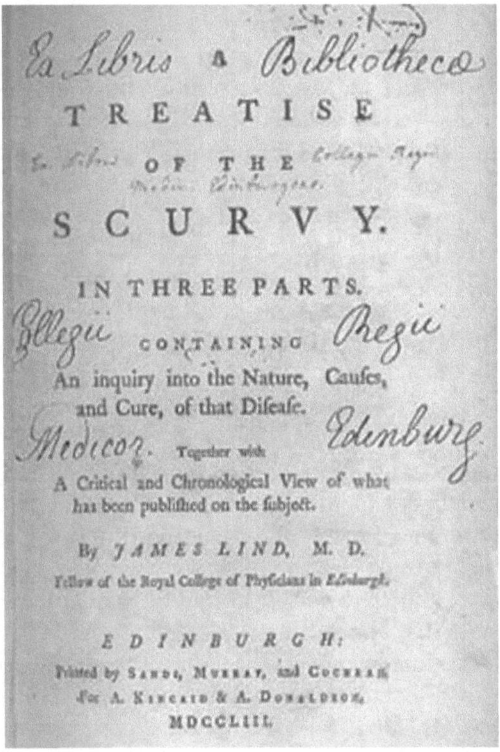

A
TREATISE
OF THE
SCURVY.
IN THREE PARTS.
CONTAINING
An inquiry into the Nature, Cauſes, and Cure, of that Diſeaſe.
Together with
A Critical and Chronological View of what has been publiſhed on the ſubject.
By JAMES LIND, M. D.
Fellow of the Royal College of Phyſicians in Edinburgh.
EDINBURGH:
Printed by SANDS, MURRAY, and COCHRAN.
For A. KINCAID & A. DONALDSON.
MDCCLIII.

Figure 6.1 James Lind's *A Treatise of the Scurvy* (1753).

James Lind's treatment for scurvy is one of the first trials recorded that comes close to present-day clinical trials. However, even if Lind realised that two oranges and one lemon a day were superior to any other treatment for scurvy, it was to take almost 50 years before the Royal Navy supplied its ships with lemon juice for prophylactic purposes. Another couple of hundred years would pass before the first known controlled double-blind study was performed in the 1940s, when Austin Bradford Hill (1951) directed a study testing a pertussis vaccine.

The need for controlled and blinded trials stems from the recognition that all rational treatment and prevention depend upon aetiological knowledge, and that the assessment of causality can be easily influenced by subjective attitudes and bias. The word 'rational' implies that the aetiology is based upon a recognisable and describable web of factors, logically ending in overt clinical disease. The essence of any aetiological reasoning is that exposure to a particular variable will have a specific effect on a human body. Such exposure may be any factor produced outside this body. The effect may be either an increased probability of disease or a reduced risk of a clinical event. Thus, both environmental factors and means of treatment are included among such aetiological agents. One of the major problems of aetiological reasoning in medicine, which distinguishes it from physical science, is that a cause of a disease, or an effective drug, has to be defined in terms of factors affecting the probability of disease. Only rarely (maybe never) are we in a position to state that a causal factor will always be followed by certain, defined disease, or that all subjects treated with a particular drug will benefit from that treatment. Add to this that most diseases are caused by multiple factors, where each may have a necessary but not a sufficient impact upon the final outcome. This implies that we have to assess statistical associations and decide whether we accept that these associations imply causal relationships. A set of methodologies has been developed to aid our assessment, among which trials and experiments constitute an increasingly important strategy.

Experiments and trials

Physical experiments are traditionally set up as models in which all factors except those being tested remain constant during the experimental period. This kind of model differs from the clinical trial, where it is not possible to control all external factors. The only way to overcome the influence of other, uncontrolled factors on the outcome is to nullify their effects by distributing them randomly across the different treatment strata in the trial. The randomisation procedure clearly does not guarantee identical distribution of the disease or effect determinants between the allocated groups. The tendency towards identical distribution, however, does increase with increasing numbers of individuals allocated (Rothman 1977). A symmetrical distribution is less likely to occur where only a few observational units such as communities or blocks of patients are randomly allocated. This can have profound effects upon the interpretation of community intervention studies.

We can envisage three different situations in which clinical experiments or controlled trials are useful in the assessment of a causal issue. One is to determine whether a certain exposure to an external factor is associated with a specific pathological effect, another to assess whether a certain treatment has a superior effect compared to another regime, and a third to assess whether a health promotion measure or public health intervention may affect disease risk at a community level. Even if the purpose differs, all these situations may be described as aetiological assessments. The statistical analyses and the causal inferences are always based upon comparing two or more groups with regard to the outcome variable (e.g. disease, or intermediary factors such as blood pressure, blood lipids or even behaviour) where the influences of other factors have been neutralised. A distinction will be drawn, however, between experiments aimed at demonstrating aetiological biological associations and clinical trials aimed at testing the effectiveness and efficacy of a certain treatment or prevention procedure.

When to use clinical trials

Trials can act as instruments of guidance when there are doubts about the best treatment or the best advice to reduce the probability of harmful effects or disease. Thus trials should be started only if there are doubts about whether a certain regime differs from another or whether some preventive action should be undertaken. The doubt may arise with regard to the effect on the disease incidence, case fatality rate, secondary attacks, or whether one treatment regime is associated with more side effects than another. Doubts usually arise when the difference in expected effect is small or moderate. The chances are that a large effect will have impressed the medical community sufficiently to reduce doubts to nil, thereby reducing the incentive for conducting a trial. Large effects are thus usually identified by methods other than controlled trials, such as non-randomised observational studies. The clinical trial usually takes months or even years to complete. It has been extensively studied and described with regard to planning, organisation, implementation, analyses, reports and inference (Yusuf *et al.* 1984; Hulley and Cummings 1988; Anon. 1996).

The causal concept

An epidemiological experiment is based on the assumption that the exposure, be it to therapy or to some other sort of intervention, will affect the causal web leading to overt disease. While the mechanism does not necessarily have to be fully understood, a likely causal association between the treatment in question and the disease must exist before one embarks upon a clinical trial. Figure 6.2 shows a simplified pathway of disease from the obvious environment and gene interaction, leading to pathogenic gene products as well as gene–gene interactions, and finally clinically overt disease. Even this simplified version of a pathogenic mechanism shows that a number of factors must be included in the causal chain or web. Some of these are assumed to be sufficient to cause disease, whereas others are contributing as necessary causal elements, but by themselves are not sufficient to result in a clinical event. The likely interaction or effect modification that exists between the different factors is a valid argument for adopting a multifactorial approach to affect the disease risk.

Epidemiological trials and experiments according to observation units and methods

Whether one approaches single individuals, communities, workplaces or other population subgroups will determine a number of the trial parameters, the experimental design and the inferences that can be drawn from the results. Epidemiological experiments and trials may therefore be categorised according to both observation units and intervention methods. Table 6.1 on page 77 gives the main features.

The observation unit – the unit to be studied – in a clinical trial is usually the individual participant. There are exceptions to this, where communities or population subgroups are allocated to different regimes or interventions aimed at reducing their risk of disease. The methods of intervention go from public health measures to reduce exposure to external environmental factors through individual advice to the use of tailor-made drugs aimed at well-defined pathogenic mechanisms. The assessment of screening is also included in this overview. The different categories listed in Table 6.1 are not mutually exclusive: combinations may occur both of

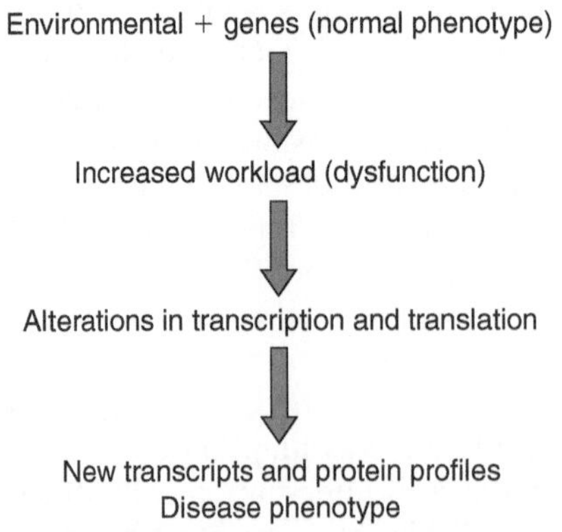

Figure 6.2 Disease pathway.

Table 6.1 Trial designs

Design	*Intervention method*	*Observational units*
Multifactorial design	Advice and health promotion measures	Individuals
Multifactorial design	Advice and health promotion measures	Communities
Single-factor design	Advice and health promotion measures	Individuals
Single-factor design	Advice and health promotion measures	Communities
Multifactorial design	Pharmaceutical drugs	Individuals
Single-factor design	Pharmaceutical drugs	Individuals
Single-factor design	Screening	Individuals
Single-factor design	Screening	Communities

methods used and of units of observation. It is important to realise, however, that the choice of observation units determines the power of the study and thereby the possibility of reaching a valid result.

The major asset of clinical trials compared to observational studies is the control over extraneous factors that the randomisation process gives. Even with the randomisation, however, the influence of extraneous factors cannot be excluded, and the final analyses of the study may be performed very much along the lines of traditional longitudinal observational studies. One of the major sources of error that may arise in an observational study is differential misclassification, which can result in a bias in the estimate of the magnitude of the risk association. This may be the case if one exposure group is also exposed to more intensive medical attention than another. Such differential exposure can lead to subclinical and minor health effects, which would otherwise remain unrecognised, being noted and recorded, resulting in turn in the rates of both endpoints and side effects being inflated. This systematic error may exaggerate the health consequences of a certain exposure or treatment. The only way to ensure that such differential misclassification does not influence the results is to keep both participants and investigators uninformed about the allocation to different treatment groups, i.e. blinded. The blinding procedure is clearly feasible when it comes to assessments of various drug regimes. It is, however, virtually impossible to keep the participants uninformed about dietary changes or other lifestyle intervention. Thus, health promotion measures such as advice about healthy diets, non-smoking, physical activity or allocation to a screening programme cannot be done blindly. Similarly, surgical and other invasive procedures usually cannot escape the impact of observer and/or participant bias. Both participants and investigators will be aware of the group into which the participants have been allocated. This is also the case in community interventions, leading to decreased validity of the observed results.

Multiple factor intervention trials aimed at individuals

Epidemiological studies assessing single intermediary factors, such as blood pressure, blood lipids and (later) blood glucose, have provided insights in the causal web leading to a number of chronic disorders, especially within the field of preventive cardiology (Holme *et al.* 1988; Solberg *et al.* 1985). Knowledge gained from such studies has been transformed into public health actions aimed at identifying high-risk individuals and initiating single-factor interventions (Hypertension Detection and Follow-up Program Cooperative Group 1979; Lipid Research Clinics Program Prevalence Study 1980 – see Williams *et al.* 1980).

As the multifactorial causal mechanisms became evident, it was argued that a multifactorial trial aimed at exposure variables, e.g. smoking, diet or physical activity, would be more effective. There were plans in the United States to undertake a major study on cardiovascular diseases using factorial design aimed at assessing the independent contributions of single factors such as physical activity, smoking and diet, as well as the joint effects from the same factors. The study (entitled Jumbo!) was never implemented, which implies that in the field of cardiovascular prevention we do lack large controlled studies on the most important exposure variables for one of the main incapacitating disease groups worldwide.

The alternative to Jumbo became known as the Multiple Risk Factor Intervention Trial (MRFIT), which involved dietary advice, anti-smoking advice and blood pressure treatment, including a pharmaceutical intervention, thereby combining interventions against direct exposure variables and the intermediary risk factors of blood pressure and the total serum cholesterol group (Multiple Risk Factor Intervention Trial Research Group 1982). This study was based on screening 361,662 American men for coronary risk factors and a subsequent intervention aimed at 12,866 high-risk men allocated to a Special Intervention (SI) group or Usual Care (UC).

Even before the completion of the study and the revelation of the results, voices were raised that even inconclusive results could not be used as arguments against the hypothesis that lifestyle intervention among middle-aged men might reduce their cardiovascular risk. The results of this very large study showed a 7.1 per cent reduction in coronary mortality in the SI group compared to the UC group, but total mortality was slightly higher in the SI group. The results were not significant, even with broad confidence limits. The expected difference had been calculated at 26.6 per cent. Thus, the goal missed the target by a factor of more than 3. The results of MRFIT raise a number of questions concerning the aetiological thinking underlying the hypothesis to be tested, the study design and the intervention methods. The observed coronary mortality and the coronary risk factor levels were lower by a third in the UC group, resulting in loss of statistical power. The increased total mortality in the SI group might have been related to certain drugs used in the high-risk subjects, some of whom might have been adversely affected. Reduced smoking or decreased cholesterol levels might then not have outweighed these effects.

A two-factor study with a discrepant result

The results of MRFIT are in seeming contrast to the much smaller Oslo Diet and Antismoking Trial, in which a substantial reduction in cardiovascular risk was observed after participants were given individually orientated advice (Hjermann *et al.* 1986). One might speculate that MRFIT could have had similar results provided one had stratified for blood pressure before randomisation and had thus excluded the hypertensives from some of the groups. There is a discrepancy between observational studies on blood pressure as a coronary risk factor and the effect of drug-induced blood pressure reduction upon subsequent coronary risk. The latter may not have been taken into consideration in the planning of MRFIT during the 1970s (Collins *et al.* 1990). A number of dietary intervention studies have shown a lipid-lowering effect from dietary changes, but the effect on coronary risk has been small, and considerably smaller than that observed in the Oslo study (Brunner *et al.* 1997). We are thus faced with a number of risk-factor intervention studies in the field of preventive cardiology where the observational data are not fully corroborated by intervention trials. Some of them even go in the wrong direction after an extended follow-up (Strandberg *et al.* 1991). This situation changed completely when statins yielded the benefits that could be expected from the observational studies. The consequences of these discrepant results, the failure of MRFIT, as well as some of the other lifestyle intervention studies have led to a broader and more encompassing view on both the aetiology of coronary heart diseases and the design of intervention studies (Kornitzer 1998).

Discrepant results: what went wrong?

The seemingly discrepant results between MRFIT and the Oslo Trial can be explained by different inclusion criteria, such as the exclusion of hypertensives in the latter. There are, however, other discrepant results that may be more difficult to explain in terms of study design and inclusion criteria. Two examples will be given here: the effect of quitting cigarette smoking and the use of antioxidants.

The excess mortality for smokers has been well established for a long time (Paffenbarger *et al.* 1978; Erikssen and Enger 1978). Observational studies also show that both men and women who report having quit smoking have a mortality that decreases with time since quitting. After five years it falls almost to the level of those who have never smoked (Tverdal *et al.* 1993). On the basis of these observations and the obvious non-physiological nature of tobacco smoke, the 'medical establishment' quickly came to the conclusion that quitting smoking was likely to decrease mortality rates. Thus, very little doubt existed with regard to the aetiological role of tobacco smoking as an important health threat. Nonetheless, a randomised controlled trial of anti-smoking advice was undertaken after screening for high-risk subjects among 1,445 male smokers working as civil servants in Whitehall, London (Rose and Hamilton 1978). After one year, 51 per cent of the intervention group reported that they were not smoking any cigarettes, while most of the others reported a reduction in number smoked. Compared with the 'normal care' group, the men in the intervention group showed a decline in the prevalence of sputum production and dyspnoea; ventilatory function did not improve, but its rate of decline was significantly slowed. There were no evident effects on sickness absence over one year or on mortality over an average of 7.9 years. The authors concluded that the risk of cigarettes to the smoker's life might have been overestimated in observational studies. Twenty years after the original intervention, however, total mortality was 7 per cent lower, fatal coronary heart disease was 13 per cent lower and lung cancer 11 per cent lower. None of the results, however, was statistically significant (Rose and Colwell 1992). At this stage, the authors concluded that the results were consistent with observational studies, implying that smoking cessation by middle-aged men substantially improves their chances of avoiding lung cancer or a fatal heart attack, even if the results were not statistically different. The 'normal care' group was obviously contaminated by the intervention measures. Thus, when it comes to smoking cessation we do not have *any* controlled trial that actually demonstrates a statistically significant impact on mortality, even if the long-term results are going in the 'right' direction.

More importantly, the study demonstrates the difficulty in designing and performing a lifestyle intervention trial. The major issues were the wide confidence intervals, which reflect the lack of sufficient numbers of participants in the trial; the diluting effects of lack of compliance in the intervention group; and the progressive reduction in smoking by the control group.

Was the HOT study necessary?

The Multiple Risk Factor Intervention Trial (MRFIT) demonstrated that subjects with ECG changes and other signs of cardiovascular disease did not benefit from active antihypertensive treatment, whereas otherwise healthy hypertensives obviously did so. At the same time, Stewart (1979) discussed whether considerable blood pressure reduction might increase the risk of coronary heart disease (CHD). This was supported by Collins and co-workers, who reported that antihypertensive drug treatment did not reduce the CHD risk as much as would be expected from epidemiological studies (Collins *et al.* 1990). These findings gained further support from other formal meta-analyses as well as longitudinal studies (Holme 1988; Thürmer *et al.* 1994; Thelle 1995).

This represents some of the background to the Hypertension Optimal Treatment (HOT) study, which was a randomised unblinded trial set up to assess whether there was a level for blood pressure reduction below which there was no more to gain, thereby defining optimal blood pressure (Hansson *et al.* 1998). This would have to be the level of blood pressure associated with the lowest risk of blood pressure-associated disease and death risk.

The HOT study randomised 18,790 persons with diastolic blood pressure between 105 and 115 mmHg to three groups, in whom the pressure was to be reduced to 90 mmHg, 85 mmHg and 80 mmHg respectively. The participants were treated with felodipin and, depending on the effect, with other drugs. There was no placebo group.

The trial was not an attempt to show the effect of antihypertensive treatment, or to provide information about the effect of blood pressure treatment in this risk segment. The three groups reached different targets, and the average difference between the groups was 2 mmHg. From previous studies (Selmer 1992), this implies a cardiovascular risk difference of about 4–6 per cent between each group. Differences of that magnitude are too small to be statistically significant in a sample of this size. In fact, there were no such differences between the groups with regard to cardiovascular morbidity and mortality. The risk of coronary heart disease, however, was clearly lowest in the group with the lowest blood pressure target. This was mainly due to the diabetics, who showed a remarkably low risk. The CHD risk among non-diabetics in this group was not reduced compared to other blood pressure target groups, and the total CVD death risk was highest in this group, though the difference was not statistically significant. There are two conclusions to be drawn from the HOT study. First, there was no detectable difference in the risk of complications from blood pressure between the different blood pressure target groups. Second, diabetics obtained a remarkably good effect by having their diastolic blood pressure reduced below 85 mmHg.

The second part of the HOT analyses is in reality a prospective cohort analysis where the principle of analysing according to 'intention to treat' has been abandoned. The blood pressure achieved is now used as an explanatory variable for morbidity and mortality. This analysis cannot provide information about the effect of treatment, as the changes in blood pressure are not taken into account. The results did, however, provide insight into the relationship between blood pressure and risk. The risk curves differed slightly for the different end points, but it has been impossible – even with this extensive material – to argue for or against a so-called J curve (see Figure 6.3). The cardiovascular mortality rates do not increase in the interval 80–95 mmHg. There is an increase in total CVD risk in the area below 75 mmHg, but this does not hold for other endpoints such as stroke.

Did the HOT study provide new insights? The risk curves show that the pressure corresponding to minimum risk has wide confidence intervals, as the curves are close to zero from 80 to 95 mmHg diastolic pressure. The main conclusion seems to be that clinicians treating hypertensives should be satisfied with a diastolic blood pressure between 80 and 90 mmHg, but more inference than that is hard to draw. The major aim, to distinguish between the blood pressure target groups, would have required a much larger study. So the question arises: was the study unnecessary?

Trial results differ from the observational data

A remarkable set of negative results from intervention studies arises in the field of antioxidants. There is today a huge market for antioxidant diet supplementation, but the evidence for any beneficial effect is, to say the least, doubtful. The theoretical background stems from 1931, when it was shown that univalent reduction of molecular oxygen results in an oxygen radical (the oxygen molecule receives an electron and becomes a superoxide, which transforms to hydrogen peroxide and hydroxyl radical). It took a long time, however, to become clear that this mechanism might have important biological consequences. In 1969, superoxide dismutase, which removes superoxide, was discovered. This led to an intensive search for reactive molecules, and it was soon established that hydrogen peroxide in the presence of iron or copper transformed to a hydroxy radical. Other radicals with biological effects were derivatives of polyunsaturated fatty acids, sulphhydryl compounds and quinone-like substances.

It was established thereafter that a large number of protective and defence mechanisms involving, *inter alia*, selenium and vitamins existed. Observational studies supported the theory that an intake of dietary products high in antioxidants was protective against cancer and cardiovascular diseases (Hercberg *et al.* 1998). This theory also gained support from the basic sciences in explaining a number of then still inadequately understood disease mechanisms such as carcinogenesis, atherogenesis, thrombosis, heart failure and remodelling, chronic pain, as well as rotting and decay. The controlled trials, though, have not supported these observational findings, in the sense that additional antioxidants have provided no protection against either cardiovascular diseases or cancer. The very ambitious ATBC study involving 27,271 Finnish smokers aged 50–69 who were given 50 mg of vitamin E, 20 mg of beta-carotene or a placebo (Virtamo *et al.* 1998; Albanes *et al.* 1996) concluded that among smokers beta-carotene

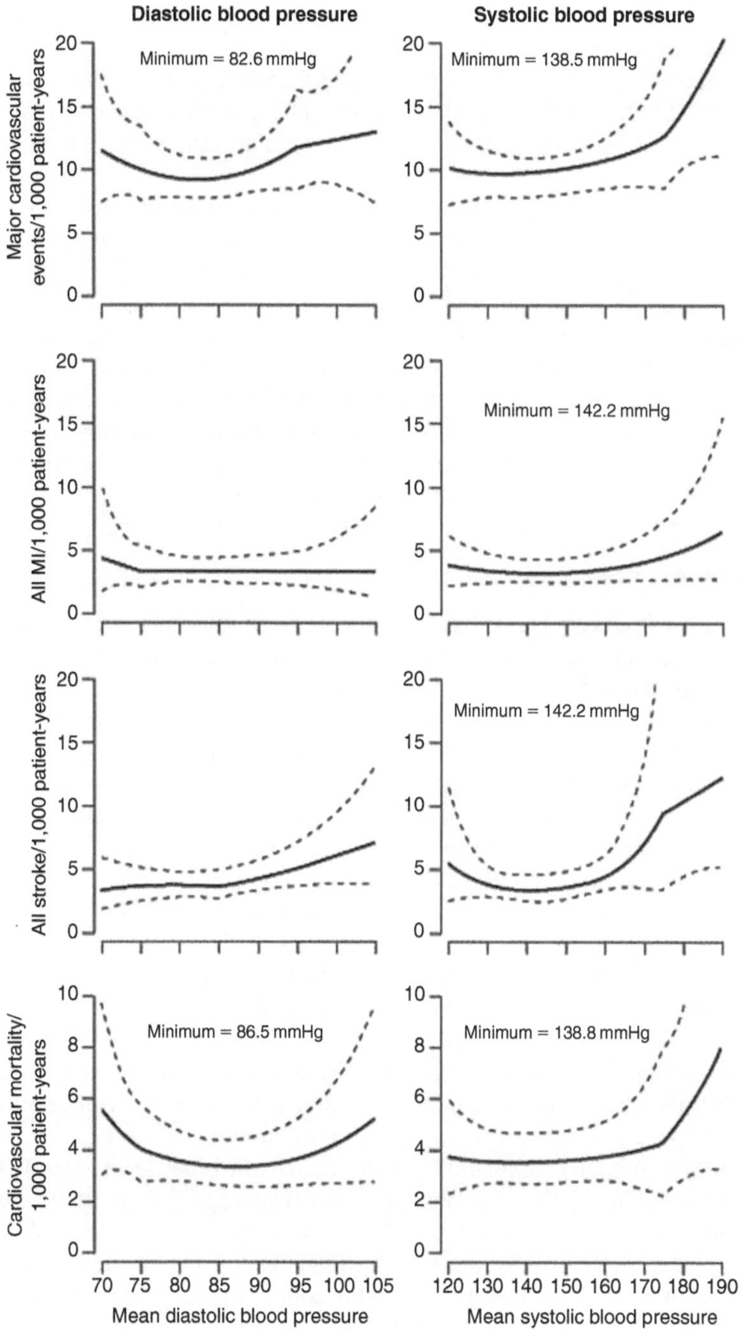

Figure 6.3 Relation between blood pressure and cardiovascular events (from Hansson *et al.* 1998; reproduced with permission from Elsevier (*The Lancet*, 1998, 351: 1955–62)).

had no effect on risk of myocardial infarction (MI), whereas vitamin E did have a marginal effect on fatal MI. The risk of lung cancer increased by 18 per cent in the beta-carotene group. The Cambridge Heart Antioxidant Study (CHAOS), which involved 2,002 CHD patients, showed that the risk of MI was reduced, but the mortality remained the same (Stephens *et al.* 1996).

Why did the trials give results that differed dramatically from the consistent and biologically valid data obtained in observational studies? The probable biological explanations lie beyond the scope of this chapter, but the conflicting evidence emphasises the need for a solid aetiological basis in addition to the use of valid study instruments when embarking upon trials of this kind. The conflict is more than a pure intellectual exercise. It raises the question of what kind of public health message should be conveyed to the public. This leads to the assessment of community interventions as being a special kind of experiment, more often than not being non-randomised or so-called pseudo-experimental.

Community interventions

Community interventions differ in principle from the above trials not only because they are not randomised, are unblinded and aim at the public rather than the individual, but also because of the fact that almost no one is excluded from the experiments for any formal reasons. Clinical trials are often 'exclusive' in the sense that a number of conditions may prevent the potential participants from taking part in the study. The major consequence of this selection is usually that the study population are at a lower risk than the general population from which the study population has been selected. This implies that the results from the clinical trials may not be as easily transferred to the public as might have been anticipated from the trial itself. Community interventions or the assessment of public health efforts, however, have to undergo the same scientific scrutiny as any trial before one can draw conclusions or generalise from the observations. This was the case in the 1990s when the Swedish Medical Technical Bureau assessed the effects of community interventions aimed at cardiovascular diseases. The study concluded that there was no scientific basis for starting new community- or population-focused programmes similar to those that had been implemented in the 1970s and 1980s (SBU 1997). The researchers claimed that the changes seen with regard to cardiovascular mortality rates were nothing more than secular changes that were already taking place. These conclusions are seemingly in contrast to other observational studies, such as the international collaborative project MONICA (Kuulasmaa *et al.* 2000). The Swedes, on the other hand, applied stringent scientific criteria to their analysis, and disregarded the concomitant changes in mortality rates and risk-factor levels. These conflicting conclusions thus reflect the difficulties in assessing cause and effect at a population level, and show that such conclusions must involve far more than a pure formal assessment of the observed statistical changes. Trials are never proofs; they only provide indications for associations. The aetiological conclusions must follow a discussion that takes all the criteria of causality into consideration. Figure 6.4 shows that the community may also want to decide for themselves whether they should take the existing evidence seriously or not. The sign was spotted in Sausalito, just outside San Francisco.

Ethics in epidemiology and trials

Epidemiologists as well as other researchers involved in clinical trials and intervention projects have a moral and professional obligation to follow ethical guidelines based upon maximising benefits to individuals and society, and minimising the risks (Coughlin and Beauchamp 1996). Further discussion of these ethical issues falls outside the scope of this chapter, but some comments are needed on the question of whether any research hypothesis should be tested by a controlled trial. The controlled study on the effects of stopping smoking which was cited on p. 80 could be discussed in the light of the impact of the results. The authors state in their paper 20 years after the trial was initiated that 'This is the only

Figure 6.4 A community intervention in health care.

randomised single factor trial ... of antismoking advice, and is likely to remain so' (Rose and Colwell 1992).

The arguments in favour of the study are now more than 30 years old, and the study was undertaken at a time when the results of large observational studies had only just become available (Hammond 1971). The reason for doing the trial must therefore have been that there were doubts about the effects of stopping smoking, based upon these studies. One may question whether the investigators asked themselves what they would have done had the results been negative or inconclusive. How should one proceed from this result? Should this study be repeated today? Were the beneficial effects of stopping smoking seen in observational studies due only to confounding variables? If the last were the case, so much stronger would have been the imperative to identify these health-promoting confounders. The major reason for the inconclusive results is most likely the lack of power, which again draws attention to the importance of planning to include assessment of the effects, as well as the implementation of the study and the risk of contaminating the control group. A study that lacks the power to show the expected results should not be undertaken. It is a waste of resources and exposes subjects to unnecessary burdens. Additionally, the impact of inconclusive results on the domain in question may contribute in a negative way by increasing the uncertainty regarding the research issue.

This is not to say that negative or inconclusive results from randomised clinical or intervention studies are not to be trusted. The other example quoted earlier on the antioxidant controversy shows a consistent pattern of intervention studies disagreeing with the results of the observational studies, implying that vitamin supplements do not have the impact on disease risk that would be expected from observational studies.

Closing comments

The formal assessment of causal relationships based upon scientific reasoning is a relatively new concept in medical science. Most of the actions taken before the second half of the nineteenth century, when the germ theory provided the basis for treatment and prevention, were based upon empiricism, imagination and direct observation. The observation and reality principle – you can believe what you see, as long as you see what I see – was a guiding principle.

We have seen in this chapter that there are medical and public health issues that are unlikely to be solved by randomised, controlled or blinded trials, and where the above principle remains relevant. This is characteristic of lifestyle interventions as well as community actions; whereas doubts about the effects that different drug regimens have need to be assessed by randomised controlled trials. The constraints on observational studies when it comes to drawing causal inference are well known in the epidemiological literature. Randomised controlled trials may also lead us astray.

The bottom line is that in medical science there is no such thing as a causal proof. Any conclusion drawn from causal inference must be based upon a comprehensive discussion of the available evidence concerning the issue in question. The results from experiments, trials and observational data are only a part of this evidence.

References

Albanes, D., Heinonen, O.P., Taylor, P.R. *et al.* (1996) Alpha-tocopherol and beta-carotene supplements and lung cancer incidence in the alpha-tocopherol, beta-carotene cancer prevention study: effects of base-line characteristics and study compliance, *Journal of the National Cancer Institute*, 88: 1560–70.

Asilomar Working Group on Recommendation for Reporting of Clinical Trials in the Biomedical Literature (1996) Checklist of information for inclusion in reports of clinical trials, *Annals of Internal Medicine*, 124: 741–3.

Brunner, E., White, I., Thorogood, M., Bristow, A., Curle, D. and Marmot, M. (1997) Can dietary interventions change diet and cardiovascular risk factors? A meta-analysis of randomized controlled trials, *American Journal of Public Health*, 87: 1415–22.

Collins, R., Peto, R., MacMahon, S. *et al.* (1990) Blood pressure, stroke and coronary heart disease. Part 2. Short-term reductions in blood pressure: overview of randomized drug trials in their epidemiological context, *Lancet*, 335: 827–8.

Coughlin, S.S. and Beauchamp, T.L. (1996) *Ethics and Epidemiology*, Oxford: Oxford University Press.

Erikssen, J. and Enger, S.C. (1978) Smoking, lung function, physical performance and latent coronary heart disease in presumably healthy middle-aged men, *Acta Medica Scandinavica*, 203: 509–16.

Hammond, E.C. (1971) Smoking in relation to diseases other than cancer: total death rates, in R.C. Richardson (ed.) *The Second World Conference on Smoking and Health*, pp. 24–34.

Hansson, L., Zanchetti, A., Carruthers, S.G. *et al.* (1998) Effects of intensive blood-pressure lowering and low-dose aspirin in patients with hypertension: principal results of the Hypertension Optimal Treatment (HOT) randomised trial, *Lancet*, 351: 1755–62.

Hercberg, S., Galan, P., Preziosi, P., Alfarez, M.J. and Vazquez, C. (1998) The potential role of antioxidant vitamins in preventing cardiovascular diseases and cancers, *Nutrition*, 14: 513–20.

Hill, A.B. (1951) http://www.brookes.ac.uk/schools/bms/medical/synopses/hill2.html.

Hjermann, I., Holme, I. and Leren, P. (1986) Oslo Study Diet and Antismoking Trial: results after 102 months, *American Journal of Medicine*, 80 (2A): 7–11.

Holme, I., Helgeland, A., Hjermann, I., Leren, P. and Mogensen, S.B. (1988) Correlates of blood pressure change in middle-aged male mild hypertensives: results from the untreated control group in the Oslo hypertension trial: the Oslo Study, *American Journal of Epidemiology*, 127: 742–52.

Hulley, S.B. and Cummings, S.R. (1988) *Designing Clinical Research*, Baltimore: Williams and Wilkins.

Hypertension Detection and Follow-up Program Cooperative Group (1979) Five-year findings of the hypertension detection and follow-up program. I. Reduction in mortality of persons with high blood pressure, including mild hypertension, *Journal of the American Medical Association*, 242: 2562–71.

Kornitzer, M. (1998) Primary and secondary prevention of coronary artery disease: a follow-up on clinical controlled trials, *Current Opinion in Lipidology*, 9: 557–64.

Kuulasmaa, K., Tunstall-Pedoe, H., Dobson, A. *et al.* (2000) Estimation of contribution of changes in classic risk factors to trends in coronary-event rates across the WHO MONICA Project populations, *Lancet*, 355: 675–87.

Lind, J. (1757) *A Treatise of the Scurvy. In Three Parts. Containing an Inquiry into the Nature, Causes and Cure, of that Disease. Together with a Critical and Chronological View of what has been Published on the Subject,* London: A. Millar.

Multiple Risk Factor Intervention Trial Research Group (1982) Multiple risk factor intervention risk factor change and mortality results, *Journal of the American Medical Association*, 248: 1465.

Paffenbarger, R.S., Brand, R.J., Sholtz, R.I. and Jung, D.L. (1978) Energy expenditure, cigarette smoking, and blood pressure level as related to death from specific diseases, *American Journal of Epidemiology*, 108: 12–18.

Rose, G. and Colwell, L. (1992) Randomised controlled trial of anti-smoking advice: final (20 year) results, *Journal of Epidemiology and Community Health*, 46: 75–7.

Rose, G. and Hamilton, P.J. (1978) A randomised controlled trial of the effect on middle-aged men of advice to stop smoking, *Journal of Epidemiology and Community Health*, 32: 275–81.

Rothman, K.J. (1977) Epidemiologic methods in clinical trials, *Cancer*, 39: 1771–5.

SBU (1997) To prevent illness [in Swedish]. Stockholm: SBU.

Selmer, R. (1992) Blood pressure and twenty-year mortality in the City of Bergen, Norway, *American Journal of Epidemiology*, 136: 428–40.

Solberg, L.A., Strong, J.P., Holme, I. *et al.* (1985) Stenoses in the coronary arteries: relation to atherosclerotic lesions, coronary heart disease, and risk factors: the Oslo Study, *Laboratory Investigation*, 53: 648–55.

Stephens, N.G., Parsons, A., Schofield, P.M., Kelly, F., Cheeseman, K. and Mitchinson, M.J. (1996) Randomised controlled trial of vitamin E in patients with coronary disease: Cambridge Heart Antioxidant Study (CHAOS), *Lancet*, 347: 781–6.

Stewart, I.M. (1979) Relation of reduction in pressure to first myocardial infarction in receiving treatment for severe hypertension, *Lancet*, 1: 861–5.

Strandberg, T.E., Salomaa, V.V., Naukkarinen, V.A., Vanhanen, H.T., Sarna, S.J. and Miettinen, T.A. (1991) Long-term mortality after 5-year multifactorial primary prevention of cardiovascular diseases in middle-aged men, *Journal of the American Medical Association*, 266: 1225–9.

Thelle, D.S. (1995) Is blood pressure treatment as effective in a population setting as in controlled trials? Results from a prospective study (letter), *Journal of Hypertension*, 13: 567–9.

Thürmer, H., Lund-Larsen, P.G. and Tverdal, A. (1994) Is blood pressure treatment as effective in a population setting as in controlled studies? Results from a prospective study, *Journal of Hypertension*, 12: 481–90.

Tverdal, A., Thelle, D., Stensvold, I., Leren, P. and Bjartveit, K. (1993) Mortality in relation to smoking history: 13 years' follow-up of 68,000 Norwegian men and women 35–49 years, *Journal of Clinical Epidemiology*, 46: 475–87.

Virtamo, J., Rapola, J.M., Ripatti, S. *et al.* (1998) Effect of vitamin E and beta carotene on the incidence of primary nonfatal myocardial infarction and fatal coronary heart disease, *Archives of Internal Medicine*, 158: 668–75.

Williams, O.D., Mowery, R.L. and Waldman, G.T. (1980) Common methods, different populations: the Lipid Research Clinics Program Prevalence Study, *Circulation*, 62: 18–23.

Yusuf, S., Collins, R. and Peto, R. (1984) Why do we need some large, simple randomised trials?, *Statistics in Medicine*, 3: 971–80.

7 Number needed to treat – number needed to cheat?

Ivar Sønbø Kristiansen

Introduction

Considerable proportions of doctors' time are devoted to interventions for chronic disease processes such as atherosclerosis (which causes adverse events such as myocardial infarction and stroke) or osteoporosis (causing bone fractures). To the extent that such interventions slow or halt the disease processes, the adverse consequences are postponed. If the postponement is longer than the remaining life span, the outcome is 'avoided'. Even though postponement and the time dimension are crucial to the understanding of the intervention effects, it is impossible to measure postponement of death or other adverse events directly. What we *can* do is to observe, typically in clinical trials, the timing of adverse events in either treated or untreated groups of patients and then compare the *proportions* of individuals with the adverse event in the two groups. Figure 7.1 depicts the results of a clinical trial aimed at exploring survival benefits from enalapril (a drug for hypertension) in patients who have had a heart attack. If the proportion of fatal events is denoted by D_c in the control group and by D_i in the intervention group, the effect of the therapy can be expressed in several ways:

$$D_c - D_i = \text{absolute risk reduction (ARR)} \qquad (1)$$

$$(D_c - D_i)/D_c = \text{relative risk reduction (RRR)} \qquad (2)$$

$$D_i{*}(1 - D_c)/D_c{*}(1 - D_i) = \text{odds ratio (OR)} \qquad (3)$$

In 1988, Laupacis and co-workers published a paper in which they proposed the use of the reciprocal of the absolute risk reduction as a measure of effectiveness of therapies. They called this measure the number needed to treat (NNT) (Laupacis *et al.* 1988):

$$1/(D_c - D_i) = \text{number needed to treat (NNT)} \qquad (4)$$

In Figure 7.1, the risk of fatal outcomes after five years is about 44 per cent in the intervention group and 51 per cent in the control group. The

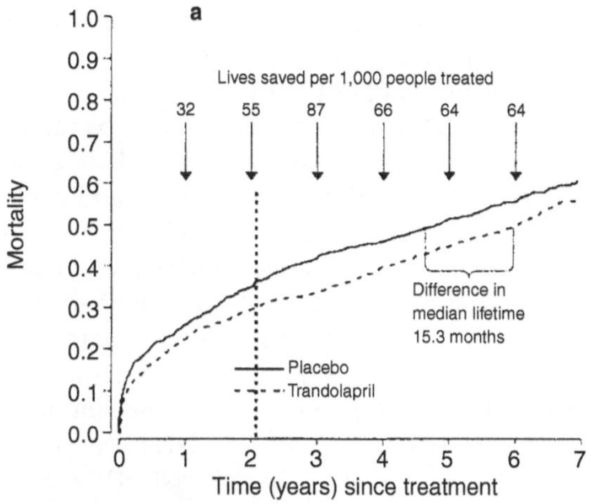

Number of patients at risk

Placebo	873	647	564	497	463	416	373
Trandolapril	876	677	615	576	524	475	431

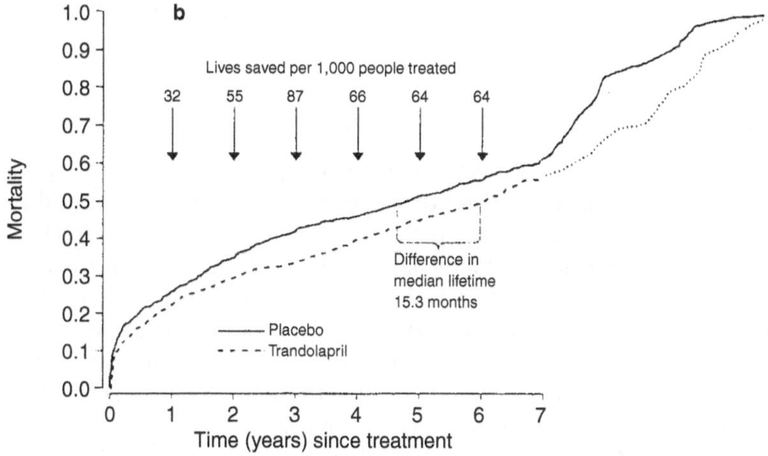

Number of patients at risk

Placebo	873	647	564	497	463	416	373
Trandolapril	876	677	615	576	524	475	431

Figure 7.1 (a) Survival in patients with reduced left ventricular function after an acute myocardial infarction (heart attack). The dotted line represents patients who received a drug (trandolapril), while the continuous line represents a similar control group. The vertical dotted line indicates a point in time (two years from the start of therapy) at which number needed to treat (NNT) might be estimated. The publication (Torp-Pedersen and Kober 1999) presents data for seven years' follow-up. (b) A hypothetical prolongation of the study until all patients are dead. The area between the survival lines for the treatment group and the control group represents the gain in mean survival time (life expectancy).

absolute risk reduction is then 7 per cent (51 per cent − 44 per cent = 7 per cent), or more precisely 6.4 per cent according to the publication (Torp-Pedersen and Kober 1999). This means that NNT is 1/0.064 = 15.6.

Since the invention of the statistic NNT it has been embraced by many, not least by advocates of evidence-based medicine (EBM) (Black *et al.* 1995; Cook and Sackett 1995; Jaeschke *et al.* 1995; McCormack and Levine 1993; Schulzer and Mancini 1996). Some claim that the 'number needed to be treated (NNT) to prevent one event is the most useful measure of clinical effort ... patients must expend in order to help them avoid bad outcomes' (Sackett *et al.* 2000). It is further claimed that NNT is 'a currency for making decisions' (McQuay and Moore 1997), that it is 'easily understood by clinicians' (Laupacis *et al.* 1988) and that it 'has intuitive meaning' (Riegelman and Schroth 1993). The use of NNT has been expanded to encompass harm ('number needed to harm' – NNH), screening ('number needed to screen' – Rembold 1998), education ('number needed to educate' – Gallefoss 2001), exposure ('number needed to expose' – Bender and Blettner 2002) and offence ('number needed to offend' – Stone *et al.* 2002). In this chapter we will first explore the properties of NNT and then look at the evidence that NNT helps decision makers (patients, doctors, policy makers, etc.) to make better decisions.

Properties of NNT

The main problem with using NNT stems from the fact that interventions for chronic diseases have a crucial time dimension that is not captured by metrics measured at one single point in time. In Figure 7.1, ARR is represented by the vertical distance between the two survival curves. NNT is 31, 18, 11, 15, 16 and 16 after 1, 2, 3, 4, 5 and 6 years respectively of follow-up. Which NNT is best suited as the basis for medical decisions? The end of a clinical trial may be seen as a 'natural' measuring point, but is still arbitrary. When NNT is presented for a therapy, it is crucial to know when in the course of the therapy NNT is measured, and whether NNT varies with time. A quick browse through some medical journals reveals several survival curves from clinical trials in which the vertical distance between the curves, and hence NNT, varies with time.

To avoid the time dependence of NNT it has been proposed that NNT should be multiplied by the number of years of treatment in order to estimate how many patients need to be treated for one year in order to avoid one adverse outcome. Suppose, for example, that NNT is 30 after 3 years for treatment A, while it is 40 after 2 years for treatment B. Which treatment is the more effective? When 'we have to treat 30 patients for 3 years with A to avoid one bad outcome', the method would suggest that 'we have to treat 30 × 3 = 90 patients for one year' for the same benefit. For treatment B, the similar number would be 40 × 2 = 80, which would indicate that treatment B is more effective. This simple method for comparison of therapies only makes sense if ARR increases proportionally with time. A glance at survival curves from some clinical trials would indicate that this is seldom the case. Figure 7.1 may be more typical with NNTs that vary up and down over time. It can happen that survival curves can even cross each other, in which case the 'best' therapy will depend on when NNT is measured.

In the EBM handbook by Sackett *et al.* (2000), NNT was defined as 'the number of patients we need to treat with the experimental therapy in order to prevent one of them from developing the bad outcome'. In a study of GPs' skills in EBM, NNT is defined as 'the number of patients needed to be treated to achieve one good outcome' (Young *et al.* 2002). Or in the words of McLaren (2002), '66 patients would have to take ramipril [a drug] for 4.5 years to prevent one stroke'. These statements have two important shortcomings. First, they fail to state explicitly that NNT is time dependent. This may induce users of NNT to believe that it is a general measure. Second, the definitions may leave the impression that events are totally avoided in a few patients while others are not affected by the therapy. In their 'invention paper', Laupacis and co-workers state that 'a number needed to be treated of 11 means that 10 out of 11 patients either do not need therapy or will not respond to it' (Laupacis *et al.* 1988). This interpretation would imply that the likelihood of being helped by the therapy is 1/NNT. A similar interpretation of the NNT has been adopted by others (ibid.; McAlister *et al.* 2000; Misselbrook and Armstrong 2002; San Laureano *et al.* 1999). This would mean that the treatment is like a lottery in which a few (one out of NNT) 'win a prize' while the others receive no benefit. Unfortunately, these interpretations of NNT are unlikely to be correct for interventions aimed at chronic disease processes. This can easily be seen from a graphic explanation.

In Figure 7.2a, the survival times of 20 pairs of patients in a hypothetical trial are represented by horizontal lines. Patients in each pair are identical except that one receives treatment and the other does not. The effect of the therapy can therefore be measured as the difference of survival time for each pair. To ease understanding, patients are ordered according to survival time. From the ordered presentation of survival times one can imagine that survival curves in fact represent the survival times of the individual patients. The vertical line indicates a point in time when we wish to measure the effect of the therapy. Since one fewer patient is alive in the control group and we started to treat 20, ARR is 1/20 = 0.05 and NNT is 1/0.05 = 20. From Figure 7.2a, we see that all 20 patients have their survival times affected by the therapy even though NNT is 20. In other words, we cannot infer the proportion of patients who (dis-)benefit from a therapy by using NNT or indeed any other metric that is measured at a single point in time. The characteristics of NNT as explained in Figure 7.2 would be the same whether the intervention is delaying death or other adverse outcomes such as heart attack, stroke or fractures.

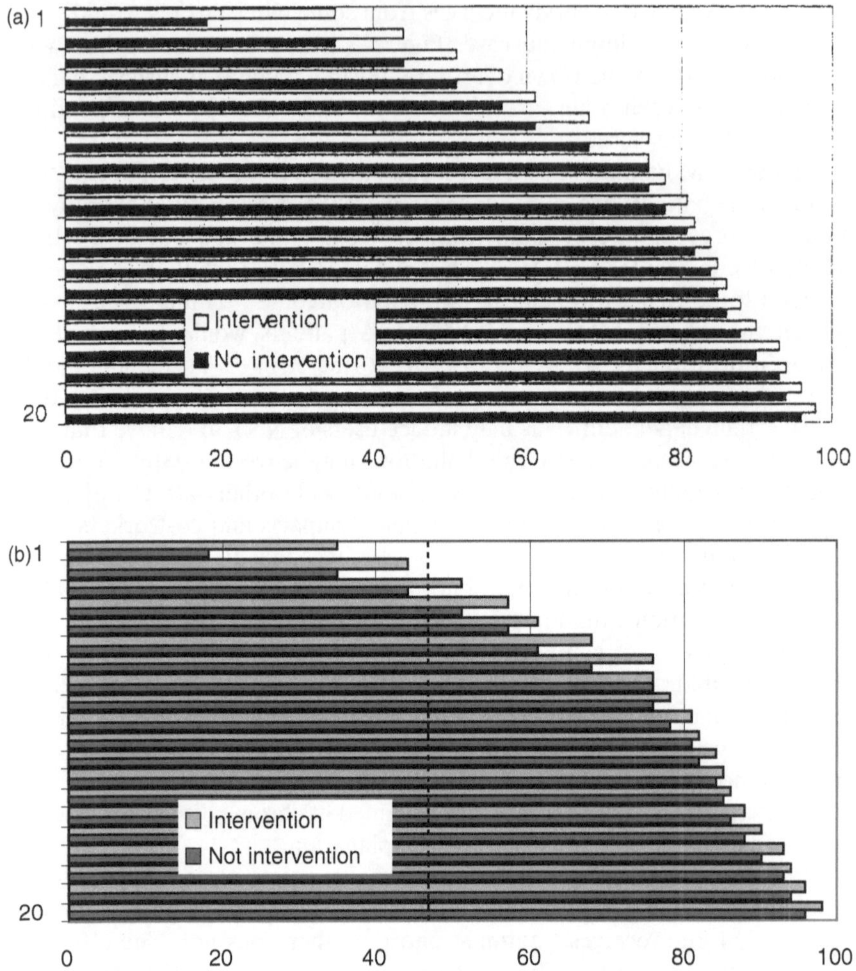

Figure 7.2 Survival times in pairs of identical patients with and without intervention.

Figure 7.2b depicts another hypothetical trial in which 1 out of 20 patients is influenced by the therapy while the others are not. Early in the trial, one patient is cured, with a substantial increase in survival time, and NNT is consequently 20 during most of the trial.

The question is, then, which of the two scenarios of Figure 7.2 is more likely in real life? Computer simulations of survival times indicate that it is in practice impossible to judge what proportions are influenced by an intervention. In real-life trials we do not have pairs of identical patients, and the survival curves become 'blurred' by patients who drop out from therapy or are lost to follow-up. From clinical trials, the mean postponement of the adverse event (e.g. mean increased lifespan) can be estimated, but the distribution of the effect across patients remains unknown. From a biological point of view, it seems plausible that Figure 7.2a comes just as close to the truth as Figure 7.2b. For example, angiographic studies of patients taking statins for hypercholesterolaemia show that there was an impact on the majority of the patients with respect to the width of their coronary arteries. Where this occurred, there may be a postponement of death in the majority of those taking statins (Brown *et al.* 1990). In a study of osteoporosis, the majority of those taking a bisphosphonate had improvements in their bone mineral density (Hochberg *et al.* 1999). Again, one would imagine that this translates into postponements of the adverse event (bone fracture). However, in the osteoporosis case, falls are a causal factor, in addition to fragile bones. Since severe falls are infrequent, one could hypothesise that only a fraction of patients – namely, some of those who fall – benefit from the therapy. Another reason that not everyone will benefit from osteoporosis interventions is simply that some osteoporotic people die from other causes before they sustain a fracture.

Another type of problem relates to the fact that ARR and NNT are dependent on the baseline risk (D_c in equations (1)–(4)) (Smeeth *et al.* 1999) – that is, the risk of adverse events without intervention. Assuming that the relative risk reduction is independent of the baseline risk, as suggested by advocates of EBM (Sackett *et al.* 2000), the greater the baseline risk, the greater the ARR, and hence the smaller the NNT. This means that an intervention effect cannot generally be described by a single NNT. Rather, NNT is specific for a specific therapy, in a specific group of patients, after a specific period of follow-up.

Even if we knew with certainty NNT for an intervention, this does not mean that we 'avoid one bad outcome' each time we treat NNT patients. Chance comes into play, and the number of patients 'avoiding' an event when NNT patients have treatment will vary from none up to NNT. In other words, NNT is an average number only, even when we know the true value of ARR. In reality, since we are left with uncertainty when estimating NNT, that uncertainty should be expressed through some measure such as confidence intervals. This raises problems, however. First, even though NNT is the reciprocal of ARR, the reciprocal of the confidence limits for the ARR may yield biased estimates of the confidence limits for NNT (Hutton 2000). Second, there are pitfalls when the confidence interval of ARR encompasses zero. If, for example, the confidence interval for ARR is $[-0.01, +0.02]$, the confidence interval for NNT is not $[-100, 50]$ even if we disregard the bias introduced by the simple inversion technique. NNT cannot take values in the interval $[-1, 1]$, because one has to treat at least one patient to avoid or induce one event, and because probabilities cannot take values greater than 1.0. Additionally, NNT has two confidence intervals when the confidence interval for ARR includes 0: one at $[-\infty, -100]$ and the other at $[50, \infty]$.

All these issues point to the need for a change in the usual definition of NNT. An NNT of, for example, 11 does not mean that 'if 11 patients are treated for 3 years, one bad outcome is avoided'. Rather, it means that 'if 11 patients are treated for 3 years, on average one less bad outcome is observed by the end of the 3-year period for patients with a specific risk level'. NNT *does not* say anything about the proportion of patients affected by the therapy, and it *does not* indicate whether outcomes are avoided for ever or not.

Alternatives to NNT

All measures of effectiveness according to equations (1)–(4) (NNT, RRR, etc.) are based on comparisons of proportions in an intervention and a control group at a specific point in time. These proportions can be measured by drawing a vertical line in the survival plot (see the dotted line in Figure 7.2b). These effectiveness measures may be called vertical measures. An alternative is to use horizontal effect measures, i.e. to measure along the horizontal line that divides the patient groups into two. One could look, for example, at the survival time for the first 50 per cent who die in the control group and the first 50 per cent who die in the intervention group. If the death that leads to that 50 per cent in the control group occurs after 30 months (i.e. median survival time is 30 months), and it occurs after 35 months in the intervention group, the gain in median survival time is 5 months. Percentages other than 50 per cent may be used for computing horizontal effect measures. This measure is frequently used in cancer studies, when some patients die soon while others have very long survival times. In Figure 7.1 the gain in median survival would be 15.3 months.

By combining vertical and horizontal effect measures, survival probabilities across time are captured. Gain in life expectancy is the most frequently used combination measure. It is estimated as the area between the survival curves, and represents the mean delay in death across all patients having therapy. In many cases, we are interested not only in increased lifespan, but postponement of adverse events such as hip fracture or heart attack. Such postponements can be estimated from curves of event-free survival in the same way as ordinary survival (Christensen *et al.* 2002).

To calculate the gain in (event-free) survival time, we need to continue the clinical trial until all patients either have had the adverse event or are dead. In most cases we are unable to get such data because trials are discontinued before all patients are dead (see Figure 7.1, for example). In such cases, we could in principle disregard any (dis-)benefits beyond the trial period and estimate the increased lifespan on the basis of the trial period alone. This would tend to bias the effects up or down. By extrapolating survival curves into the future, we can estimate total effects of an intervention, although with some degree of uncertainty. Figure 7.1b is an example of how we could estimate life year gains by extrapolating from the study data.

Does NNT help in making better decisions?

From the section 'Properties of NNT' (p. 92), it is clear that some of those who advocate the use of NNT do not fully understand the concept themselves. In one case, an editorial suggested a new concept called the 'personal probability of benefit' (PPB) (Misselbrook and Armstrong 2002). This was defined as the reciprocal of NNT (which is equal to ARR). Some of us pointed out, on the basis of a simple numerical example, that NNT does not predict the probability of benefit, but the authors still 'stand by [their] comments on the NNT and the personal probability of benefit statistics' (Kristiansen *et al.* 2002a). When advocates of EBM and of the use of NNT misunderstand the concept and its limitations, one could hardly expect non-experts to do any better. So what is the evidence that NNT really helps doctors, patients or policy makers in making better decisions?

To address this question, we would first and ideally need to define what we mean by the term 'better decisions'. When a patient considers taking a cholesterol-lowering drug, for example, the patient would need to know and understand the risk of a heart attack with and without the drug, the consequent relative risk reduction, and how these risk reductions reflect the timing of heart attack. She would therefore need to know how much the therapy – on average – would delay the heart attack. She would also need to appreciate that evidence from the clinical trial cannot inform her about the distribution of this average across those taking the drug. Whether the fully informed patient then opts for therapy is a decision based on subjective valuation of the costs and the benefits. There exists no decision that is optimal for all. Even if all patients have the same baseline risk and obtain the same effect from therapy, the optimal decision may vary across patients depending on cost, alternative uses of income and other resources, preferences for the outcomes and other factors.

For the individual patient, it is seldom possible to obtain all information that is needed for the optimal decision as defined above, and busy clinicians would not have the time to collect it and then provide the patients with all the information that is necessary to make an optimal decision. In practice, doctors would use one or two estimates such as, for example, baseline risk of the event, the relative risk reduction or NNT. If NNT were the best way of informing the patient, this would mean that this measure would result in decisions that are closer to the 'optimal decision' than other effect measures. Unfortunately, no studies have been undertaken to explore this issue. There is ample evidence, however, that patients, doctors and policy makers are more likely to accept a therapy when its effects are presented in terms of relative risk reduction rather than absolute risk reduction, NNT or postponement of adverse events (Bobbio *et al.* 1994;

Christensen *et al.* 2003; Cranney and Walley 1996; Fahey *et al.* 1995; Forrow *et al.* 1992; Hux and Naylor 1995; Nexoe *et al.* 2002). This does not prove that NNT is better than the others, because no gold standard for the 'optimal decision' is used in any of these studies. When some claim that, for example, relative risk reduction 'overstates' the effect of a therapy (Bucher *et al.* 1994), one could equally well claim that NNT 'understates' it. All of the vertical effect measures (equations (1)–(4)) are based on the same two proportions (expressing two different probabilities). It is therefore difficult to see why one would be better than the others. They are simply different statistics with different properties. One *single* statistic is unable to provide *all* the information that is contained in the two probabilities, but one may complement the others. While statisticians may prefer the log of the odds ratio because the parameter space is unbounded and because of the properties of the estimation method for it, some doctors prefer NNT because they have difficulties in understanding decimals (Hutton 2000), or they feel that at the bedside NNT slips more easily off the tongue (Sackett 1996).

In the absence of direct evidence that NNT helps people to make better decisions, what indirect evidence is available? In a Canadian study, doctors were asked to rank seven therapies in terms of clinical usefulness. In general, NNT better reflected doctors' ranking of therapies than relative risk reduction. The therapies varied, however, not only with respect to NNT, but also in other important characteristics. It is therefore not necessarily the case that NNT was the decisive characteristic. In the Canadian study the authors did not discuss whether NNT would be different if other time periods had been chosen. Nor do we know whether the ranking according to NNT was the same as the ranking based on, for example, improvements in life expectancy. In another Canadian study the authors compared the effectiveness of 66 different therapies using NNT and quality-adjusted life years (QALYs) (Chong *et al.* 2002). The QALY measure is an aggregate measure of health benefits across time and supposedly less susceptible to variation in ARR over time. The correlation between NNT and QALY was moderate. The authors concluded that NNTs should be used with caution when evaluating treatment benefits.

The Odense Risk Group is a multidisciplinary group of researchers exploring various aspects of risk and risk concepts. The group has performed several empirical studies to try to elucidate the extent to which experts and lay people comprehend NNT. In one study, lay people were offered a hypothetical therapy for heart attack (Kristiansen *et al.* 2002b). The respondents were randomised to NNT of 10, 25, 50, 100, 200 and 400. An NNT of 10 represents an ARR of 10 per cent and would clearly be interpreted as a substantial difference in survival, while an NNT of 400 represents an ARR of 0.25 per cent. We would need a clinical trial of some 10,000 patients to detect this latter effect. Interestingly, the proportions consenting to therapy were high, and surprisingly similar for all levels of effectiveness (83 per cent, 87 per cent, 85 per cent, 85 per cent, 81 per cent and 74 per cent, respectively). In another study, respondents were offered a hypothetical osteoporosis intervention with NNT in the range of 10 to 400 (Christensen *et al.* 2003). Here, the proportions consenting to therapy were lower (about 60 per cent), but again there was no significant trend towards lower levels of consent with greater NNT.

Why, then, were the respondents so insensitive to variations in NNT? To the extent that one believes that the effectiveness of a therapy will influence therapeutic decisions, the findings are consistent with the hypothesis that lay people do not understand the concept of NNT. This comes as no great surprise, as there is a rich literature documenting the fact that people have difficulties in understanding concepts of risk and probability. The insensitivity to the magnitude of NNT has been found in other studies of decision making among lay people (Nexoe *et al.* forthcoming), and patients have been reported to understand RRR and ARR better than NNT (Sheridan *et al.* 2003).

In a study of heart attack (Kristiansen *et al.* 2002b), we asked those who would not accept the therapy why they wouldn't. About one-third stated that they thought that only one in NNT gained benefit from the therapy. In other words, they thought that they could infer the probability of receiving benefit from a therapy by means of NNT. In the study of hip fracture, all respondents were asked directly about their understanding of NNT (Christensen *et al.* 2003). While 43 per cent felt uncertain about the meaning of NNT, 23 per cent claimed that it meant that one out of NNT would benefit from the therapy.

While lay people seem to be relatively insensitive to the magnitude of NNT (or simply do not understand it) when considering consenting to a therapy, doctors do better. In a randomised study of Norwegian doctors, 72 per cent said they would recommend a therapy if NNT were 50, but only 52 per cent if it were 200 (Halvorsen *et al.* 2003). But again, considerable proportions of the doctors thought that NNT expresses the probability of receiving benefit from a therapy. This was also the case in a study of Danish doctors (Nexoe *et al.* 2002). Difficulties in understanding NNT have also been reported among medical students (Sheridan and Pignone 2002).

Discussion

NNT has been proposed as a statistic that is both easy to understand and intuitively meaningful. Such claims may be warranted when NNT is used to measure the effectiveness of therapies whose effect is instantaneous. For example, when treating ventricular fibrillation, an immediately life-threatening heart condition, the patient will either be cured of the condition within minutes, or he or she will die. When comparing therapies for such conditions, NNT poses no major problems. The effects can be expressed by saying that 80 per cent die with therapy A and 100 per cent with therapy B, or that five patients need to be treated with A rather than B to avoid one immediate death. When there is a crucial time dimension involved – typically, interventions for chronic disease processes – the consequence of the therapy is to postpone adverse outcomes. Then, NNT is no longer such a simple concept because postponement of events involves a time dimension while NNT captures the outcome only at a single point in time. Estimation of postponements requires information on time as well as the probability of adverse outcomes (i.e. survival curves). NNT captures the probability. NNT can be improved (though not perfected) by estimating it on the basis of hazards and expressing the statistic in terms of years of therapy needed to treat. Such a statistic still requires assumptions about hazards being constant over time. It is also less easy to compute. Other metrics measured at one single point in time suffer from some of the same limitations as NNT, and there is little evidence that these or other metrics are better understood than NNT. The other metrics, however, have not been promoted as easily understood.

The story about NNT and its adoption in the medical community is an intriguing one. It is clear that several of those who have proposed the metric do not fully understand it themselves. Second, problems and limitations of NNT have been repeatedly highlighted in the scientific literature (Dowie 1998; Hutton 2000; Altman and Andersen 1999; Kristiansen 2000; Lesaffre and Pledger 1999; Lubsen *et al.* 2000; Smeeth *et al.* 1999; Wu and Kottke 2001). Yet still NNT is advocated as a simple measure, with little mention of its limitations. Third, NNT continues to be proposed by advocates of EBM as an excellent measure of effectiveness without any direct evidence that it helps patients or doctors in making better decisions. It has been adopted with the same enthusiasm that EBM advocates condemn when clinicians adopt therapies on the basis of hope rather than hard evidence. It may well prove just as hard to make the advocates understand the limitations of NNT as it is to make enthusiastic clinicians lose confidence in therapies lacking evidence of clinical effectiveness. Fourth, it has proved difficult to get studies published when their results indicate problems with NNT, even in journals that otherwise promote EBM.

Why has NNT been adopted with such optimism – as a 'huge advance on what we had before' (Moore and McQuay 1999)? One reason lies in the name of the metric: 'number needed to treat'. While doctors may have difficulties in understanding risk measures such as absolute or relative risk reduction (Young *et al.* 2002), NNT is seemingly easy to understand. One can only speculate whether a more correct abbreviation such as 'RARR–APIT' (Reciprocal Absolute Risk Reduction – Arbitrary Point In Time) might become as popular as NNT. Also, NNT may be seen as a measure of effectiveness that does not 'overstate' the therapeutic benefits. There are widespread concerns about the use and costs of pharmaceutical interventions for chronic conditions such as hyperlipidaemia, osteoporosis, etc., and NNT may be seen as a measure with which to avoid unfounded therapeutic optimism among patients and clinicians. In a paper about physician–industry interactions, the authors criticise newspapers that 'presented benefits in relative terms only – an approach that has been shown to increase the enthusiasm of doctors and patients for long-term preventive treatments and that could be viewed as potentially misleading' (Moynihan *et al.* 2000). Most surprisingly, and seemingly coming close to contradicting themselves, the same authors then go on to state:

> In the case of public health interventions, such as vaccination ... it is difficult to impart effective messages by reporting only on absolute reductions in risk, which would tend to minimize important population-wide benefits. In such cases, media reports might emphasize the relative benefits.
>
> (ibid.)

One wonders whether such judgements are 'evidence based'.

The problems and limitations of NNT are not necessarily unique to this metric. All metrics that capture effect at a single point in time (ARR, NNT, RRR, odds ratio, etc.) have the same time-dependent limitations, and we know of no evidence that any of them helps people better than NNT in making clinical decisions. Postponement of adverse events has been proposed as an alternative to single-point measures as NNT and RRR (Christensen *et al.* 2002). We are all used to the concept of time and have experience in distinguishing between, for example, a duration of one month as against one year. One would therefore expect people to understand what is meant by one month of life extension as opposed to, for example, one year. Indeed, in a study of lay people's perceptions of

Box 7.1 Limitations of number needed to treat (NNT)

- NNT may vary considerably according to when it is measured.
- NNT may vary considerably according to the baseline risk of an adverse event.
- NNT gives no information about the individual probability of receiving benefit.
- NNT gives information about the *average* number of patients who need to be treated.
- NNT is not an evidence-based measure of effectiveness.
- NNT has been widely misunderstood by those who advocate or use it.
- NNT may induce people to make other decisions than, for example, relative risk reduction (RRR).
- NNT may be a misleading name for the measure.

osteoporosis therapies when considering a hypothetical therapy, the respondents were sensitive to the length of time of the postponement (Christensen *et al.* 2003). However, there is so far no direct evidence that postponement of adverse events helps people make better decisions than NNT or other metrics.

In conclusion, NNT is not easily understood, nor is it intuitively meaningful. If NNT is superior to other measures, that remains to be proven, and the measure's limitations should be acknowledged (Box 7.1). Choice of measures of effectiveness should be based on evidence rather than beliefs or ideologies.

References

Altman, D.G. and Andersen, P.K. (1999) Calculating the number needed to treat for trials where the outcome is time to an event, *British Medical Journal*, 319: 1492–5.

Bender, R. and Blettner, M. (2002) Calculating the 'number needed to be exposed' with adjustment for confounding variables in epidemiological studies, *Journal of Clinical Epidemiology*, 55: 525–30.

Black, W.C., Nease, R.F. and Tosteson, A.N. (1995) Perceptions of breast cancer risk and screening effectiveness in women younger than 50 years of age, *Journal of National Cancer Institute*, 87: 720–31.

Bobbio, M., Demichelis, B. and Giustetto, G. (1994) Completeness of reporting trial results: effect on physicians' willingness to prescribe, *Lancet*, 343 (8907): 1209–11.

Brown, G., Albers, J.J., Fisher, L.D. *et al.* (1990) Regression of coronary artery disease as a result of intensive lipid-lowering therapy in men with high levels of apolipoprotein B, *New England Journal of Medicine*, 323: 1289–98.

Bucher, H.C., Weinbacher, M. and Gyr, K. (1994) Influence of method of reporting study results on decision of physicians to prescribe drugs to lower cholesterol concentration, *British Medical Journal*, 309: 761–4.

Chong, C.A.K.Y., Naglie, I.G. and Krahn, M.D. (2002) Number needed to mislead? NNT does not accurately predict health benefit or efficiency, *Medical Decision Making*, 22: 531.

Christensen, P.M., Brixen, K., Brøsen, K., Andersen, M. and Kristiansen, I.S. (2003) A randomised trial of laypersons' perception of the benefit of osteoporosis therapy: Number needed to treat versus postponement of hip fractures?, *Clinical Therapeutics*, 25: 2275–85.

Christensen, P.M., Brøsen, K., Brixen, K. and Kristiansen, I.S. (2002) Expressing effects of osteoporosis interventions in terms of postponing of fractures, *European Journal of Clinical Pharmacology*, 58: 629–33.

Cook, R.J. and Sackett, D.L. (1995) The number needed to treat: a clinically useful measure of treatment effect, *British Medical Journal*, 310: 452–4.

Cranney, M. and Walley, T. (1996) Same information, different decisions: the influence of evidence on the management of hypertension in the elderly, *British Journal of General Practice*, 46: 661–3.

Dowie, J. (1998) The 'number needed to treat' and the 'adjusted NNT' in health care decision-making, *Journal of Health Services Research Policy*, 3: 44–9.

Fahey, T., Griffiths, S. and Peters, T.J. (1995) Evidence based purchasing: understanding results of clinical trials and systematic reviews, *British Medical Journal*, 311: 1056–9.

Forrow, L., Taylor, W.C. and Arnold, R.M. (1992) Absolutely relative: how research results are summarized can affect treatment decisions, *American Journal of Medicine*, 92: 121–4.

Gallefoss, F. (2001) Cost-effectiveness of self-management in asthmatics: a one-year follow-up randomised, controlled trial, *European Respiratory Journal*, 17: 206–13.

Halvorsen, P.A., Kristiansen, I.S., Aasland, O.G. and Førde, O.H. (2003) Medical doctors' perception of the 'number needed to treat' (NNT), *Scandinavian Journal of Primary Health Care*, 21: 162–6.

Hochberg, M.C., Ross, P.D., Black, D. *et al.* (1999) Larger increases in bone mineral density during alendronate therapy are associated with a lower risk of new vertebral fractures in women with postmenopausal osteoporosis: Fracture Intervention Trial Research Group, *Arthritis and Rheumatism*, 42: 1246–54.

Hutton, J.L. (2000) Number needed to treat: properties and problems, *Journal of the Royal Statistical Society*, 163: 403–19.

Hux, J.E. and Naylor, C.D. (1995) Communicating the benefits of chronic preventive therapy: does the format of efficacy data determine patients' acceptance of treatment?, *Medical Decision Making*, 15: 152–7.

Jaeschke, R., Guyatt, G., Shannon, H., Walter, S., Cook, D. and Heddle, N. (1995) Basic statistics for clinicians: 3. Assessing the effects of treatment: measures of association, *Canadian Medical Association Journal*, 152: 351–7.

Kristiansen, I.S. (2000) Helping patients integrate research evidence, *Journal of the American Medical Association*, 284: 2595.

Kristiansen, I.S., Gyrd-Hansen, D., Nexoe, J. and Nielsen, J.B. (2002b) Number needed to treat: easily understood and intuitively meaningful? Theoretical considerations and a randomized trial, *Journal of Clinical Epidemiology*, 55: 888–902.

Kristiansen, I.S., Nexoe, J., Gyrd-Hansen, D. and Nielsen, J.B. (2002a) NNT is not easily understood, *Family Practice*, 19: 566.

Laupacis, A., Sackett, D.L. and Roberts, R.S. (1988) An assessment of clinically useful measures of the consequences of treatment, *New England Journal of Medicine*, 318: 1728–33.

Lesaffre, E. and Pledger, G. (1999) A note on the number needed to treat, *Controlled Clinical Trials*, 20: 439–47.

Lubsen, J., Hoes, A. and Grobbee, D. (2000) Implications of trial results: the potentially misleading notions of number needed to treat and average duration of life gained, *Lancet*, 356: 1757–9.

McAlister, F.A., Straus, S.E., Guyatt, G.H. and Haynes, R.B. (2000) Users' guides to the medical literature: XX. Integrating research evidence with the care of the individual patient: Evidence-Based Medicine Working Group, *Journal of the American Medical Association*, 283: 2829–36.

McCormack, J.P. and Levine, M. (1993) Meaningful interpretation of risk reduction from clinical drug trials, *Annals of Pharmacotherapy*, 27: 1272–7.

McLaren, H. (2002) Doctors' self rating of skills in evidence based medicine, *British Medical Journal*, 325: 280.

McQuay, H.J. and Moore, R.A. (1997) Using numerical results from systematic reviews in clinical practice, *Annals of Internal Medicine*, 126: 712–20.

Misselbrook, D. and Armstrong, D. (2002) Thinking about risk: can doctors and patients talk the same language?, *Family Practice*, 19: 1–2.

Moore, A. and McQuay, H. (1999) Numbers needed to treat derived from meta analysis: NNT is a tool, to be used appropriately, *British Medical Journal*, 319: 1200.

Moynihan, R., Bero, L., Ross-Degnan, D. *et al.* (2000) Coverage by the news media of the benefits and risks of medications, *New England Journal of Medicine*, 342: 1645–50.

Nexoe, J., Gyrd-Hansen, D., Kragstrup, J., Kristiansen, I.S. and Nielsen, J.B. (2002) Danish GPs' perception of disease risk and benefit of intervention, *Family Practice*, 19: 3–6.

Nexoe, J., Kristiansen, I.S., Gyrd-Hansen, D. and Nielsen, J.B. (forthcoming in *Family Practice*) Lay people's preferences for heart attack prevention: the influence of outcome type, costs and effect size in terms of number needed to treat.

Rembold, C.M. (1998) Number needed to screen: development of a statistic for disease screening, *British Medical Journal*, 317: 307–12.

Riegelman, R. and Schroth, W.S. (1993) Adjusting the number needed to treat: incorporating adjustments for the utility and timing of benefits and harms, *Medical Decision Making*, 13: 247–52.

Sackett, D.L. (1996) On some clinically useful measures of the effect of treatment, *Evidence Based Medicine*, 1: 37–8.

Sackett, D.L., Straus, S.E., Rosenberg, W. and Haynes, R.B. (2000) *Evidence-Based Medicine: How to Practice and Teach EBM*, New York: Churchill Livingstone.

San Laureano, J.A., Briganti, E.M. and Colville, D.J. (1999) Number needed to treat: a useful new method of assessing the magnitude of treatment effect and its application to the management of diabetic retinopathy, *Australian and New Zealand Journal of Ophthalmology*, 27: 137–42.

Schulzer, M. and Mancini, G.B. (1996) 'Unqualified success' and 'unmitigated failure': number-needed-to-treat-related concepts for assessing treatment efficacy in the presence of treatment-induced adverse events, *International Journal of Epidemiology*, 25: 704–12.

Sheridan, S.L. and Pignone, M. (2002) Numeracy and the medical student's ability to interpret data, *Effective Clinical Practice*, 5: 35–40.

Sheridan, S.L., Pignone, M. and Lewis, C.L. (2003) A randomized comparison of patients' understanding of number needed to treat and other common risk reduction formats, *Journal of General Internal Medicine*, 18 (1): 884–92.

Smeeth, L., Haines, A. and Ebrahim, S. (1999) Numbers needed to treat derived from meta-analyses: sometimes informative, usually misleading, *British Medical Journal*, 318: 1548–51.

Stone, J., Wojcik, W., Durrance, D. *et al.* (2002) What should we say to patients with symptoms unexplained by disease? The 'number needed to offend', *British Medical Journal*, 325: 1449–50.

Torp-Pedersen, C. and Kober, L. (1999) Effect of ACE inhibitor trandolapril on life expectancy of patients with reduced left-ventricular function after acute myocardial infarction: TRACE Study Group: Trandolapril Cardiac Evaluation, *Lancet*, 354: 9–12.

Wu, L.A. and Kottke, T.E. (2001) Number needed to treat: caveat emptor, *Journal of Clinical Epidemiology*, 54: 111–16.

Young, J.M., Glasziou, P. and Ward, J.E. (2002) General practitioners' self ratings of skills in evidence based medicine: validation study, *British Medical Journal*, 324: 950–1.

8 Decision analysis, evidence-based medicine and medical education

A case study in the diffusion of innovation within academic medicine

Arthur S. Elstein

Introduction

Decision analysis (DA) and evidence-based medicine (EBM) arrived on the medical scene at approximately the same time, in the 1980s. *Clinical Decision Analysis* (Weinstein *et al.* 1980) quickly became the standard text in that field for 20 years. The EBM series in the *Canadian Medical Association Journal* (later *CMAJ*) began in 1983 (Sackett 1983). It was shortly followed by a textbook (Sackett *et al.* 1985) and then in the 1990s by a series of articles in the *Journal of the American Medical Association*, first "The rational clinical examination" and then "The user's guide to the medical literature," which continues to be published at irregular intervals. A series of papers on innovations in clinical decision analysis beginning with Klein and Pauker (1981) and a "how to" series by Detsky *et al.* (1997) were published over roughly the same time.

Both DA and EBM emphasize a quantitative approach to decision making to provide guidance to clinical decision makers. Despite their similarities, they have received quite different responses in the medical community. EBM has become a major curricular movement within academic medicine while DA has remained the interest of a relatively small scholarly community and is used primarily by health policy analysts, who tend not to be in the faculty of a medical school. How and why did this happen? What were the strategies and ideological commitments that led to these outcomes? This chapter explores these questions. It has four goals:

- to identify the problems in clinical practice that provided the impetus for developing both EBM and DA;
- to make explicit the underlying similarities between EBM and DA;
- to identify the important differences between these approaches;
- to relate these similarities and differences to the fates of these innovations.

Forces and issues underlying their development

EBM and DA both arose in a particular social and psychological context and both respond to perceived problems in providing health services. What was this context? What were these problems? If EBM and DA are answers, what were the questions? To what problems in the health care system, especially in developed, industrialized countries, did these innovations respond?

Practice variation

Variations in clinical practice that could not be accounted for by variations in clinical features of the patients (co-morbidities, contra-indications) were first identified by Wennberg and his colleagues (e.g. Wennberg and Gitelsohn 1973), and have since been the topic of hundreds of studies. These studies have demonstrated: (a) overutilization of treatments when compared with generally accepted guidelines (e.g. Ottesen *et al.* 2001); (b) underutilization of treatments of demonstrated effectiveness (e.g. Ghosh *et al.* 2002; Hart 1999); (c) practice variations related to the specialty or clinical training of physicians (Fowler *et al.* 2000); (d) variations related to geography or local clinical culture that are difficult to account for on strictly clinical grounds (O'Connor *et al.* 1999a); (e) variations related to the type of clinical setting (e.g. teaching hospitals versus community hospitals); and (f) variations related to age, socio-economic status or ethnicity of the patients.

The recurrent question in these studies is whether the observed variation is acceptable practice. Should age-related variation be attributed to clinically relevant contra-indications, such as co-morbidities that are more likely to occur among the elderly? Or should it be attributed to rationing, age discrimination, and social attitudes that are unfavorable toward the elderly (Rose *et al.* 2000; Soumerai *et al.* 1997)? Practice variation related to specialty training is illustrated by a study that found that urologists and radiation oncologists disagreed in their recommendations for managing a hypothetical case of localized prostate cancer: urologists overwhelmingly recommended prostatectomy, and about the same proportion of radiation oncologists recommended the treatment they provide (Fowler *et al.* 2000). Since there is no convincing evidence that one treatment is better than the other, the preference differences are probably associated with training and self-interest.

Three general strategies have been proposed for dealing with practice variation: clinical guidelines, EBM and DA (Eddy 1996; Elstein *et al.* 2002). The problem with guidelines, at least in the United States, has been that many physicians do not trust them. They are seen either as inappropriately challenging professional authority (Greco and Eisenberg 1993) or as a not particularly subtle effort to ration care (Inouye *et al.* 1998). Either way, they have generally not been popular with the intended users, although they continue to be advocated by policy makers, government departments of health, academic training centers, and third-party payers (Cabana *et al.* 1999).

EBM and DA, by contrast, leave authority for decision making largely in the hands of the clinician. Both provide advice about how to approach the decision problem, but they do not mandate the decision maker's choice. Increasingly, EBM and decision analysis principles are used to develop clinical guidelines and policies. EBM has been used to develop criteria for appropriateness of utilization of a diagnostic technology or a treatment strategy. Decision analysis has been extensively used to explore the probable consequences of different approaches to the same clinical situation. The results of this analysis can be formulated as a flow chart or as a clinical guideline of the form "Under the following clinical circumstances, the best thing to do is . . ." The decision analysis explains the rationale of the recommended strategy in quantitative terms.

Technology explosion

The rapid expansion of diagnostic and therapeutic technologies in the past three decades has significantly increased the range of options available for a wide range of clinical problems. This means that physicians and patients are offered choices that were not previously available. Some options are very costly, and it is not necessarily true that the more expensive option is better. For example, new drugs for managing hypertension are generally more expensive than older therapies, but the evidence that they are markedly better is limited. Yet pharmaceutical companies market new drugs more vigorously, for obvious reasons. If a new therapy is both better and more expensive, is the added benefit worth the additional cost? How should these decisions be made, particularly when many of them offer complex mixes of benefits and harms? The clinical literature frequently addresses, or at least recognizes, the problem. The questions to be asked are "How should this balancing be done?," "How good is unaided clinical judgment at figuring out the correct answer?" and "What tools can be applied?." Both EBM and DA address these questions directly.

Patient empowerment

In the United States and most developed countries, the past three decades have also seen a significant increase in the role of patients and their families in clinical decision making. This trend is seen in the development of shared decision-making tools (O'Connor *et al.* 1999b), decision aids intended for patients to read and discuss with health professionals, and especially in the growth of courses and training in medical ethics. Patient autonomy, and therefore informed consent, is arguably the first principle in medical ethics, at least as taught in the United States, Canada and European countries. Both EBM and DA respond to these themes: EBM focuses attention on outcome probabilities, but clearly recognizes that patients' values and preferences should play a part in clinical decision making. DA asks that probabilities and values (utilities) be explicitly assigned to each possible clinical outcome and then provides a rule for calculating the expected utility of each option. DA further tries to identify whether a clinical choice should be driven primarily by the probabilities of various outcomes, in which case the evidence is of primary concern, or whether the choice ought to be driven by patient preferences and values, in which case the evidence is subordinate to preferences and values, and we have to be concerned with being sure that the patient's preferences are properly understood and incorporated into the decision. This understanding has led to numerous studies of the problems inherent in assessing patients' preferences (Bleichrodt *et al.* 2001; Stiggelbout 2000)

Decision psychology

Experts in all fields trust their judgment. Yet for the past 30 years, the analysis of cognitive limitations, shortcomings and flaws has been a major theme in psychological research on clinical judgment and decision making. Within the problem-solving paradigm, humans have been recognized to be operating with limited or bounded rationality. The size of working memory is relatively small, while the size of long-term memory is huge. Consequently, complex problems have to be represented in simplified problem spaces, and problem solvers, constrained by their cognitive limitations, seek satisfactory rather than optimal solutions; they endeavor to "satisfice" rather than to "optimize" (Newell and Simon 1972). Other investigators have demonstrated that clinical problem solvers are much affected by prior specific clinical experiences, and less affected by logical reasoning than would be optimal, so that practice variation might be understood in part as a result of inevitable variations in prior clinical experience – no two clinicians, even if trained within the same specialty program within the same hospital, ever see precisely the same patients (Elstein and Schwartz 2002; Schmidt *et al.* 1990; Gruppen and Frohna 2002).

The decision-making paradigm has emphasized statistical decision theory as an idealized account of rational choice, rather than an account of actual decision making. Departures from the rules and axioms of this theory have been demonstrated in practically every area that the theory identifies as crucial to decision making: estimating probabilities when statistical frequency data are unavailable; revising probabilities with imperfect or uncertain information; quantifying values (utilities are moderately affected by the method of elicitation, contrary to theory); and choice itself (framing effects). The departures from ideal rationality have been identified as cognitive heuristics and psychological biases (Kahneman *et al.*

1982; Elstein and Schwartz 2002) and have been investigated in literally hundreds of studies. Heuristics are seen as ways of simplifying very complex tasks, similar to their role in problem solving. They are useful rules of thumb that are often correct but do not guarantee a correct solution. Biases are seen as features inherent in the "wiring" of the human cognitive machine, akin to optical illusions. Psychologists and clinicians have explored the implications of these heuristics and biases for clinical decision making. The theme of this work has been that decision makers are more affected by psychological factors and less purely rational than we might wish to be or think we are. Human decision making is seen as reasonable most of the time, but rarely perfectly rational, as rationality is defined by the standard of maximizing expected utility. Useful discussions of heuristics and biases are provided by Hogarth (1987), Baron (2000), Russo and Schoemaker (1990) and Chapman and Elstein (2000)

All of these factors have been shown to affect clinical decision making, and DA and EBM both endeavor to respond to them via a range of technical fixes that fall short of providing specific directions about what to do in every circumstance and yet share an approach to decision making under uncertainty. I now turn to sketching the fundamentals of the common approach.

Underlying similarities (common fundamentals)

Diagnostic reasoning, 2×2 tables, and Bayes's theorem

Both decision analysis and evidence-based medicine conceptualize the problem of reaching a diagnosis as a matter of probability revision with imperfect information. Both represent the accuracy of a diagnostic test by two measures, sensitivity and specificity, that can be converted into measures of the strength of evidence: positive and negative likelihood ratios. Both understand that the predictive value of a positive (or negative) test is a function of two variables, prior probability (either prevalence or belief) and the strength of the evidence, and both try to communicate this understanding to users. Both are explicit about the uncertainty inherent in diagnosis because of imperfect evidence, and both recommend some form of Bayes's theorem as the correct way to deal with these problems.[1] Thus, both present 2×2 tables and a (Bayesian) nomogram as convenient implementations of these fundamental concepts.

These fundamental concepts are all discussed in standard texts on decision analysis and EBM (e.g. Weinstein *et al.* 1980; Hunink *et al.* 2001; Sackett *et al.* 1991; Sackett *et al.* 1997). But the two decision analysis texts index an additional term that is missing in the EBM texts: Bayes's theorem. This is just one example of an important point: The decision analysis texts make a consistent effort to relate the concepts and the technical implementation (in 2×2 tables, nomograms, probability trees, etc.) to a larger framework of inference and decision that is applicable not only to medicine but to all situations involving uncertainty – we might call it a theory. The EBM texts stay closer to the ground and are more "practical," less concerned with the broader theory from which particular tools find their origin and justification.

PICO: the answerable clinical question and the decision tree

One aim of EBM is to provide busy clinicians with a set of practical tools for finding and interpreting the clinical literature relevant to actual clinical problems. This literature search is quite different than the review of the literature conducted by research scientists because it is intended for clinical use. The clinician must be able to decide whether and how to apply the results of a focused literature search to a particular patient.

I use the word "practical" in two senses of the term. First, EBM advocates claim that the tools provided for search and interpretation can in fact be employed within the realistic constraints of everyday clinical practice. The literature search must be rapid and focused, not necessarily exhaustive, and need not review the historical development of a clinical problem. (The rise of the Cochrane Collaboration and their Reports suggests that this goal is more an ideal than a reality, but that is not essential to this discussion.) Second, the tools are practical in the sense that they do not aim primarily at increasing the physician's knowledge, a common objective of much reading and study. Although advocates of EBM would agree that knowledge is preferable to ignorance, EBM has a more ambitious aim: to change the decisions and actions taken by the clinician – that is, it aims to change practice.

EBM advocates repeatedly stress that one does not practice EBM by simply "reading papers." The clinician must "read the right papers at the right time" and then alter clinical practice in the light of what has been learned (Greenhalgh 1997). But how does one ensure that the right papers have been read at the right time? How can readers possibly know that they have found the right papers? Maybe the very best paper has been missed in a quick search?

One might think that the way to do this is to have a deep understanding of the structure of the medical knowledge base (MESH) so as to optimize search strategy, but EBM does not focus the reader's attention on this issue. Rather, it directs the clinician's attention to formulating the search question in such a way as to help the reader relate whatever is found to the clinical problem that motivated the search. The search is thus organized around an "answerable clinical question" (ACQ), which has four parts, summarized in the mnemonic *PICO*.

- P What is the **patient's problem**?
- I The clinical **intervention** contemplated (a diagnostic test, a treatment, a prognostic marker).

- C **Compare** the contemplated intervention with at least one relevant alternative (for example, a new diagnostic test can be compared with the current standard, or a new treatment can be compared with the standard of care or placebo).
- O The clinical **outcome** of interest. What standard is used to compare the two interventions? Examples of useful outcome measures include reduced length of stay in hospital, decreased incidence of influenza following administration of flu vaccine, decreased incidence of acute myocardial infarction (AMI) with daily small doses of aspirin, etc.

In short, the ACQ provides a semi-formal structure applicable, in principle, to any clinical problem where a question arises about what should be done next. Interestingly, this structure contains precisely the same elements as a basic decision tree. Every decision tree specifies:

- the clinical situation or context of the decision (P);
- the options from among which an action must be selected (I and C);
- the outcome or outcomes (in the case of multiple objectives) that the decision maker is trying to satisfy or maximize (O).

It is true that a formal decision analysis requires some crucial details about the outcomes. The probabilities and utilities (values) of each outcome must be specified. Conflicts among probabilities derived from various studies must be taken into account and techniques have been developed for quantifying subjective valuations. Further, the analysis is not complete unless it is accompanied by a sensitivity analysis, in which the analyst explores whether the recommended action might be changed by plausible variations in the more uncertain parameters. But these differences should not obscure the fundamental similarity between the two approaches.

This similarity is seen most clearly in the first edition of *Clinical Epidemiology* (Sackett *et al.* 1985). The first half of that book is an elementary textbook of decision analysis, while part 2 is devoted to critical appraisal of the literature. As time passed, the DA theme waned in EBM writing, and critical appraisal became more prominent. A good example of the trend is Greenhalgh's (1997) book, where decision analysis is mentioned only to refer the reader to other sources. Thus, we see that from 1985 to 1997 these two family members grew further apart. More recently, decision analysis texts (Hunink *et al.* 2001) have placed more emphasis on searching the literature to find relevant probabilities and outcome data, and for these purposes EBM methods are understandably recommended.

Dependence on desktop computing

The advance of EBM has been enormously aided by the availability of powerful desktop computers. When we compare how we conducted MEDLINE searches in the early 1970s with the speed and flexibility of current PubMed searches, it is evident that even if the EBM framework had been available then, it could not have been applied in real clinical work. EBM advocates motivated the development of PubMed, a version of the National Library of Medicine's internationally used database of the world's medical literature that employs EBM-derived filters to guide the selection of literature.

Similarly, early clinical decision analyses were necessarily quite simplified representations of the problem, because the computations had to be carried out by hand or with a pocket calculator. *Clinical Decision Analysis* (Weinstein *et al.* 1980) was written and published before desktop computers were available. By 1983 the invention and marketing of these machines, along with spreadsheets, made it possible to construct more complex models, including Markov processes (Beck and Pauker 1983; Sonnenberg and Beck 1993). More recent publications (Rouse and Owen 1998) discuss Markov models, and the newest decision analysis text (Hunink *et al.* 2001) comes with a CD-ROM to implement computer-based exercises. The link with computer technology could not be clearer!

Differences

Emphasis

EBM has moved increasingly toward critical appraisal, emphasizing the "quality" of literature, and stressing a hierarchy of research methods leading to trustworthy findings. The pinnacle of research methodology is the randomized clinical trial; case studies are the least trustworthy, and other methods rank in between. Meta-analysis is the primary statistical method for combining the results of several studies into one overall estimate of effect size. DA has consistently worried less about the trustworthiness of individual studies, perhaps because it relies more on sensitivity analysis to identify which variables in a complex problem are crucial determinants of the decision and to explore the effects of plausible variations on the recommended path. The method enables the analyst to identify whether the range of results in several studies indeed affects the decision or whether the decision is "insensitive" to these variations. Hence, the trustworthiness of any one study is less of an issue than it is for EBM.

Status of human judgment

For EBM, lack of knowledge is the fundamental problem. Conventional methods of keeping up with the increasing volume of published clinical literature can easily be demonstrated to be inadequate. But the problem can be remedied by searching the medical literature in a focused, directed fashion and critically evaluating what is found. The recommended method of identifying the answers that are available in the literature becomes all the more important and constitutes a "new approach to the practice of medicine." Advocates acknowledge that there are medical situations for which answers are simply unavailable in the literature, that ignorance of these answers is not simply a personal defect. In other words, not all clinical questions are "answerable" (Naylor 1995), and informed judgment still has an important place.

For EBM, clinical judgment is not the problem; physicians' judgments are trustworthy provided they are informed by current knowledge. For example, judging whether the results of a study apply to a patient who is not exactly like the study's cohort is not seen as particularly problematic, and neither is determining how much the results need to be adjusted. These acts of judgment are left in the hands of the physicians who are using EBM methods to search the literature for answers to their questions or who are reading the Cochrane review that pertains to their question.

For DA, judgment is itself a problem, as shown by the psychological literature. The only question is, how big is this problem? Here, despite some defense of the adequacy of human judgment, the general consensus is that the more complex or multivariate a problem is, the more likely it is that combining evidence by a formal rule will be helpful. Even if the result of this exercise is not viewed as a clinical mandate, it does give insight into the problem and it may make us think more deeply about the reasons for our choices. That is why it is worth doing a decision analysis. Discrepancies between what people intuitively want to do and what they ought to do if they were expected-utility maximizers are noted, discussed and argued about.

Status of formal models

The model of a clinical problem can take many forms: a flow chart, an algorithm, a decision tree, an influence diagram, an equation. The model provides guidance in several ways. For the most part, algorithms and flow charts point to "what to do next" under given conditions. Decision trees, influence diagrams and equations provide guidance about how complex, probabilistic information should be combined. In decision analysis, the criterion for recommending an option is that it maximizes expected utility. The model takes into consideration every factor or variable that the decision analyst has put into it, and combines probabilities and utilities of all outcomes so as to identify a strategy that maximizes expected utility.

For decision analysis, building a model of a clinical problem is time-consuming but is absolutely necessary. Every variable that should be taken into account in making the clinical decision should be in the model, for if it is omitted it will play no part in generating the model's prescription. The model is thus an explicit representation of everything that goes into making a decision. Decision makers are advised to consider the recommendations of the model in making a decision, and in particular to consider reasons why their intuitive choice conflicts with the model's preferences, but they are not required to follow the model's recommendations. There may be reasons for not following this recommendation, but they too should be made explicit and justified.

Early decision-analytic models were relatively simple, and could be constructed literally "on the back of an envelope." For examples, see the decision trees given by Weinstein *et al.* (1980). As time passed, models became increasingly complex. To model more accurately complex clinical situations that unfold over time, analysts turned to Markov models (Beck and Pauker 1983; Sonnenberg and Beck 1993), as already mentioned. Cost-effectiveness analysis was introduced and became a dominant mode of analysis of health policy issues (Russell *et al.* 1996; Russell 2000). Few clinicians outside of the decision-analytic, public health and health policy communities had the quantitative and statistical background to understand these models. Yet decision analysis said that modeling was an essential part of the process, that the numbers in the literature were only as good as the model which used them.

On the issue of modeling, EBM offers a mixed message. One message is that clinicians can do the needed modeling on their own. Formal models are time-consuming and not really needed. Clinicians can quickly find the studies needed to answer ACQs and can figure out how the results apply to their patients. It is true that randomized controlled trials (RCTs) provide more trustworthy data than other types of studies; nevertheless, "Do the results of these studies apply to my patient?" is a question answered by informed clinical judgment. The second message is: Formal combination of the results of conflicting studies is needed, and that is why systematic literature reviews and meta-analysis are the methods of choice. At this point, EBM moves from the desk of the practicing clinician to that of the academic researcher, since few practicing clinicians have acquired the skills or have the time to do a systematic review and a meta-analysis on an urgent clinical question. The Cochrane Collaboration was formed to provide a mechanism for regularly updating reviews of studies on important clinical questions and for disseminating the results to a broad readership.

EBM also left cost-effectiveness to the side, while in decision-analytic circles it has become an increasingly visible theme. This is especially ironic, considering that Canada and the United Kingdom, where EBM has been most extensively developed, are both countries with national health schemes that require global budgeting and explicit resource allocation. But this has had the effect of aligning EBM more closely with the interests of individual clinicians and their patients.

Status of utility theory

The "normative nucleus" (Hilden and Habbema 1990) of decision analysis is utility theory. Techniques of utility elicitation are described in a variety of articles and texts (Hunink *et al.* 2001; Sox *et al.* 1988). The assumption that actions should be chosen so as to maximize expected utility has led to extensive exploration of the theoretical foundations of the approach as well as numerous studies of psychological, social and methodological factors that affect the numbers that represent the evaluations of outcomes (Miyamoto 2000; Stiggelbout 2000; Bleichrodt *et al.* 2001) and the conditions under which choices are found to systematically violate expected utility.

Maximizing an outcome is essential for EBM as well. The use of meta-analysis to move toward a single aggregated estimate of the effect of a treatment shows that measuring outcomes is a crucial aspect of EBM. For the most part, EBM has focused on "objective" outcomes (e.g. development and progression of diabetic neuropathy or number of adverse events prevented, as in the reduction of the incidence of influenza following a campaign of vaccination). A standard textbook of EBM (Sackett *et al.* 1997) describes using a visual analog scale (a value "thermometer") to evaluate various possible outcomes of treatment, as well as the patient's current health, on a common scale. But the authors caution that none of them has found they have the time required to carry out this elicitation and analysis in more than 1 per cent of their patients.

A major problem has been the status of recommendations based on maximizing expected utility. From the standpoint of decision theory, the same recommendation applies to one patient from a cohort and to the entire cohort. Yet clinicians, even those who know decision analysis techniques, have found it difficult to implement this principle (Cohen 1996). Somehow, a single case looks different than a cohort of very similar people in a similar situation. Policy analysts have referred to this as the difference between individual and statistical lives (Schelling 1968).

Behavioral study of decision making has shown that reasonable decision makers – that is, people whose choices most of us would regard as "reasonable" – are not necessarily rational in the sense of obeying the principles and axioms of rational choice theory. The dominant descriptive theory of choice is prospect theory and its variants (Kahneman and Tversky 1979; Tversky and Kahneman 1981, 1986). In particular, choices are affected by even minor variations in the wording of the problem (framing effects). In clinical medicine, focusing on outcomes as either survival or mortality or lives saved versus lives lost can lead to marked shifts in preferences, although the outcomes considered are formally identical. Since survival and mortality are major outcomes in health care decisions, framing effects can lead to discrepancies between the recommendations of a decision-analytic model and intuitive, but reasonable, choices.

Spirit of the innovation

For EBM, the problem is the balance between knowledge and ignorance, between sound evidence and mere opinion. The solution to this problem is to be found by consulting the medical literature. Thus, while practice patterns and habits based on ignorance of the scientific evidence border on sinfulness, the way to repentance and redemption is open to all.

The use of religious terminology is deliberate. Several critics have noted the evangelical tone of much EBM advocacy. One British physician, self-described as "dissenting from the orthodoxy of evidence-based medicine," noted that EBM offers "a holy message," and said that because of his criticism, he had been "cast as a heretic" (Grahame-Smith 1998). Another, reviewing Greenhalgh's book, referred to "the new medical deity" and compared EBM to other "new cults" (Blaney 1998).

Other critics have seen EBM as an attack on academic medicine. "Evidence based medicine is a neologism for informed decision making, and this example of newspeak would have delighted George Orwell" (Fowler 1995). Another critic argued that coining the term "evidence-based medicine" was one of the worst political decisions ever made by the academic community, since it suggested that all other medical practice was not evidence based. In fact, what has distinguished academic medicine from the time of Harvey to the present is the insistence that diagnosis and treatment be based on the best available evidence and our scientific understanding (K. Ludmerer, in a lecture at UIC, 1 June 2000 (a paraphrase from my notes)).

Clearly, something in the tone of advocates has been off-putting. But it has also carried the day. Its success, in my opinion, has been due to several factors:

It seems to me no accident that EBM was developed in predominantly Protestant countries (Canada, the United Kingdom, the United States), for it emphasizes individual autonomy by promoting the doctrine that salvation of the medical profession is to be found by individual physicians consulting the medical literature, reading it thoughtfully and then acting independently, according to their conscience.

By contrast, the decision analysis community has been cautious and non-exhortative, largely lacking evangelistic fervor, and has become increasingly concerned with the social context of decisions, as evidenced by the growing prominence of cost-effectiveness analyses. The spirit of decision analysis is perhaps best characterized as argumentative, rather than evangelical, in the sense that proponents are more interested in the back-and-forth of the argument than in the answer to the question. Proponents prefer logical consistency and coherence to rapid availability of a satisfactory solution. They concede that judgment and decision making are complex, that any model may well exclude variables that are important to some decision makers, and that decision makers should be cautious and explore the decision from a variety of viewpoints, using sensitivity analysis, quality-adjusted life years, discounting. If the decision makers cannot approach the problem from different perspectives, they should be explicit about the perspective employed. Decision makers are more like a jury that deliberates over complex evidence for several days than a jury that renders a decision within one hour. As a result, the DA community bifurcated into those interested in clinical decision making and those focused on policy issues. These developments did not enhance the marketability of the innovation; most people do not get enthusiastic about arcane methodological/scientific issues they do not understand.

Critics of decision analysis have generally focused on three issues:

1. Model building takes too much time to be clinically realistic.
2. The preferred methods of utility assessment (standard gamble and time trade-off) are too complicated for many patients to understand what is being asked (Goldstein and Tsevat 2000).
3. The principle of maximizing expected utility is not the only consideration in choice; fairness and equity are also relevant. For example, many people strongly prefer giving priority to treating seriously ill patients even if this allocation of resources is not cost-effective. Conflicts arise between what seems best for a cohort and what seems best or fair for an individual (Ubel *et al.* 1996, 2000).

Regardless of the content of the criticisms, however, the tone has generally been much less passionate than the response to EBM.

Outcome; consequences

These differences in emphasis have led to the current situation: In the clinical community, both in and outside of academic medicine, decision analysis is viewed as impractical in the everyday clinical setting. It takes too much time, utility assessment is too complicated for many patients, and it is unclear what to do when the results of an analysis conflict with clinical judgment and intuition. Even decision analysts themselves offer the technique and its recommendations as a way of gaining insight into a clinical problem, not as a prescription to be taken whether the decision maker likes it or not (Dolan 1997). Decision analysis has found its place in cost-effectiveness analysis, guideline development and health policy debate, all applications that view clinical medicine from a societal or population perspective. Its role in the clinician's bag appears to be small and not growing.

On the other hand, EBM has disseminated itself broadly in academic medicine. It is the current fashion in curriculum reform: just about every medical school in the United States has found a place in its curriculum for some type of EBM experience. The argument has now shifted to what kind of EBM experience has positive effects on clinical practice and patient outcomes, not whether there should be an EBM experience in either the preclinical curriculum or the clinical clerkships or both.

In my opinion, the main forces leading to these two outcomes were the different answers of these innovative movements to the issues outlined in the previous section of this chapter, and the responses of the clinical community to their answers. These differences in content and emotional tone ultimately outweighed the underlying similarities sketched earlier.

Ultimately, the EBM message empowers individual clinicians in a way that decision analysis has not. EBM places in their hands the same knowledge base used by academic specialists and authorizes them to interpret this literature and apply it to their patients. Ironically, it downplays the importance of social and community aspects of practice and the role of community standards and norms in determining practice standards and the diffusion of guidelines. Although it was developed in a country with comprehensive national health insurance and the problems of global budgeting, it does not emphasize the societal perspective on resource allocation. EBM's case was further strengthened by emphasizing its roots in science and clinical trials, not subjective beliefs and values, thereby avoiding the thorny issue of biases in assessing beliefs, methodological difficulties in assessing values and preferences, and the problems of information integration and judgment that have dominated decision psychology for the past 25 years.

In my opinion, both innovations must change to relate them better to clinical practice. EBM needs to take more serious account of the role of patients' preferences and values in decision making. As long as there are treatments that entail both benefits and possible harms, some consideration of how patients view the potential harms in relation to benefits will be necessary. These consideration are the ultimate act of clinical judgment, and the psychological literature should foster humility about the quality of those judgments. They can be facilitated by exploring values and preferences along the lines suggested by utility theory. While this exploration is not needed for every ailment and for every possible treatment, pleading that there is simply not enough time to do this, or that the task is too complex for most patients, seems an inadequate response to the challenge when the occasion does arise.

DA, on the other hand, needs to become more accessible and useful to practitioners. Models too complex to be trusted or understood are unlikely to be helpful, even if they are faithful representations of the clinical situation, and experience shows that most clinicians are unlikely to master the art of tree building. So what can be done? A possible solution to this problem is an Internet library of decision trees for common clinical situations, designed so that they provide both literature-based probabilities and representative utilities obtained from patients in various clinical settings. These trees would be analogous to the Cochrane Library and should be designed so that clinician users can input probabilities and utilities from their own patients, see a decision-analytic recommendation based on these personalized inputs, and then compare the structured recommendation with their own judgment and the patient's expressed wishes. One would not be obliged to follow the recommendation, but at a minimum one would have to justify why not, thus making the basis of a decision more clear and explicit. This procedure would, in my judgment, enhance the conversation that should occur between clinicians and their patients, thereby contributing importantly to achieving informed consent. In this way, decision analysis could become as useful to clinical practice as EBM has been to date.

Acknowledgments

Earlier versions of this chapter were presented at the Institute for Clinical Epidemiological Sciences, Sunnybrook Hospital, Toronto; at Medical Education Grand Rounds, University of Toronto Faculty of Medicine; at the Department of Medical Decision Making, Leiden University Medical Center (Netherlands); and at the Institute of Public Health, University of Southern Denmark, Odense. I am grateful to these audiences for many useful comments, criticisms and suggestions. Any errors of fact or interpretation in this chapter are my responsibility.

Note

1 Bayes's theorem is the mathematical rule for revising diagnostic opinion with imperfect evidence, such as laboratory tests. The key parameters are the pre-test probability of disease and the strength of the evidence. Pre-test probability can be based either on population-based data, such as can be provided by clinical epidemiology, or on the clinician's understanding of and beliefs about the patient. The strength of the evidence is represented quantitatively by test sensitivity and specificity or a likelihood ratio derived from these measures. For further details, see Sackett *et al.* (1997) and Hunink *et al.* (2001).

References

Baron, J. (2000) *Thinking and Deciding*, 3rd edn, Cambridge: Cambridge University Press.

Beck, J.R. and Pauker, S.G. (1983) The Markov process in medical prognosis, *Medical Decision Making*, 3: 419–58.

Blaney, D. (1998) Review of Greenhalgh, T., How to Read a Paper: The Basics of Evidence Based Medicine, *Medical Education*, 32: 444.

Bleichrodt, H., Pinto, J.P. and Wakker, P.P. (2001) Making descriptive use of prospect theory to improve the prescriptive use of expected utility, *Management Science*, 47: 1498–514.

Cabana, M.D., Rand, C.S., Powe, N.R. *et al.* (1999) Why don't physicians follow clinical practice guidelines? A framework for improvement, *Journal of the American Medical Association*, 282: 1458–65.

Chapman, G.B. and Elstein, A.S. (2000) Cognitive processes and biases in medical decision making, in G.B. Chapman and F. Sonnenberg (eds) *Decision Making in Health Care: Theory, Psychology, and Applications*, Cambridge: Cambridge University Press.

Cohen, B.J. (1996) Is expected utility theory normative for clinical decision making?, *Medical Decision Making*, 16: 1–6.

Detsky, A.S., Naglie, G., Krahn, M.D., Naimark, D. and Redelmeier, D.A. (1997) Primer on medical decision analysis. I. Getting started, *Medical Decision Making*, 17: 123–5.

Dolan, J.G. (1997)A survey of clinicians' opinions regarding the value of published decision analyses as sources of clinically useful information, *Medical Decision Making*, 17: 427–30.

Eddy, D.M. (1996) *Clinical Decision Making: From Theory to Practice,* Boston: Jones & Bartlett.

Elstein, A.S. and Schwartz, A. (2002) Clinical problem solving and diagnostic decision making: selective review of the cognitive literature, *British Medical Journal*, 324: 729–32.

Elstein, A.S., Schwartz, A. and Nendaz, M. (2002) Medical decision making, in G. Norman, C. van der Vleuten and D. Dolmans (eds) *International Handbook of Medical Education*, Boston: Kluwer.

Fowler, F.J., Collins, M.M., Albertsen, P.C., Zietman, A., Elliott, D.B. and Barry, M.J. (2000) Comparison of recommendations by urologists and radiation oncologists for treatment of clinically localized prostate cancer, *Journal of the American Medical Association,* 283: 3217–22.

Fowler, P.B.S. (1995) Evidence-based medicine (letter), *Lancet*, 346 (8978): 838.

Ghosh, S., Ziesmer, V. and Aronow, W.S. (2002) Underutilization of aspirin, beta blockers, angiotension-converting enzyme inhibitors, and lipid-lowering drugs and overutilization of calcium channel blockers in older patients with coronary artery disease in an academic nursing home, *Journals of Gerontology A: Biological Sciences and Medical Sciences*, 57: M398–400.

Goldstein, M.K. and Tsevat, J. (2000) Applying utility assessment at the bedside, in G.B. Chapman and F. Sonnenberg (eds) *Decision Making in Health Care: Theory, Psychology, and Applications*, Cambridge: Cambridge University Press.

Grahame-Smith, D. (1998) Evidence-based medicine: challenging the orthodoxy, *Journal of the Royal Society of Medicine*, 91 (Suppl. 35): 7–11.

Greco, P.J. and Eisenberg, J.M. (1993) Changing physicians' practices, *New England Journal of Medicine*, 329: 1271–4.

Greenhalgh, T. (1997) *How to Read a Paper: The Basics of Evidence Based Medicine*, London: BMJ Books.

Gruppen, L.D. and Frohna, A.Z. (2002) Clinical reasoning, in G.R. Norman,

C.P.M. van der Vleuten and D.J. Newble (eds) *International Handbook of Research in Medical Education*, Dordrecht: Kluwer Academic.

Hart, R.G. (1999) Warfarin in atrial fibrillation: underused in the elderly, often inappropriately used in the young, *Heart*, 82 (5): 539–40.

Hilden, J. and Habbema, J.D.F. (1990) The marriage of clinical trials and clinical decision science, *Statistics in Medicine*, 9: 1243–57.

Hogarth, R.M. (1987) *Judgment and Choice: The Psychology of Decision*, 2nd edn, New York: Wiley.

Hunink, M., Glasziou, P., Siegel, J. *et al.* (2001) *Decision Making in Health and Medicine: Integrating Evidence and Values*, New York: Cambridge University Press.

Inouye, J., Kristopatis, R., Stone, E., Pelter, M., Sandhu, M. and Weingarten, S. (1998) Physicians' changing attitudes toward guidelines, *Journal of General Internal Medicine*, 13: 324–6.

Kahneman, D. and Tversky, A. (1979) Prospect theory: an analysis of decision under risk, *Econometrica*, 47: 263–91.

Kahneman, D., Slovic, P. and Tversky, A. (eds) (1982) *Judgment Under Uncertainty: Heuristics and Biases*, New York: Cambridge University Press.

Klein, K. and Pauker, S.G. (1981) Recurrent deep venous thrombosis in pregnancy: analysis of the risks and benefits of anticoagulation, *Medical Decision Making*, 1: 181–202.

Miyamoto, J.M. (2000) Utility assessment under expected utility and rank-dependent utility assumptions, in G.B. Chapman and F.A. Sonnenberg (eds) *Decision Making in Health Care: Theory, Psychology, and Applications*, New York: Cambridge University Press.

Naylor, C. (1995) Grey zones of clinical practice: some limits to evidence-based medicine, *Lancet*, 345: 840–2.

Newell, A. and Simon, H.A. (1972) *Human Problem Solving*, Englewood Cliffs, NJ: Prentice-Hall.

O'Connor, A.M., Rostom, A., Fiset, V. *et al.* (1999b) Decision aids for patients facing health treatment or screening decisions: systematic review, *British Medical Journal*, 312: 731–4.

O'Connor, G.T., Quinton, H.B., Traven, N.D. *et al.* (1999a) Geographic variation in the treatment of acute myocardial infarction: the Cooperative Cardiovascular Project, *Journal of the American Medical Association*, 281: 627–33.

Ottesen, M.M., Kober, L., Jorgensen, S. and Torp-Pedersen, C., for the TRACE Study Group (2001) Consequences of overutilization and underutilization of thrombolytic therapy in clinical practice, *Journal of the American College of Cardiology*, 37: 1581–7.

Rose, J.H., O'Toole, E.E., Dawson, N.V. *et al.* (2000) Age differences in care practices and outcomes for hospitalized patients with cancer, *Journal of the American Geriatric Society*, 48 (5 Suppl.): S25–32.

Rouse, D.J. and Owen, J. (1998) Decision analysis, *Clinical Obstetrics and Gynecology*, 41: 282–95.

Russell, L.B. (2000) Cost-effectiveness analysis, in G.B. Chapman and F. Sonnenberg (eds) *Decision Making in Health Care: Theory, Psychology, and Applications*, Cambridge: Cambridge University Press.

Russell, L.B., Gold, M.R., Siegel, J.E., Daniels, N. and Weinstein, M.C., for the Panel on Cost-Effectiveness in Health and Medicine (1996) The role of cost-effectiveness analysis in health and medicine, *Journal of the American Medical Association*, 276: 1172–7.

Russo, J.E. and Schoemaker, P.J.H. (1990) *Decision Traps*, New York: Simon & Schuster.

Sackett, D.L. (1983) Interpretation of diagnostic data: 1. How to do it with pictures, *Canadian Medical Association Journal*, 129: 429–32.

Sackett, D.L., Haynes, R.B. and Tugwell, P. (1985) *Clinical Epidemiology: A Basic Science for Clinical Medicine*, Boston: Little, Brown.

Sackett, D.L., Haynes, R.B. and Tugwell, P. (1991) *Clinical Epidemiology: A Basic Science for Clinical Medicine*, 2nd edn, Boston: Little, Brown.

Sackett, D.L., Richardson, W.S., Rosenberg, W. and Haynes, R.B. (1997) *Evidence-Based Medicine: How to Practice and Teach EBM*, New York: Churchill Livingstone.

Schelling, T.C. (1968) The life you save may be your own, in S.B. Chase (ed.) *Problems in Public Expenditure Analysis*, Washington, DC: Brookings Institution.

Schmidt, H.G., Norman, G.R. and Boshuizen, H.P.A. (1990) A cognitive perspective on medical expertise: theory and implications, *Academic Medicine*, 65: 611–21.

Sonnenberg, F.A. and Beck, J.R. (1993) Markov models in medical decision making: a practical guide, *Medical Decision Making*, 13: 322–8.

Soumerai, S.B., McLaughlin, T.J., Spiegelman, D., Hertzmark, E., Thibault, G. and Goldman, L. (1997) Adverse outcomes of underuse of beta-blockers in elderly survivors of acute myocardial infarction, *Journal of the American Medical Association*, 277 (2): 115–21.

Sox, H.C. Jr., Blatt, M.A., Higgins, M.C. and Marton, K.I. (1988) *Medical Decision Making*, Boston: Butterworth.

Stiggelbout, A.M. (2000) Assessing patients' preferences, in G.B. Chapman and F. Sonnenberg (eds) *Decision Making in Health Care: Theory, Psychology, and Applications*, Cambridge: Cambridge University Press.

Tversky, A. and Kahneman, D. (1981) The framing of decisions and the psychology of choice, *Science*, 211: 453–8.

Tversky, A. and Kahneman, D. (1986) Rational choice and the framing of decisions, *Journal of Business*, 59: S251–78.

Ubel, P.A., Nord, E., Gold, M., Menzel, P., Prades, J.-L.P. and Richardson, J. (2000) Improving value measurement in cost-effectiveness analysis, *Medical Care*, 38: 892–901.

Ubel, P.L., Dekay, M.L., Baron, J. and Asch, D.A. (1996) Cost-effectiveness analysis in a setting of budget constraints: is it equitable?, *New England Journal of Medicine*, 334: 1174–7.

Weinstein, M.C., Fineberg, H.V., Elstein, A.S. *et al.* (1980) *Clinical Decision Analysis*, Philadelphia: Saunders.

Wennberg, J. and Gitelsohn, A. (1973) Small area variations in health care delivery, *Science*, 182: 1102–8.

9 Randomised controlled trials in drug policies

Can the best be the enemy of the good?

Kjeld Møller Pedersen

Introduction

The study question determines the relevant design. The policy question, the intended decision makers and their objective functions determine the relevant data and evidence.

These two homegrown truths are all too often overlooked. Many discussions about the merits of randomised controlled trials (RCTs) disregard these simple observations and are often accompanied by confusion about the exact role of scientific evidence in the policy-making process. This is even more the case at a time when 'evidence-based' this or that is the obvious, tempting and almost politically correct catchword. Clearly, this arises most frequently in the context of evidence-based medicine (Sackett *et al.* 1996; Sackett and Rosenberg 1995), which is the focus of this book, and extensions to evidence-based policy (Ham *et al.* 1995; Klein 2000; Innvaer *et al.* 2002). This last is exemplified by the WHO in its *World Health Report 2000* on improving the performance of health systems, which raises doubts about what, according to the WHO, constitutes evidence (WHO 2000). The WHO also maintains a special section on its Web site about evidence and information for policy, and has a global programme on evidence for health policy. WHO is co-sponsoring the European Observatory on Health Care Systems, which supports and promotes evidence-based health policy making through comprehensive and rigorous analysis of the dynamics of health care systems in Europe. More generally, in the United Kingdom the government is trying to create a culture of 'evidence-based policy' that will apply to all policy areas, including public health and health care (Strategic Policy Making Team 1999). It is likely, indeed, that governments worldwide subscribe to the use of evidence in policy making, including the pharmaceutical area. Logically, all this requires a clear definition of what constitutes evidence – who could be against evidence? – and what policy and policy making are, and how evidence enters such processes.

Policy, policy making and evidence

The chapter title indicates this chapter's scope and focus, namely RCTs and the use of evidence from drug trials in policy (making). With such a broad heading, it is necessary to limit the scope of inquiry considerably.

'Drug policies' is a broad term that more generally encompasses the regulation of pharmaceuticals and pharmaceutical markets. The scope is immense and fascinating: see, for instance, EudraNet (www.eudra.org), a network in the field of European human and veterinary pharmaceuticals. EudraNet helps to undertake the collaborative business processes in pharmaceuticals, from submission and evaluation of marketing authorisation applications to pharmacovigilance of products on the market.

Since 1985, many EEC and, later, EU directives have been adopted with the aim of achieving a single, EEC-wide market for pharmaceuticals. This single market should also strengthen the European pharmaceutical industry's competitiveness and research capability. From the first European Community pharmaceutical directive, issued in 1965, to the present day, Community lawmakers have striven to ensure that, first and foremost, medicinal products for human use help to maintain a high level of protection for public health.

Much of the impetus behind that first directive (65/65/EEC) stemmed from a determination to prevent a recurrence of the thalidomide disaster in the early 1960s, when thousands of children were born with limb deformities as a result of their mothers taking thalidomide as a sedative during pregnancy. This experience, which shook public health authorities and the general public's trust, made it clear that to safeguard public health, no medicinal product must ever again be marketed without prior authorisation based on evidence – that is, evidence on safety and efficacy coming from RCTs.

This takes us directly to the first drug policy issue, namely, marketing authorisation, where the RCT and policy meet. The RCT is a core part of evidence (documentation) for market authorisation, as for instance administered by the Food and Drug Administration (FDA) in the United States, and, increasingly, the European Agency for the Evaluation of Medical Products (EMEA) in Europe on behalf of the EU member countries.

The second area where evidence and policy meet is when decisions about the reimbursement of drugs are made. Here the RCT usually also has an important role, even if not as dominating as for marketing authorisation. RCTs and meta-analyses are often integrated with economic evaluations. Increasingly such evaluations are used as decision inputs for reimbursement questions (that is, government or insurance subsidy towards the cost of drugs), which in turn raises a host of issues about how to use RCTs in such analyses. Economic evaluation or not, there is also a more general issue related to RCTs used in connection with reimbursement, namely to what extent phase III trials are really relevant to the question about reimbursement.

With this as a backdrop, it is now possible to define what policy and policy making are in general – and also as applicable to drug policies.

A policy is a course of action that sets out politically legitimate rules for behaviour and actions for a specific area under the political control of a policy-making body, be that a standard political body, e.g. a parliament, or an administrative body like the FDA or EMEA, which derive legitimacy from the underlying political system. It is normally valid for a given geographical area and the people living there. A policy is thus something different from, for instance, an evidence-based treatment decision by an individual physician for a given patient. A policy concerning treatment with drugs could, for example, be that only the most cost-effective treatments should be used or reimbursed. This means of course that a policy ultimately may have consequences for an individual, but based on more general policy principles that apply, all other things being equal.

Policy making is the process leading to policy. Policy making thus involves the use of evidence about the subject matter on hand, e.g. RCT-based evidence, evidence from observational studies, evidence on costs, evidence on efficient organisational form, etc. values and implicit or explicit objective functions, i.e. what is to be pursued, for instance maximisation of quality-adjusted life years (QALYs) per monetary unit expended. Policy making thus is decision making about some future course, rules and actions. It is politically sanctioned decision making with consequences usually for many people, or high-risk groups with relatively few members.

Policy making rarely is based on evidence from one single discipline, e.g. medicine or economics, but is usually cross-disciplinary, or at least based on evidence inputs from several disciplines. Furthermore, many types of evidence are used, RCT being one piece out of several that are possible. As a logical consequence, policy making is not usually identical to, for instance, carrying out and interpreting a meta-analysis of RCTs of a particular drug, or making a cost–utility analysis of the same drug, but the two types of evidence will be important inputs to the policy-making process.

Researchers tend to be rather naïve about the policy-making process. They have a tendency to believe not only that the most relevant evidence is what they produce, but also that this is all that is needed to arrive at a policy – without, incidentally, clarifying the above terms. For this and other reasons, there is a gap between actual policy making and the research evidence produced by the scientific community (Dobbins *et al.* 2001; Elliott and Popay 2000; Harries *et al.* 1999; Hoffmann *et al.* 2002; Innvaer *et al.* 2002; Lohr *et al.* 1998; Niessen *et al.* 2000; Palmer 2000).

It is important to distinguish between means and ends in policy making. Evidence concerns the means, i.e. the effectiveness of contemplated courses of action. In principle, evidence does not come into play when ends are considered, because ends are 'pure politics' in a positive sense.

'Politics' is often, however, taken to mean something irrational, arbitrary, or something that runs counter to evidence. However, this (simplified) view – often just implying that 'they', the politicians, did not follow the advice or inclinations of the observers making the statement – overlooks the fact that the setting of objectives is the very nature of politics. The evidence-related question in policy making is to evaluate the degree of goal fulfilment that characterises the different means. In cases where several pieces of empirical evidence are used, for instance because a broad goal in reality is multidimensional, the weighting of the available evidence is also a question that belongs more in the realm of politics than science. However, politics cannot be reduced to mere setting of objectives and weights attached to different objectives. Political decision making also involves negotiation, consensus seeking, etc. (Stone 1997), in the process of which the role of evidence often seems to outsiders to play a minor role, but in a sense may underlie the whole exercise, and what is being negotiated may actually be which objectives to pursue and which weigh (not literally, but in broad terms) to use. In the space allotted here this topic unfortunately cannot be pursued further.

'Evidence' is a self-evident and yet vague term. In the evidence-based approach it is rarely stated explicitly that it is a positivistic empirical tradition as opposed to, for instance, an idealistic perspective such as phenomenology, where the preferred approach is that of making observations through participation and other typical qualitative methods. This author supports thinking along quantitative lines, mainly because many of the issues involved cannot be settled in a satisfactory way by qualitative methods.

Within the evidence-based-medicine tradition, there is a somewhat dogmatic hierarchy of (empirical) evidence placing RCTs and meta-analyses based on RCTs at the top, while observational studies and professional judgement or consensus are accorded lower credibility. However, there is a strong tendency towards dogmatism in the sense of a feeling that this type of quantified evidence alone ought to shape decisions and policy, however defined. This dogmatism seldom stops to ask: (relevant) evidence for answering which questions? Implicitly, it is assumed that all decisions and policy making can and should be supported by empirical evidence defined in this way. As soon as these modifiers are added, in many cases further admissible evidence can enter. In addition, it is still somewhat heretical thinking to note that observational studies in some instances may be considered on an equal footing with RCTs. An editorial in the *New England Journal of Medicine* (Pocock and Elbourne 2000), following the publication of two articles showing in a head-to-head comparison with RCTs that observational studies did not – as commonly believed – overestimate the size of the treatment effect (Benson and Hartz 2000; Concato *et al.* 2000), is fairly typical of the reaction pattern: 'yes, but . . . alas, the RCT is almost always to be preferred'. A considered opinion on the balance between randomised and observational studies can be found in the editorial by Ioannidis *et al.* (2001).

The point here is not to enter into a discussion of whether (well-designed) observational studies should be a 'gold standard' on an equal footing with RCTs, but rather to stress the obvious, namely that the question(s) to be answered to a considerable extent determine what is admissible and relevant evidence. This issue, however, is rarely discussed, but in a sense is the more important one. Many futile discussions could be avoided if this issue were also considered. As becomes apparent later in the chapter, first of all, RCTs seldom provide necessary and sufficient evidence for many 'real-life' decisions – but of course do so for narrow, scientific questions. Second, in policy making several types of evidence are used – and, most importantly, usually a number of rather divergent criteria/objectives need to be weighted – an attribution process that by its very nature is not dictated by (pure) scientific logic. Third, for many policy issues there is not much empirical evidence available that follows strict scientific standards, i.e. no RCT is available on the merits of leaving pharmaceutical markets free to set prices, and solid observational evidence is not readily available either. Real-life policy making is messy, but not arbitrary. It has to take place in the uncontrolled environment outside the laboratory and outside protocol-driven research projects.

RCT and evidence-based medicine

The randomised trial was originally seen as the application of the ideas of Ronald A. Fisher (1935) and Bradford Hill (1937) to the study of the efficacy of drugs. For that reason alone, RCTs and the testing of effects of drugs are closely related. The small 1972 book by Cochrane has done much to push the use of RCT-based evidence, e.g. the Cochrane Collaboration. However, his thinking was broader. He talked about 'this cost/benefit approach' (p.2), namely effectiveness (which is really efficacy; see p.132) and efficiency, by which he meant 'the vast problem of the optimum use of personnel and materials in achieving these results'. In today's parlance he probably would have talked about cost-effectiveness.

To turn to drugs, the European Commission (2002) notes that all clinical trials on medicinal products for human use should be designed, conducted, recorded and reported according to the principles of good clinical practice. The Commission issues guidelines that clarify the principles of good clinical practice in the conduct for the European Union of clinical trials on medicinal products for human use. This is a clear-cut example of regulation and policy making explicitly requiring a specific type of evidence, in particular the RCT. However, it begs the question of what constitutes necessary and sufficient evidence to support policy making and monitoring.

Drug development and RCT

The RCT is an indispensable tool during the drug development phases. Hence, some of the issues related to RCTs as used in policy making in reality do not apply to phases I–III in describing the development and testing of a new drug. Here the focus is research, not policy. However, phase III studies raise a number of issues, because here we approach the stage of policy making.

Following the handbook published by the US agency, the Center for Drug Evaluation and Research (CDER) (2002), the three stages can be described concisely as follows. Phase I includes the initial introduction of an investigational new drug in humans. These studies are closely monitored and may be conducted in patients, but are usually conducted in healthy volunteers. They are designed to determine the metabolic and pharmacological actions of the drug in humans, to discover the side effects associated with increasing doses, and, if possible, to gain early evidence on effectiveness. During phase I, sufficient information about the drug's pharmacokinetics and pharmacological effects should be obtained to permit the design of well-controlled, scientifically valid phase II studies. The total number of subjects included in phase I studies varies with the drug, but is generally in the range of 20–80.

In phase I studies, the regulatory authorities can usually impose a clinical hold (i.e. prohibit the study from proceeding or stop a trial that has started) for reasons of safety, or because of a sponsor's failure to disclose accurately the risk of study to investigators.

Phase II includes the early controlled clinical studies conducted to obtain some preliminary data on the efficacy of the drug for a particular indication or indications in patients with the disease or condition. This phase of testing also helps to determine the common short-term side effects and risks associated with the drug. Phase II studies are typically well controlled, i.e. RCTs, closely monitored, and conducted in a relatively small number of patients, usually involving several hundred people.

Phase III studies are expanded controlled trials. They are performed after preliminary evidence suggesting efficacy[1] of the drug has been obtained in phase II and are intended to gather the additional information about efficacy and safety that is needed to evaluate the overall benefit–risk relationship of the drug. Phase III studies usually involve several hundred to several thousand people.

The RCTs from the three phases, but in particular from phases II and III, are used when drug companies apply for marketing authorisation – to the FDA in the United States, to EMEA in the EU, or to the various national medicines agencies.

Example of marketing authorisation

The following is the concluding section from a 27-page EMEA review of a product, an ointment called Protopy, for a skin disease, atopic dermatitis – a chronic relapsing inflammatory skin disease – that was granted marketing authorisation in February 2002 (EMEA 2002). The example was randomly picked from among the published evaluations from EMEA. The idea behind the inclusion of this example is to give a concrete illustration of how RCTs are used in reaching something that in essence is a policy conclusion, namely a marketing authorisation that holds for all EU countries – markets that in total have a greater population than does the United States.

A total of six phase III RCTs had been conducted in Europe and the United States with a total of 2,737 adults and children in the trials, i.e. on average 450 in each trial. All had a multi-centre, randomised, double-blind, parallel group design. Four phase II studies were carried out to assess the optimal dose, two with children and two with adults. A total of 452 patients participated. The design was randomised, multi-centre, double-blind.

> Based on the CPMP [Committee for Proprietary Medicinal Products] review of data on quality, safety and efficacy, the CPMP considered by consensus that the benefit/risk profile of Protopy (0.03% and 0.1%) in the treatment of moderate to severe atopic dermatitis in adults who are not adequately responsive to or are intolerant of conventional therapies was favourable as well as the benefit/risk profile of Protopy 0.03% in the treatment of moderate to severe atopic dermatitis in children (2 years of age and above) who failed to respond adequately to conventional therapies, and therefore recommended the granting of the marketing authorisation.
>
> (EMEA 2002)

Accordingly, the product is thus deemed ready for introduction to the market. However, there is at least one question that was not addressed directly in the authorisation process – a question that is a curious mixture of health professional opinion and a political issue, namely whether a documented effect is big enough to warrant use in the treatment of patients. It is a question that sits on the border between science and policy making.

Another issue strictly related to the authorisation process it how quality, safety and efficacy are weighted in reaching a decision. It is probably fair to expect that the weightings vary according to which drug is considered. It would still be of interest, however, to have a debate about the relative size of the (implicit) weights used. The point is that as soon as such issues are introduced, one leaves the realm of objective science and enters the world of judgements that are based on experience and knowledge, and, of course, purely subjective aspects. Scientists should not be the only people involved here.

It is an old truth that a treatment effect can be statistically significant without necessarily being clinically significant (Bailar and Mosteller 1992). When samples are very large, small differences may be statistically significant even though they have no importance in clinical practice or possibly even in public health. At the other extreme, small samples may produce large differences so imprecisely determined that they are not statistically significant. RCTs are designed to be able to detect a specified difference in effect. However, no clear rules exist for any threshold size of this effect. Is a 10 per cent difference big enough to be of interest? Who should decide on the relevant effect size to be pursued in RCTs? To these issues one should probably add a question about the burden or welfare loss associated with the particular disease to modify or amplify the questions of size of effect.

One could say that this should be a health professional question, but if the drug is going to receive (considerable) reimbursement from public funds, e.g. Medicare in the United States or from tax-funded health care systems as in northern Europe, it is an issue that should be part of the political decision-making process. It would be possible to argue then that the decision about effect in phase III is a matter of professional judgement, based, however, on transparent criteria, and that the issue is to be considered again when deciding on reimbursement. However, if the RCTs that are used as inputs to the reimbursement decisions are the same ones, there is a danger that the question will not be addressed explicitly.

For obvious reasons, P values and (in particular) confidence intervals are important in RCTs. However,

> one should not equate P values or the results of hypothesis testing with *decisions*. P values are a way of reporting the results of statistical analysis. Similarly, the result of a hypothesis test might be best described as a *conclusion*, rather than a decision, to emphasize that the results of the hypothesis test are another way of reporting data. *Decisions* depend on conclusions but also on such factors as costs, risks, size of effect, consequences, and *policy consequences*. Issues of *institutional decision making* and many other factors can also affect the decision.
>
> (Bailar and Mosteller 1992: 198; emphasis added)

Experienced researchers of course recognise the above, but may forget it in specific cases, and the insights of the quotation emphasize what ideally should take place during the authorisation process, and illustrate that, albeit important, an RCT is not the only type of evidence that is relevant.

Effectiveness versus efficacy

When results from RCTs are used in economic evaluations, they ideally should document effectiveness, not efficacy. It is usually thought that phase II and III RCTs are primarily concerned with efficacy.

Efficacy can be defined as performance of treatment under ideal and controlled circumstances (Bombardier and Maetzel 1999; Revicki and Frank 1999). This research is designed to explore biomedical end points and to answer questions about the difference in efficacy and safety between two treatments under highly controlled experimental conditions. Efficacy studies focus on internal validity, i.e. being valid for the universe studied as set out in the protocol rather than with external validity and hence generalisability to clinical practice settings.

Effectiveness can be defined as the performance of a treatment under usual or real-world conditions. Thus, effectiveness studies are designed to evaluate treatment outcome under usual care conditions. They answer questions about policy or management decisions. Some internal validity may be sacrificed to obtain greater external validity.

The differences between efficacy and effectiveness studies are summarised in Table 9.1.

Phase II and III studies are primarily concerned with efficacy. In view

Table 9.1 Summary of differences between efficacy and effectiveness studies

	Efficacy studies	*Effectiveness studies*
Objective	Does it work under optimal circumstances?	Does it work under real-world circumstances?
Motivation	Regulatory approval – marketing authorisation	Reimbursement
Intervention	Fixed/very well-defined regimen, controlled circumstances	Flexible regimen – adjustment to individual needs of patients, more uncontrolled, less standardised. Blinding is not used
Comparator	Placebo – or often somewhat arbitrarily chosen	Usual care
Design	RCT – 'according to the book'	RCT or open label – less control
Outcomes	Condition-specific. Short-term time horizon. Strong link to mechanism of action	A wide range, comprehensive, for instance QALY. Long(er) time horizon. Weak(er) link to mechanism of action
Analysis	Protocol adherence	Intent to treat

Source: Modified after Bombardier and Maetzel (1999).

of the policy issues involved in both market authorisation and the granting of reimbursement, evidence on effectiveness is the more relevant type of evidence. Without being able to document it firmly, this author would claim that users of efficacy studies often (also) consider them to be effectiveness studies.

It is sometimes claimed that effectiveness data are collected in 'phase IV', namely as part of the important post-marketing surveillance. However, as defined by, for instance, the FDA's Center for Drug Evaluation and Research,

> the goal of CDER's Post-Marketing Surveillance (PMS) system is to monitor the ongoing safety of marketed drugs. This is accomplished by reassessing drug risks based on new data learned after the drug is marketed, and recommending ways of trying to most appropriately manage that risk.
>
> (Center for Drug Evaluation and Research 2002: section on post-market surveillance)

In part, the need for post-marketing surveillance arises from the fact that RCTs are seldom designed to capture rare and/or harmful adverse effects of a drug, again showing the limited set of issues for which RCTs provide both necessary and sufficient evidence.

The limited relevance of efficacy studies in pharmacoeconomic evaluations

By their very nature, efficacy-orientated RCTs are of limited relevance as evidence in pharmacoeconomic evaluations. Yet these are increasingly used when making reimbursement decisions. There are two issues in this context: the use of efficacy data in economic evaluations, and the nature of the decision leading to the granting or the denying of reimbursement for a particular drug.

Data from RCT have high internal validity, but are constrained in terms of length of follow-up period, strict adherence to protocol and a narrowly defined patient group (indication and some relevant patient characteristics), and occasionally also the range of outcomes used, e.g. intermediate end points. From a narrow scientific point of view, i.e. focusing on the documentation of effects based on clearly defined cause–effect thinking, this is of course desirable, and the efficacy data produced are relevant. However, when transferred to the policy context and the everyday setting of patient treatment, there are important shortcomings.

The highly controlled and somewhat ideal circumstances in which RCTs are conducted do not accord well with the real world. Once a drug is approved, it will then be used in far more uncontrolled 'everyday circumstances'. For that reason alone, a relatively high threshold value for detectable effect should be set, because the effects in everyday use undoubtedly will be less than the results produced under the ideal circumstances of efficacy studies.

In many situations, economists, when conducting economic evaluation of pharmaceuticals, have to extrapolate beyond the period observed in RCTs because the follow-up period used is short. For instance, life years saved is generally a more relevant outcome measure for pharmacoeconomic evaluations than, say, the percentage surviving x days. In many instances, the whole of the remaining lifespan has to be considered to capture those dimensions that are economically meaningful. For these and other reasons, elaborated in what follows, models are often used in pharmacoeconomics not as a substitute for RCTs but to alleviate the shortcomings of most available RCTs – be they efficacy or effectiveness studies.

However, modelling also has dangers and is still the subject of debate, but is nevertheless a fact of life in pharmacoeconomic evaluations (Buxton *et al.* 1997; Hay *et al.* 1999; Weinstein *et al.* 2001). There remains nonetheless a need for clarification of the purpose of models. That is, are they intended to predict future events, to aid in making better decisions, or to organise and use available data – be they RCTs or evidence from observational studies? Similarly, there is a need for rules for validating models, in particular if disease/aetiology dimensions are included (Weinstein *et al.* 2001).[2]

Pharmacoeconomic evaluations and reimbursement

Reimbursement decisions are increasingly expected to be supported by pharmacoeconomic evaluations – a development that started in Australia and Ontario in the early 1990s. Considerable experience has been accumulated (Freund 1996; Glennie *et al.* 1999; Hailey 1997; Henry 1992; Hill *et al.* 2000; Langley 1996; Menon *et al.* 1996; Torrance *et al.* 1996).

From the earlier discussion of effectiveness studies, it follows that phase III trials have limitations in decision making about reimbursement. In addition, it should be noted that cost-effectiveness analyses should be based on a comparison of the new intervention with current practice, rather than with a placebo, as is often the case in such trials (even though this is changing). In addition, phase III trials are mainly efficacy (explanatory) trials rather than effectiveness (pragmatic/naturalistic) trials, thereby restricting their value for making decisions about resource allocation.

In a United Kingdom context there have recently been discussions about how organisations such as the National Institute for Clinical Excellence (NICE) should make recommendations on reimbursement where there is a lack of relevant RCT evidence. The proposal is to develop an explicit framework in which it is recognised that decisions need to be made despite uncertainty about costs and effects. The recommended approach is what the authors call 'decision analysis', but this is in fact the same as what has been termed modelling in this chapter (Claxton *et al.* 2002).

Decision analysis is with some justification claimed to provide an explicit method for deciding on reimbursement by integrating the decisions to adopt a new drug (or technology in general) and to demand additional information by doing further research. The relevant tasks include extrapolation of costs and benefits over the relevant time period and from surrogate endpoints to ultimate health outcomes, generalisations of cost-effectiveness assessment across clinical settings and populations of patients, and comparisons of the costs and benefits of alternative strategies for the management of patients. Most importantly, decision modelling needs all relevant inputs to the decision to be identified explicitly, and enables data to be synthesised from various sources.

All this, however, is based on a normative presumption that reimbursement decisions in practice follow this path. Yet in all countries more or less explicit rules exist, and in many instances these prevent these ideals being followed (see the recent series on pricing and reimbursement of drugs in European countries in the *European Journal of Health Economics*). Consider the case of Denmark (Pedersen 2003).

To receive general reimbursement, two primary criteria have to be fulfilled: first, that the drug has a documented safe and therapeutically valuable effect for well-defined medical indications; and second, that the price of the drug has a reasonable relationship to the therapeutic value. The latter point should ideally lead to an opening up for more pharmacoeconomic evaluations, which in Denmark currently are submitted purely on a voluntary basis. Instead, some rather primitive price per defined daily dose (DDD) is used to capture the 'reasonable relationship'.

In nine situations, general reimbursement is not granted.[3] In the current context, the most important ones are:

1 There is a risk that the medicinal product will be used outside its approved indication.
2 The effect of the medicinal product is not clinically documented.
3 There is a risk that the medicinal product will be used as a first-line choice.
4 It is not clear whether the medicinal product should be used as a first choice.

If one or more of these points exist, even good pharmacoeconomic evaluations are disregarded, basically showing the primacy of efficacy-orientated thinking. There is no doubt that according to this line of thinking, the product used above as an example of marketing authorisation will not receive general reimbursement in Denmark.

The point here is not to argue for the overriding importance of adopting the sorts of ideas recently outlined in relation to NICE or just that a greater role should be allowed for cost-effectiveness and cost–utility analyses. Instead, what this shows is how efficacy permeates thinking even when we move to reimbursement policy making. As an aside, it seems that the issue of first- versus second-line choice is an important one when considering reimbursement. Even strong supporters of the increased use of pharmacoeconomic evaluations would admit that this feature is not currently captured by such analyses. Also, RCT-based evidence will rarely, if ever, be present for all nine points, or just the four points mentioned here, again pointing to the limited, albeit important, role of RCT-based evidence in policy making.

Conclusions

Randomised controlled trials are an indispensable part of drug development and testing. There is no doubt about this. However, evidence from RCTs is never both necessary and sufficient for decision and policy making, particularly in the case of efficacy-orientated trials. Effectiveness studies should be used far more widely.

In the discussions surrounding evidence-based medicine, much more attention ought to be paid to clarifying the nature of the decisions or policy making involved. In this connection, one should be careful to make the implicit objective function explicit. If one considers the standard definition of evidence-based medicine, as for instance given by Sackett, several questions arise:

> Evidence based medicine is the conscientious, explicit, and judicious use of current best evidence in making decisions about the care of *individual patients*. The practice of evidence based medicine means integrating individual clinical expertise with the best available external clinical evidence from systematic research.... Evidence based medicine is not restricted to randomized trials and meta-analyses ... [but] it is when asking questions about therapy that we should try to avoid the non-experimental approaches, since these routinely lead to false positive conclusions about efficacy. Because the randomized trial, and especially the systematic review of several randomized trials, is so much more likely to inform us and so much less likely to mislead us, it has *become the 'gold standard'* for judging whether a treatment does more good than harm.
>
> (Sackett *et al.* 1996: 71–2; emphasis added)

First of all, should decisions be based on the individual-patient ethic of efficacy or effectiveness or on the population-health ethic of efficiency? In response to Maynard (1997), Sackett concedes that considerations for groups based on cost-utility are the more relevant: 'I reckon that the fundamental approach constitutes the best way forward at present' (Sackett 1997). Second, as a consequence of the above, the strict reliance on RCTs in some cases can and should be relaxed.

Furthermore, as with the hierarchy of evidence with RTC at the top, there is a hierarchy, although more fuzzy, of health and drug policy questions: choice of treatment, choice of reimbursement/financing, choice of (for instance) hospital structure ... and choice of organizational form, e.g. market versus hierarchy in publicly integrated systems, choice of price and market regulation for pharmaceuticals, and choice of means to reduce, for instance, inequality in health or drug utilisation. There is no clear one-to-one mapping from the evidence hierarchy to policy hierarchy, and it is obvious that the RCT simply is not and will not be available for many structural questions, from hospital structure (Edwards and Harrison 1999), to reduction of inequality of health (Macintyre 2003). The exact nature of available and desirable evidence changes with the policy issue. This is one simple but important lesson from this chapter, along with the question of when the RCT is both necessary and sufficient for policy making at the group or societal level, as opposed to the patient level.

Notes

1 Actually, 'effectiveness' is used by CDER, but to keep things clear, efficacy has been substituted. In any case, this is probably what is meant by CDER.

2 A fairly transparent example of model-building for Alzheimer's disease is given by Caro *et al.* (2001). Morris provides a good example of a comparison of economic modelling and clinical trials (Morris 1997).

3 In view of the earlier discussion of politics, it should be noted that these nine points are set out in legislation, i.e. they have political legitimacy and reflect political objectives, and as such are not up for discussion. However, the precise weights attached to the objectives were not stated in the legislative process, thereby leaving some 'political' space to the Danish Medicines Agency and the associated advisory board on reimbursement. This case also illustrates the grey zone between politics and the execution of political decisions – a zone that leaves some leeway for the weighting not only of objectives but also of evidence.

References

Bailar, J.C. and Mosteller, F. (eds) (1992) *Medical Uses of Statistics*, 2nd edn, Boston: NEJM Books.

Benson, K. and Hartz, A.J. (2000) A comparison of observational studies and randomized, controlled trials, *New England Journal of Medicine*, 342: 1878–86.

Bombardier, C. and Maetzel, A. (1999) Pharmacoeconomic evaluation of new treatments: efficacy versus effectiveness studies?, *Annals of Rheumatic Diseases*, (Suppl.) 58: 182–5.

Buxton, M.J., Drummond, M.F., van Hout, B.A. *et al.* (1997) Modelling in economic evaluations: an unavoidable fact of life, *Health Economics*, 6: 217–27.

Caro, J.J., Gatsius, B.A., Migliaccion-Walle, K., Raggio, K. and Ward, A. (2001) Assessment of health economics in Alzheimer's disease (AHEAD) based on need for full-time care, *Neurology*, 57: 964–71.

Center for Drug Evaluation and Research (2002) *The CDER Handbook* (on New Drug Development and Review, Generic Review, OTC Review, Post-Drug

Approval Process), Washington, DC: Internet version of handbook, http://www.fda.gov/cder/handbook/ (accessed 29 December 2002).
Claxton, K., Schulpher, M. and Drummond, M. (2002) A rational framework for decision making by the National Institute for Clinical Excellence (NICE), *Lancet*, 360: 711–15.
Cochrane, A.L. (1972) *Effectiveness and Efficiency: Random Reflections on Health Services*, London: Nuffield Provincial Hospitals Trust.
Concato, J., Shah, N. and Horwitz, R.I. (2000) Randomized, controlled trials, observational studies, and the hierarchy of research designs, *New England Journal of Medicine*, 342: 1887–92.
Dobbins, M., Cockerill, R. and Barnsley, J. (2001) Factors affecting the utilization of systematic reviews: a study of public health decision makers, *International Journal of Technology Assessment in Health Care*, 17: 203–14.
Edwards, N. and Harrison, A. (1999) Planning hospitals with limited evidence: a research and policy problem, *British Medical Journal*, 319: 1361–3.
Elliott, H. and Popay, J. (2000) How are policy makers using evidence? Models of research utilisation and local NHS policy making, *Journal of Epidemiology and Community Health*, 54: 461–8.
European Agency for the Evaluation of Medical Products (EMEA) (2002) Scientific discussion of Protopy. EMEA Document http://www.emea.eu.int/humandocs/PDFs/EPAR/protopy/109602en6.pdf (accessed 29 December 2002).
European Commission (2002) *E. D. G. Detailed Guidelines on the principles of good clinical practice in the conduct in the EU of clinical trials on medicinal products for human use*, Draft 5.1, Brussel, July.
Fisher, R.A. (1935) *The Design of Experiments*, 9th edn, Edinburgh: Macmillan.
Freund, D.A. (1996) Initial development of the Australian guidelines, *Medical Care*, 34 (12 Suppl.): DS211–15.
Glennie, J.L., Torrance, G.W., Baladi, J.F. *et al.* (1999) The revised Canadian Guidelines for the Economic Evaluation of Pharmaceuticals, *Pharmacoeconomics*, 15: 459–68.
Hailey, D. (1997) Australian economic evaluation and government decisions on pharmaceuticals, compared to assessment of other health technologies, *Social Science and Medicine*, 45: 563–81.
Ham, C., Hunter, D.J. and Robinson, R. (1995) Evidence based policymaking, *British Medical Journal*, 310: 71–2.
Harries, U., Elliott, H. and Higgins, A. (1999) Evidence-based policy-making in the NHS: exploring the interface between research and the commissioning process, *Journal of Public Health Medicine*, 21: 29–36.
Hay, J., Jackson, J., Luce, B., Avorn, J. and Ashraf, T. (1999) Methodological issues in conducting pharmacoeconomic evaluations: modelling studies, *Value in Health*, 2: 78–81.
Henry, D.A. (1992) The Australian guidelines for subsidisation of pharmaceuticals, *Pharmacoeconomics*, 2: 422–6.
Hill, B.A. (1937) *Principles of Medical Statistics* (9th edn, 1971), London: Oxford University Press.
Hill, S.R., Mitchell, A.S. and Henry, D.A. (2000) Problems with the interpretation of pharmacoeconomic analyses: a review of submissions to the Australian Pharmaceutical Benefits Scheme, *Journal of the American Medical Association*, 283: 2116–21.

Hoffmann, C., Stoykova, B.A., Nixon, J., Glanville, J.M., Misso, K. and Drummond, M.F. (2002) Do health-care decision makers find economic evaluations useful? The findings of focus group research in UK health authorities, *Value in Health*, 5: 71–8.

Innvaer, S., Vist, G., Trommald, M. and Oxman, A. (2002) Health policy-makers' perceptions of their use of evidence: a systematic review, *Journal of Health Services Research and Policy*, 7: 239–44.

Ioannidis, J.P.A., Haidich, A.B. and Lau, J. (2001) Any casualties in the clash of randomised and observational evidence?, *British Medical Journal*, 322: 879–80.

Klein, R. (2000) From evidence-based medicine to evidence-based policy?, *Journal of Health Services Research and Policy*, 5: 65–6.

Langley, P.C. (1996) The November 1995 revised Australian guidelines for the economic evaluation of pharmaceuticals, *Pharmacoeconomics*, 9: 341–52.

Lohr, K.N., Eleazer, K. and Mauskopf, J. (1998) Health policy issues and applications for evidence-based medicine and clinical practice guidelines, *Health Policy*, 46: 1–19.

Macintyre, S. (2003) Evidence based policy making (editorial), *British Medical Journal*, 326: 5–6.

Maynard, A. (1997) Evidence-based medicine: an incomplete method for informing treatment choices, *Lancet*, 349: 126–8.

Menon, D., Schubert, F. and Torrance, G.W. (1996) Canada's New Guidelines for the Economic Evaluation of Pharmaceuticals, *Medical Care*, 34 (12 Suppl.]: DS77–86.

Morris, S. (1997) A comparison of economic modelling and clinical trials in the economic evaluation of cholesterol-modifying pharmacotherapy, *Health Economics*, 6: 589–601.

Niessen, L.W., Grijseels, E.W. and Rutten, F.F. (2000) The evidence-based approach in health policy and health care delivery, *Social Science and Medicine*, 51: 859–69.

Palmer, G.R. (2000) Evidence-based health policy-making, hospital funding and health insurance, *Medical Journal of Australia*, 172: 130–3.

Pedersen, K.M. (2003) Pricing and reimbursement of drugs in Denmark, *European Journal of Health Economics*, 4: 1670–4.

Pocock, S.J. and Elbourne, D.R. (2000) Randomized trials or observational tribulations, *New England Journal of Medicine*, 342: 1907–9.

Revicki, D.A. and Frank, L. (1999) Pharmacoeconomic evaluation in the real world, *Pharmacoeconomics*, 15: 423–34.

Sackett, D.L. (1997) Evidence-based medicine and treatment choices, *Lancet*, 349: 570.

Sackett, D. and Rosenberg, W. (1995) On the need for evidence-based medicine, *Health Economics*, 4: 249–54.

Sackett, D.L., Rosenberg, W.M., Gray, J.A., Haynes, R.B. and Richardson, W.S. (1996) Evidence based medicine: what it is and what it isn't, *British Medical Journal*, 312: 71–2.

Stone, D.L. (1997) *Policy Paradox: The Art of Political Decision Making*, New York: W.W. Norton.

Strategic Policy Making Team (1999) Professional Policy Making for the Twenty First Century. London: Cabinet Office.

Torrance, G.W., Baker, D., Detsky, A. *et al.*, for the Canadian Collaborative

Workshop for Pharmacoeconomics (1996) Canadian guidelines for economic evaluation of pharmaceuticals, *Pharmacoeconomics*, 9: 535–59.
Weinstein, M.C., Toy, E.L., Sandberg, E.A. *et al.* (2001) Modeling for health care and other policy decisions: uses, roles, and validity, *Value in Health*, 4: 348–61.
World Health Organization (2000) *The World Health Report 2000. Health Systems: Improving Performance*, Geneva: WHO.

10 Evidence-based health care and international health

Good, but not good enough

Aileen J. Plant

There have been many who, not knowing how to mingle the useful with the pleasing in the right proportions, have had all their toil and pains for nothing.

(Miguel de Cervantes, *Don Quixote*, 1620)

Introduction

Evidence-based medicine (EBM) has become a well-known and well-accepted concept in the past decade. The concept that the best evidence can be used to make the best decisions for health has origins at least as far back as the mid-nineteenth century in Paris (Sackett *et al.* 1996). At one point defined in the following terms: 'evidence-based medicine is the conscientious, explicit and judicious use of current best evidence in making decisions about the care of individual patients' (ibid.), increasingly the term 'evidence-based medicine' is being used to encompass evidence-based health care and evidence-based health policy. Evidence-based health care and evidence-based health policy have implications wider than the direct clinical questions EBM seeks to answer concerning individual patients; they also seek to answer questions on the explicit and judicious use of current best evidence for populations. For ease of reading, in this chapter EBM will include evidence-based health care and evidence-based health policy. EBM is based on the premise that evidence can be graded by quality to ensure not only that the best decision for any given situation can be made, but also that evidence gaps become apparent.

Using an evidence base has intuitive benefits for both providers and recipients of health care. For providers, the concept that evidence can be used to determine the best way of providing health care is attractive: it can save money, prevent criticism and provide comfort that the approach is right. For recipients, the EBM approach suggests they are getting the best care, regardless of their capacity to assess the technical expertise of the provider.

In this chapter I will consider a range of issues surrounding EBM focusing on population health and health policy and the impact that EBM has on international health, especially on the health of people in developing countries, and consider what can be done to maximise the usefulness of EBM in developing countries. The recognition of the different roles that the private and public sectors play in different countries is also important. In developing countries there is generally a relatively unregulated private sector delivering health care, and the public sector often takes a significant public health approach, e.g. the provision of vaccines, and may also be involved in direct patient care. In contrast, developed countries often have a strong but regulated private sector and a parallel public sector that is a combination of public health services and provision of acute care for the more disadvantaged in society. These differences lead to particular challenges in ascertaining what is 'best care' and even greater challenges in deciding 'best care and for whom?'.

EBM: the conflict between evidence for the individual and the community

EBM has been challenged to a minor extent, mostly from within the sector most written about in terms of EBM. This mainly includes clinicians, who have challenged the 'cookbook' nature of EBM, the potential for its use to contain resources and the focus on quantitative evidence, especially randomised controlled trials. These arguments have been well dealt with by Sackett *et al.* (1996), and for the purposes of this chapter the arguments for 'cookbook' approaches are accepted – that is, that guidelines and protocols are designed to help decision making, and where individual patient characteristics require variation to the protocol, then that should be part of the evidence used to make a decision. Sackett *et al.* suggest that resources may be increased or decreased when best evidence is taken into account. The issues surrounding quantitative data are hard to refute, especially when the authors acknowledge that quantitative methods and randomised controlled trials are not suitable for every occasion.

In total, the argument around the value of EBM for individual patients has been relatively unchallenged, and on one level rightly so. If the converse is considered, who would want to receive or deliver care that is not in accordance with the best that the evidence offers? Obviously no one, yet it is naïve to think that EBM is the sole means of determining the best ways that health can be delivered in any circumstances. This is especially true when population health is one consideration and the care of an individual another, and when the EBM choice for the individual may not be the best option for the whole community. For instance, to use a simple example, a particularly expensive medication may be the best treatment for a sick child. However, the spending of that money (if it comes from the public purse) may preclude immunisation for many children. The evidence base for the illness demands one choice while the evidence base for the community demands a different choice.

The EBM approach appears at least partly congruent with the usual criteria for bio-ethics in health situations. These criteria include autonomy – that is, a respect for individual rights and freedoms; beneficence – that is, that professionals do good; non-maleficence – that is, that they do no harm; and justice – that is, that there is a fair and equitable allocation of resources without discrimination (Beauchamp 1994; Soskolne 1989). Using evidence-based decisions would at least appear to assist recipients in their decision making, thereby enhancing their autonomy. For both recipients and providers, both beneficence and non-maleficence *may* be enhanced. Although normally this would be the case, situations may arise in public health in which the good of the community and the good of the individual may not be identical. An example of this is given in the previous paragraph, and another may be when evidence determines that a certain food is causing disease and therefore the food should no longer be distributed. The result of this decision may be that the food provider goes bankrupt, with resultant health effects due to loss of income. Thus, criteria surrounding the evidence may have been met, and the health of the broader community may have benefited (i.e. professional beneficence and non-maleficence), yet the individual provider has clearly suffered harm. The final criterion, that of justice, cannot always be met in such a situation – for the individual, the financial impact may have fallen without regard for justice, even if apparently justified.

There will never be enough resources for all the health-related activity that is available; resource constraints will always exist, epitomised by the previous example of the competing resource demands of a child requiring expensive medication and the community need for a vaccine programme. Despite our desire to provide resources for all worthy health causes, this is not possible, and evidence may at least provide some information to help in appropriate decision making.

The current role of EBM in developed and developing countries

The current role of EBM is to define the quality of the evidence in any given circumstances, and to use that evidence to inform best practice in the delivery of health care. By far the majority of evidence-based research papers emanate from developed countries – a simple literature search reveals that virtually all literature is written about developed countries, despite the health care needs in the developing world. The major role of EBM has been in clear-cut, well-circumscribed clinical decisions: what is the best drug combination and timing for treating tuberculosis? Is a particular surgical decision better or worse than a medical approach?

Very often, use has been made of EBM without its being called EBM. For instance, simple approaches to fever and headache in malarial areas with limited resources have used the evidence and the probability of malaria to treat empirically for malaria, with a fixed therapeutic regime. This means that evidence has been used to determine the most likely diagnosis and the best treatment for that diagnosis. Despite the value that EBM can contribute – that is, the best answer to well-defined clinical questions – EBM has been underutilised in developing countries.

Generally, however, and despite the fact that many decisions have a limited evidence base on which to draw, the lack of progress in, for instance, controlling infectious diseases has not been due to the lack of evidence of efficacy and value of clinical treatments but rather to the lack of evidence surrounding implementation. For instance, the cause of tuberculosis has been known for over a century, and the best and most efficacious treatments for over four decades, yet 2–3 million people still die every year from tuberculosis. It is only in the past decade that considerable research effort has gone into providing the evidence surrounding implementation, with research efforts concentrating on alternative treatment delivery mechanisms, the potential for public–private provider partnerships and better methods of monitoring both individuals and public health programmes.

Should EBM have a role in developing countries?

In some ways, developing countries have much to gain from the use of evidence to direct health care, inasmuch as their resources are usually sparse and the demands on the sparse resources usually great. However, it is often just these situations in which least is being done. Very often the driver for EBM, like the push for a health outcomes approach, is economic. This is likely to be one of the reasons that developed countries have seen the rise of EBM. The increased technical capacity to intervene and the rise of health care costs have put greater pressure on health care providers. While similar pressures exist in developing countries, very often the infrastructure is not available to build the evidence base or to assess the evidence, or to implement the evidence even if it is available. Further, often the evidence does not account for the different socio-cultural, economic and political environments that exist in developing countries. To have an evidence-based response presupposes that there is sufficient (for example) clinical, epidemiological, economic, behavioural, etc., knowledge, and that there is a politically accepting environment for the evaluation and implementation of evidence. An example of this is the recent SARS epidemic; worldwide collaborations quickly identified the virus and developed protocols for stopping it spreading. What is missing is the evidence surrounding the best ways of changing health care provider behaviour in different cultural situations.

There has, however, been quite a good role for EBM in the development of standard treatments for specific situations, which in those instances where they are available and appropriate are likely to lead to most of the people who require treatment receiving appropriate treatment. Good examples of this include the use of standard protocols in Papua New Guinea which apply to the common and treatable causes of illness such as malaria and tuberculosis, and the use of protocol-driven immunisation schedules for children.

The problems of EBM in developing countries

What is considered evidence?

A major issue is, what can be considered evidence? Evidence, while often considered as a 'truth', is both context and culture dependent. For instance, if one takes merely one country and one university in that country, and two equally educated people of similar cultural backgrounds, one educated in quantitative methods and one in qualitative methods, what they consider evidence and their assessment of its quality are likely to be quite different. Current knowledge has defined very clearly the levels of evidence in the quantitative field, but the concept of different levels of evidence in other fields is less well established, and whether the best evidence in one field is equivalent to the best evidence using a different paradigm is far from established. There have been recent attempts to better evaluate non-quantitative evidence (Rychetnick) and the value of public health evidence (Brownson *et al.* 2002). While there is an acceptance that the non-availability of high-quality evidence means that evidence from the next level should be sought (Sackett *et al.* 1996; Straus and McAlister 2000), this is different from an acceptance of the validity of different types of evidence.

Problem of getting the **right** *evidence*

The most answerable questions are usually those that are narrow and well defined – but in terms of health gain, the most potential benefit may be elsewhere.

EBM is most often pursued for technological solutions to health problems rather than for the evidence necessary to implement and practise such technological solutions. This observation is even more obvious in developing countries. For instance, a randomised controlled trial may be undertaken (rightly) to determine the efficacy of a particular drug regimen against AIDS. The best constellation of factors to deliver such treatment (e.g. centralised services versus decentralised, the algorithms essential for patient safety, the interaction with local opportunistic infections, etc.), however theoretically efficacious, not only may be unclear throughout the world, but not even be considered in developing countries. At the same time, any prolonged investigations of culture and social-specific factors may end up being a reason for inaction; at a minimum, each investigation by the nature of opportunity costs precludes an alternative one. EBM, by its nature, pursues answerable, and hence often narrow, questions (Smith *et al.* 2001).

In developing countries, infectious disease may dominate both morbidity and mortality. Even in the context of EBM and taking a population health approach, the evidence when a disease does *not* occur may be less persuasive to funders than competing priorities when a concrete gain may be made for the same money (e.g. a hospital, equipment) rather than the abstract gain of fewer cases of a disease. It is particularly difficult to establish appropriate evidence for diseases whose main risk is their potential to amplify and spread. It has proven very difficult to persuade funders that there is value in having good surveillance systems. However, the recent advent of SARS has seen countries investing in surveillance.

Decisions about EBM are often clear-cut about whether a particular course of action works, but less clear-cut about the other parameters that should be considered in any health care system. Recent consideration of universal immunisation against hepatitis B in some developed countries has mostly been about the argument not 'Should we do it?' but rather 'Is it cost-effective?' The various processes whereby decisions are made are not usually explicit, leading to some infectious disease control measures being undertaken on the basis of presumed need without adequate discussion of the actual or opportunity costs, health benefits, access to health care or resource implications. All of these, of course, are important, but must be considered in total. EBM is necessary but not sufficient for decision making.

Seeking evidence that answers the right questions often requires data that are socially and economically based, not merely the evidence surrounding the underlying medical science. For instance, EBM can define appropriate drugs and length of treatment for tuberculosis, and even show that supervised therapy leads to better cure rates. However, if most tuberculosis treatment is in the hands of private providers, and the result of interventions to improve the skills for observed treatment programmes are in the public sector, as occurs in most countries, in the absence of specific action good evidence will not lead to the best or necessarily even improved health outcomes.

The geographical gap between the source of evidence and the potential application

There are two important issues in the geographical gap between the source of the evidence and its potential application. One is the issue of ensuring that drugs and vaccines are available for those communities that participate in the testing of these drugs and vaccines, thereby providing the evidence on which decisions can be made. This is an important issue for both developed and developing countries; there is frequently a gap between where the evidence is obtained, and the capacity of that community to benefit in the medium to longer term. This is particularly true for infectious diseases. Very often it is only developing countries that have a significant burden of infectious diseases which will have sufficient cases (and hence statistical power) to test a new medication or vaccine. This has been an important point of discussion between developing countries where AIDS drugs and vaccines are trialled, and the potential of these countries to buy such drugs or vaccines when the trials are over.

The recent agreement over AIDS drugs will provide at least one model of how such contributions and benefits can be better addressed, and inequity diminished (Anon. 2003). This agreement on its own, however, will be insufficient to improve health outcomes. A more comprehensive solution will be required, as the availability of evidence-based efficacious drugs, while necessary, is insufficient without appropriate distribution and delivery mechanisms.

The second issue is that where evidence is gathered in one place, the implementation of that evidence in a culturally and socially remote place may require a whole different approach to the collection of evidence and its subsequent use. It may be very difficult to determine the relevance of different information from different cultural perspectives, or to convert the evidence to an action for public health. For instance, there is very good evidence that the Ebola virus is spread by blood, and that certain funeral practices, by increasing exposure to the blood of recently deceased patients, increase the chance of further spread. This is an acceptable and reasonable explanation that can immediately lead to actions to halt the chain of transmission. However, it presupposes an acceptance of germs as a mechanism of infection and blood as a means of transmission. The population groups at risk of Ebola virus infection generally do not accept these ideas automatically, hence the evidence required to implement scientific knowledge is very different in, say, a laboratory in the United Kingdom from that in remote parts of the Democratic Republic of the Congo.

Another example is that evidence is available indicating that certain medications are equally efficacious if taken orally or by injection. Despite the scientific truth of this statement, it may count for nothing with some cultural groups. These groups may have a widespread and deeply held belief that injections are *always*, and without exception, more efficacious than tablets.

EBM and emerging and re-emerging infectious diseases

Most gains in infectious diseases have resulted from social and economic changes, developments in the delivery of safe food and water, safe disposal of human waste as well as the advent of vaccines and antibiotics. At the same time as EBM has come to the forefront, infectious diseases have returned to greater prominence in both the developed and the developing world. The existence of antibiotics, vaccines and contemporary technology meant that both governments and the public thought that infectious diseases could be controlled. Yet in the past 25 years we have seen the advent of new diseases and the re-emergence of diseases previously considered to be under control. Newly described diseases that have had a major impact on human health and trade include hepatitis C, variant Creutzfeldt–Jakob disease and HIV/AIDS. Previously described diseases that have emerged in recent years include tuberculosis, dengue, malaria, leishmaniasis and a variety of nosocomial infections.

The overwhelmingly important factors surrounding both these emerging and re-emerging diseases are that we know their causes, and by far the majority of cases could be cured with modern technology – or, at a minimum, new cases could be prevented from occurring. So, if we have the evidence to prevent or cure these diseases, why is this evidence insufficient? The answer, at least in part, is that EBM is useful but insufficient for making health care decisions. We have to examine more than the cause or treatments of health events: we have to understand the evidence for population health and how to implement the evidence, and we have to have evidence on the best methods of implementation.

Implementation implies that the evidence is available concerning the culture, political situation, economics, technical capacity, and so on. If, as societies, we do not look at the barriers to good health care from a broad perspective, we risk failing to deliver better health care.

The non-health interventions affecting health: where is the evidence?

Another issue that developing countries have had to cope with in recent years is the impact of external economic pressures, which in turn may have the biggest effect on health, yet in themselves are more ideological than subject to the kind of evidence required for delivering health. For instance, the contemporary push for 'user pays' and cost recovery as part of market economies may lead to the failure of tuberculosis treatment programmes.

Decentralisation is another economically driven change advised in many countries, mostly deriving from an ideological perspective, and rarely with any understanding of the impact on infectious disease, especially in developing country situations where the poorest individuals are those most likely to suffer from infectious diseases. For nearly all infectious diseases, poverty increases the risk. The poorest are least able to afford treatment, most of the diseases can lead to even greater poverty, and, often, changes in the economic structures of a country will benefit the poorest last. Because many infectious diseases provide risks to the broader population, not just to the individual, a strategic approach is necessary for control. In the context of decentralisation and cost recovery, the policy advice and the implications may not be available in smaller jurisdictions, and hence small problems can spread and become much bigger problems. Yet the economic advice that has led to such events has not been subjected to a randomised controlled trial with health as a measurable outcome.

What can make the evidence good for health care?

There are several approaches that can enhance the usefulness of evidence for good health care. Ensuring that evidence is culturally and socially appropriate is essential. Transfer of knowledge between cultures works best, like causality, for biologically based matters rather than culture- or socially based issues. In other words, the same bacteria will cause tuberculosis whether the individual is in Africa, the Americas or Australia. But the social and cultural predisposing factors, and the cultural and social issues in finding evidence-based solutions, may be very different.

Ensuring that the right question is asked for which evidence is sought is another key to success. Some questions are easy to define and easy to answer, whereas the questions that *need* to be answered may be quite the opposite.

Ensuring that evidence of scientific appropriateness is available is just one of the factors considered when a course of action is planned. Evidence is needed concerning implementation and intervention, not just a course of action such as a specific treatment. It is especially important that EBM be appropriate for each setting in which it is used, whether the setting be in a developing or a developed country.

Brownson *et al.* (2002) go part of the way by suggesting six steps for a public health approach:

1. Develop an initial statement of the issue.
2. Quantify the issue.
3. Search the scientific literature and organise the information.
4. Develop and prioritise programme options.
5. Develop an action plan and implement interventions.
6. Evaluate the programme (then discontinue it, remodel it or disseminate it widely).

This approach, and that of Rychetnik and Frommer (2002), form part of a useful literature that considers the evidence needed for public health approaches. However, neither deals adequately with implementation.

Conclusion

EBM can continue to contribute to health, but will not be the sole answer. This is particularly important for developing countries; as so often occurs, those who begin life with less, often benefit more slowly from societal advances. As elsewhere, developing countries require a sensible approach, recognising the benefits of EBM but at the same time recognising that EBM alone is insufficient to improve health. As well as EBM, it is essential to have a range of other information such as economic, behavioural and cultural data. Further, the best way of implementing evidence-based information itself requires evidence. EBM can contribute to better health if used appropriately, and used in conjunction with other information to the making of appropriate health care decisions. On its own, EBM is good, but not good enough to deliver better health care, whether in a developed or a developing country.

References

Anon. (2003) *Washington Post*, 23 October 2003, http://www.washingtonpost.com/wp-dyn/articles/A8763-2003Oct23.html (accessed 2 November 2003).

Beauchamp, T.L. and Childress, J.F. (1994) *Principles of Biomedical Ethics*, New York: Oxford University Press.

Brownson, R.C., Baker, E.A., Leet, T.L. and Gillespie, K.N. (2002) *Evidence-Based Public Health*, London: Oxford University Press.

Rychetnik, L. and Frommer, M. (2002) *A Schema for Evaluating Evidence on Public Health Interventions*, version 4, Melbourne: National Public Health Partnership.

Sackett, D.L., Rosenberg, W.M.C., Gray, J.A.M., Haynes, R.B. and Richardson, W.S. (1996) Evidence-based medicine: what it is and what it isn't, *British Medical Journal*, 312: 71–2.

Smith, G.D., Ebrahim, S. and Frankel, S. (2001) How policy informs the evidence, *British Medical Journal*, 322: 184–5.

Soskolne, C.L. (1989) Epidemiology: questions of science, ethics, morality, and law, *American Journal of Epidemiology*, 129: 1–18.

Straus, S.E. and McAlister, F.A. (2000) Evidence-based medicine: a commentary on common criticisms, *Canadian Medical Association Journal*, 163: 837–41.

11 Evidence-based medicine and clinical practice

Does it work?

Knut Rasmussen

What is new about psychoanalysis is not true and what is true about psychoanalysis is not new.

(Kristian Schjelderup, Norwegian bishop (1894–1980))

Introduction

Throughout the history of medicine, physicians have tried to formulate general rules based on their experience, and express them in lectures, books and journals. Over the years, however, the mass of evidence has been accumulating so rapidly in all fields of medicine that no active clinician is able to cope with it. From this situation stems the movement of evidence-based medicine (EBM), which aims at helping clinicians to systematise, analyse and draw conclusions from currently available external evidence. The process of EBM has been vastly facilitated through the 'Cochrane method' of evaluating evidence, and by modern computer technology.

Although the EBM slogan is new, the underlying ideals are not. Teachers and leaders of medicine have repeatedly formulated similar slogans in order to guide students and co-workers in the direction of medical rationality (Box 11.1) (Wulff 1981; Vandenbroucke 1996).

Box 11.1 Slogans and movements aimed at improving clinical decisions

Médecine d'observation
Clinical epidemiology
Rational clinics
Quality
Cost-effectiveness
Priority setting
Medical decision analysis
Evidence-based medicine (EBM)

This chapter contains observations on EBM made through the eyes of a clinician. Its main purpose is to underline how the best external evidence from EBM can guide, but never replace, our best clinical judgement when facing an individual patient.

The EBM terminology

The underlying broad EBM ideal is to gather and systematise all available evidence, to analyse this through a formal selection process and then to formulate general rules for good clinical medicine. This is an almost self-evident ideal to which no sensible person could object. This broad interpretation of EBM is also predominant in the current leading textbook (Sackett *et al.* 2000). The same ideals are also beautifully described in textbooks that do not use the EBM terminology (Wulff 1981; Hunink and Glasziou 2001).

Simultaneously, however, a narrower EBM concept has emerged in the Cochrane movement, giving rise to a number of critical voices (e.g. Charlton and Miles 1998). This concept seems to accept only one type of evidence, namely that based on some specific databases and meta-analyses. The narrow EBM concept may appear arrogant and prevent us from using all relevant information. In particular, it may obscure our conception of the relationship between clinical guidelines and individual decisions in medicine. This narrow concept has been applied by both health bureaucrats and the pharmaceutical industry as a means of influencing clinical decisions, thereby restricting clinical freedom. Many of the reflections in this chapter deal with the dangers inherent in this narrow EBM interpretation.

The clinical reality

Every doctor taking charge of an individual patient in a busy clinical ward faces a number of clinical decisions every day. Should any of the ten drugs the patient is on be discontinued? Should we add a few more drugs? When should we stop long-acting heparin during mobilisation of the patient? Should we electroconvert a patient with atrial fibrillation with a duration of three days directly without anticoagulation? Should we try a high-risk operation or ask the patient to go home and die in peace? When should the patient go home? What means of transportation should we choose?

Thus, if the situation is properly decoded, hundreds of such decisions are made every day in every ward. For each patient these constitute a matrix of problems that has to be negotiated with the patient in order to establish a coherent strategy for that individual. The interests of both the patient and the society or health care funder have to be appreciated. Each individual decision is based on a number of premises. Textbook knowledge, patient preferences, practical matters, resources available and the ideals of medicine come into play. Only a small fraction of the factual matters we would like to have when making the decisions are available to us.

This picture of the clinical reality shows how knowledge and evidence constitute only a part of our basis for clinical decisions. Although knowledge and evidence will hopefully play a growing role, they will always require integration into a clinical totality.

The three phases of clinical decisions

Every clinical process starts with a meeting between patient and doctor. Through this, the doctor listens to the patient's stories through a complex process of narration and intuition (Greenhalgh 2002). He or she tries to identify the patient's overt and covert problems. Gradually the doctor defines a set of hypotheses on which further diagnostics and treatments are based. This first stage of intuition and narration may be termed the pre-EBM phase. It may be the most vulnerable phase in the clinical process both for the personal relationship between doctor and patient and for the eventual clinical outcome. If in this primary contact we fail to recognise the patient's true problems and key preferences, no database or routine can help us.

When the patient's problems have been properly defined, it is then time to ask whether I as a doctor have some knowledge from other sources which may help me find some solutions. We have now entered the EBM phase. In daily practice, my first question would be whether I have some guidelines or routines that adequately cover the patient's situation. Such guidelines may be institutional or be provided by health authorities or professional societies. The EBM process has certainly been helpful in developing such guidelines. We have been able to standardise our clinical practice to a greater extent than was previously the case, and the advantages of modern medicine have been able to benefit a number of new patients. However, I must also ask whether the routines and guidelines are up to date. If the guidelines are lacking or are invalid, a broader search for evidence in textbooks, journals and EBM databases starts. This is certainly the phase to which students and young doctors most easily adapt. Help is everywhere, in libraries and from your PC.

In the third phase, the post-EBM phase, before applying the results from guidelines or from my individualised search of the literature, I must ask myself whether my patient has any special traits that make the strategy suggested inappropriate. In cooperation with the patient, I must ask whether these studies are really valid and relevant for my patient's problems. Does my patient have any concomitant disease that may affect results negatively? Are the results of the EBM research relevant to my institution and context? Does my hospital have mortality rates and cure rates for major surgery similar to those reported in the trials? Finally, do we have the resources necessary for carrying out the chosen strategy?

This description of the clinical process illustrates how the search for external evidence is preceded and followed by complicated clinical processes and judgements and why this must be so. Every time we decide that some specific general rule or routine should be used for an individual patient, we perform a 'quantum leap' in deciding that the risks and benefits that are presumed in the guidelines apply to our patient. For each patient, a number of individual traits may exist that make the chosen strategy invalid in his or her case. We should never forget that the outcome for each individual in principle is uncertain and that it is always the case that our actions may do more harm than good (Wynne 1992). The responsibility for this step can never be taken by a committee. Disclosure of this 'principled uncertainty' is an essential component of informed consent (Leeder and Rychetnik 2001; Cox 2001).

The final decisions should always be made in the patient–doctor context, on the basis of proper information. The patient can always decide to do something other than what is recommended. A young woman with severe aortic stenosis for whom a mechanical prosthetic valve is recommended may choose a biological one in order to avoid anticoagulation so that she may have children in a normal way and then accept the risk of additional surgery some years later. No EBM data indicating the superiority of a mechanical valve can overrule her informed judgement (Kerridge *et al.* 1998; Guyatt *et al.* 2000).

Checklist for sceptical clinicians

Before I accept the evidence from EBM-inspired databases or from other external sources of knowledge as relevant for my patient, it may be fruitful for me to assume the role of devil's advocate and consider some general questions:

- Is my patient truly representative of the patients studied in the trials? Do the trials adequately cover my patient's sex, age or concomitant diseases?
- How robust are the conclusions? How large are the confidence intervals? Is this really a clinical effect or only a statistical one? Are the conclusions based on only short-term trials or do we have long-term results relevant for the eventual fate of the patient?
- Is the available EBM analysis made from a number of small 'positive studies' that may be subject to heavy publication bias (Thornton and Lee 2000; Celemajer 2001)?
- Is the evidence taken from an analysis made 'too late'? Do we have new technological breakthroughs or clinical knowledge that make the results obsolete? Remember that all breakthrough technologies had an initial phase of failure. If sufficient negative reports had been made in this phase, a new technology might have been stopped prematurely by administrators.

- Who performed the analysis and who may have influenced it? Did commercial interests or 'cost-containing' health authorities influence the conclusions in a positive or negative way? Is there a hidden agenda or latent value judgement behind the analysis?
- In acute clinical conditions, the patient often leaves much of the decision to the doctor. However, the more the decision relates to long-term treatment of low-risk conditions or risk factors, the more will patient autonomy and preferences be the rule. Thus, EBM loses power in the field of prevention.

Establishing an evidence-based attitude in a clinical department

To be a doctor is to take part in a process of lifelong learning. For the clinical leader, the task is to develop a unit in which the patients are given the best possible diagnostic and therapeutic offer. Such a thing can never be made head-down, but must be achieved through involving the entire clinical department in a continuous search for optimising regimens. The following suggestions should be seen as necessary but not sufficient conditions for creating such a department:

- Curiosity and open discussion must be maintained. An atmosphere in which questions, and in particular critical ones, are appreciated as much as answers must be established. Only from such a culture can the drive to ask the right questions originate (Sackett *et al.* 2000). This must be implemented in the daily patient-oriented routines as well as in regular meetings.
- A number of obvious practical enterprises must be undertaken, including keeping an updated local library, making the central journals available to all, and establishing open access to all information sources, including EBM databases.
- Participation in local, national and international meetings should be encouraged. Meetings are certainly not an outdated form of distribution of knowledge, even though we may lack 'evidence' that doctors really learn from meetings. These may be more important for generating impressions and inspirations rather than strictly for the accumulation of knowledge.
- The interaction between the scientific programme of the department and the evidence-based routines should be maintained.
- Clinical routines should be established in important fields, should be maintained and should be made available electronically to all personnel.

EBM and teaching

Broad-version EBM is certainly necessary for all types of teaching. All teaching should definitely be evidence based. However, teaching should not be dominated by the latest therapeutic modalities. While theories about pathophysiological mechanisms may remain the same throughout one's life as a doctor, and diagnostic methods may last for decades, therapeutic regimens usually last only a few years. For medical students, it is therefore fruitful to focus on durable knowledge. Furthermore, not only facts, but understanding, attitudes, ethics and the clinical coupling of external evidence and individual factors described above should be central in all teaching of medical students. In postgraduate education, when basic mechanisms and underlying clinical assumptions are more evident, the strict EBM methods may be more applicable.

Does it work?

As all EBM enthusiasts would rapidly recognise, the only way to answer such a question properly is to perform a randomised trial with and without EBM. The control group in such a study could of course not be 'protected' from conventional types of medical information. The removal of 'strict EBM information' would therefore automatically lead to increased use of other sources. Thus, any effort to document EBM as a method in a manner accepted by the EBM movement itself is probably futile. This must be a paradox for all EBM fundamentalists. Therefore, the question should be interpreted in a much more pragmatic way. EBM should be considered as only one of the many movements that influence our diagnostic and therapeutic behaviour. In addition to the evolution of EBM, we have experienced changes in the medical schools, in postgraduate training and in the standardisation and quality work performed all over the world in medical communities. Therefore, the question should rather be whether it is possible to influence the practice of medicine through any type of information and education. The answer to this question is obviously: yes. If we follow the use of, for instance, beta-blockers, ACE inhibitors and statins in the years before and after the publications of the Timolol Trial, the Consensus I Trial and the 4S Trial, it is obvious that to cardiologists in Norway, these trials had an immediate and dramatic effect. In Norway, a number of studies indicate that virtually all patients who 'should have' these drugs in practice get them.

Such facts illustrate that the medical community can learn fast. But this does not happen all the time. Many breakthroughs are implemented only slowly, and progress is often very unevenly distributed. The reason for this probably lies not in the information process itself, but in two other factors.

First, some types of progress are much easier to implement than others. Drugs may be given as soon as they are marketed. In other fields, one may have to train personnel, purchase high-technology equipment, finance these units and maybe even build new facilities. This may require decades, and often does in practice.

Second, the possibility of financing medical advances may be a fundamental factor in deciding the implementation of progress. If tests, drugs and surgery are funded by public sources, both the implementation rate and the completeness of coverage may be high. If the patients themselves have to pay, or if other external sources must be sought, implementation and compliance will drop substantially. If progress is free of charge for the patients and beneficial for the doctor's purse, implementation will usually be quick and thorough.

Recent experience from Germany indicates that the use of EBM-based education may lead to rapid improvements in knowledge and skill regarding EBM (Fritsche *et al.* 2002). The more important question regarding whether these improvements really translated into better clinical practice was, however, not answered.

EBM and clinical research

EBM has been embraced by almost the entire research community as a method of distributing and systematising research results. The ideal of gathering evidence and asking the right questions obviously may facilitate clinical research. However, negative side effects on research from a narrow interpretation of the EBM ideals should also be considered.

- The generation of good scientific data is the core of all research. Some factions of the EBM movement are instead focusing on the rumination of old data. Endless compilations of meta-analyses are made, although it is evident that the resources would have been used much better on gathering new and better data. The EBM method may thus falsely lead researchers to think that the data are already there and you can get away with performing a new analysis.
- The EBM ideals may not be appropriate for rapid, new developments. As I have pointed out, technological advances often appear with great speed, and a meta-analysis performed too early could contribute to the premature death of a promising new technology. EBM enthusiasts should allow clinicians and inventors to develop their methods properly before they are put to the test. It should also be remembered that a number of important breakthroughs were never tested until they were already part of our routines. They now never will be.
- Similar considerations relate to older methods. As recently pointed out (Julian and Norris 2002), the evidence-based programme may overlook old and important knowledge and focus too much on marginal new results.

The worst 'EBM side effect' may be that it guides us away from pathophysiological reasoning and mechanisms towards a belief that all data are already there. Our scientific curiosity may be reduced. Like the logical empiricism of twentieth-century philosophy, the overall effect of the programme may be to restrict rather than to liberate human thought.

Bureaucratic side effects?

The ideas of EBM have been adopted not only by researchers, but also by the pharmaceutical industry and the 'health bureaucracy'. The industry may be using the movement for marketing purposes and the bureaucrat may have used it to restrict the use of new drugs and technologies. The former aims at advancing the use of new methods, while the latter seeks to restrain it. This may unpredictably affect priority setting in medicine by enhancing the use of some methods beyond reasonable limits and suppressing others (Hagcox *et al.* 2003). Even more dangerous consequences will emerge when health authorities and governments seek to exercise control through the use of EBM data for influencing health personnel. This could constitute a serious attack on the patient–doctor relationship and on the freedom of clinicians to work responsibly.

Conclusions

The EBM movement is clearly an important one which nobody should or could resist. However, EBM is to a large degree only a computerised application of what good doctors have always done: compiling medical knowledge to the benefit of the patient. The EBM movement should adapt itself to the world of clinical realities. It should look upon itself as one of many ways of achieving a lifelong, self-directed learning in medicine. There is no doubt that, conducted in this manner, EBM works. The potential side effects of the EBM method should, however, be closely observed. Clinical decision making will always be full of errors and should therefore be conducted with humility. This will remain so despite some marginal improvements in the factual basis on which the decisions are made.

References

Celemajer, D.S. (2001) Evidence-based medicine: how good is the evidence?, *Medical Journal of Australia*, 174: 293–5.

Charlton, B.G. and Miles, A. (1998) The rise and fall of EBM. *Quarterly Journal of Medicine*, 91: 371–4.

Cox, K. (2001) Evidence-based medicine and everyday reality, *Medical Journal of Australia*, 175: 382–3.

Fritsche, L., Greenhalgh, T., Falch-Ytter, Y. *et al.* (2002) Do short courses in evidence based medicine improve knowledge and skills? Validation of Berlin questionnaire and before and after study of courses in evidence based medicine, *British Medical Journal*, 325: 1338–41.

Greenhalgh, T. (2002) Intuition and evidence: uneasy bedfellows?, *British Journal of General Practice*, 52: 395–400.

Guyatt, G.H., Haynes, R.B., Jaeschke, R.Z. *et al.* (2000) Evidence-based medicine: principles for applying the users guide to patient care, *Journal of the American Medical Association*, 284: 1290–6.

Haycox, A., Bagust, A. and Walley, T. (1999) Clinical guidelines: the hidden costs, *British Medical Journal*, 328: 391–3.

Hunink, M. and Glasziou, P. (2001) *Decision Making in Health and Medicine*, Cambridge: Cambridge University Press.

Julian, D.G. and Norris, R.M. (2002) Myocardial infarction: is evidence-based medicine the best?, *Lancet*, 359: 1515–16.

Kerridge, J., Lowe, M. and Henry, D. (1998) Ethics and evidence based medicine, *British Medical Journal*, 316: 1151–3.

Leeder, S.R. and Rychetnik, L. (2001) Ethics and evidence-based medicine, *Medical Journal of Australia*, 175: 161–4.

Sackett, D.L., Straus, S.E., Rosenberg, W. and Haynes, R.B. (2000) *Evidence-Based Medicine. How to Practice and Teach EBM*, New York: Churchill Livingstone.

Thornton, A. and Lee, P. (2000) Publication bias in meta-analysis: its causes and consequences, *Journal of Clinical Epidemiology*, 53: 207–16.

Vandenbroucke, J.P. (1996) Evidence-based medicine and 'Médecine d'Observation', *Journal of Clinical Epidemiology*, 49: 1335–8.

Wulff, H.R. (1981) *Rational Diagnosis and Treatment*, Oxford: Blackwell Scientific.

Wynne, B. (1992) Uncertainty and environmental learning: reconceiving science in the preventive paradigm, *Global Environmental Change*, 2: 111–27.

Index

(P) after a page number refers to Plates. Page numbers in *italics* represent Tables. Page numbers in **bold** represent Figures or Boxed text. 'n' after a page number refers to endnotes.